M02 40002 05294

D1483153

The Last Year of Leo Tolstoy

V. F. Bulgakov

✦✦✦✦✦✦✦✦✦✦✦✦

THE
LAST YEAR
OF
LEO
TOLSTOY

✦✦✦✦

Translated from the Russian by Ann Dunnigan

With an Introduction by George Steiner

28177

The Dial Press ✦ New York

1971

PG
3395
B 7913

Frontispiece:

TOLSTOY IN 1910

SOVIET LIFE FROM SOVFOTO

Translation Copyright © 1970, 1971 by Ann Dunnigan
Introduction Copyright © 1971 by The Dial Press

All rights reserved.

No part of this book may be reproduced
in any form or by any means without the
prior written permission of the Publisher,
excepting brief quotes used in connection
with reviews written specifically for inclusion in a magazine or newspaper.

Library of Congress Catalog Card Number: 73–131182
Printed in the United States of America

First Printing

INTRODUCTION

"Most systematizers in relation to their systems," wrote Kierkegaard, "are like a man who builds an enormous castle and himself
lives alongside it in a shed; they themselves do not live in the enormous systematic building. But in the realm of mind and spirit this
is and remains a decisive objection. Spiritually understood, a man's
thoughts must be the building in which he lives—otherwise the
whole thing is deranged."

This, precisely, was the trap in which Tolstoy found himself.
From the mid-1870s on, in a rhythm of deepening intensity and
spiritual torment, Tolstoy came to regard his way of life as scan-
dalously out of tune with his moral, religious convictions. He spent
the last thirty years of his existence in an attempt, which stooped
sometimes to violence and cunning, to find personal lodging inside
the skin of his own ethical and religious creed. To move out of the
shed of aristocratic manners, spacious domesticity, literary fortune,
and world fame into the castle of poverty, chastity, and Christian
humility. The contradictions he felt between the compromises of
normal life and the absolutes of his ascetic faith were as sharp as
Kierkegaard's either/or. As he wrote to Countess Tolstoy who, with
mounting bewilderment and hysteria was seeking to oppose her
husband's mad ways, "the way you live is the very way that I have
just been saved from, as from a terrible horror, almost leading me
to suicide. I cannot return to the way I lived, in which I found
destruction, and which I have acknowledged to be the greatest evil
and misfortune. . . . Between us there is a struggle to the death.
Either God or no God."

When news spread, in the late 1870s and early eighties—*What
I Believe* appeared in 1883—of Leo Tolstoy's "conversion" to a kind
of fundamentalist, deeply anti-intellectual and anti-aesthetic Chris-

tian anarchism, the civilized world wondered. That the supreme master of the novel, the landowning aristocrat, the begetter of an immense family (Sonya Tolstoy had undergone twelve pregnancies in twenty-two years of marriage), should now proclaim himself a strict vegetarian, a wretched sinner striving to attain perfect chastity, a scorner of literature—this seemed to many a burst of histrionic madness. Suddenly, the great bear-hunter and veteran of the Crimea, the incomparable narrator of battle, preached total nonviolence, resistance to any form of military service. Almost overnight, as it seemed, the proprietor of Yasnaya Polyana, a count whose immediate household, even as late as 1884, numbered five tutors and governesses and eleven servants, declared to an incredulous world that he would rather be a beggar on the highroad, that the way to God lay through total renunciation of material values. It was as if Lear had volunteered for the storm.

In fact, this image of a sudden, apocalyptic break with the past is misleading. Like other artists or thinkers of exceeding genius, Tolstoy was formidably of a piece. The roots of spiritual crisis reach back to the very outset of his career.

In January 1847 the nineteen-year-old Tolstoy had written down rules of personal conduct which plainly anticipate those of mature Tolstoyan Christianity. In that same month he began to keep a diary, which was to become the daily witness of intense struggles between the spirit and the flesh. Two years later he founded a school for peasant children on his estate, and began experimenting with pedagogic means of spontaneous moral awakening very similar to those which were to play a central role in his old age. As early as May 1851 Tolstoy observed that the life of high society in Moscow and St. Petersburg filled him with revulsion and caused a sense of complete moral void. Already he was searching for a way out, for a meaningful spiritual and physical existence on the land. The first version of a long tale, *The Morning of a Landed Proprietor,* dates from September 1852. The hero is called Prince Nekhlyudov. His name and dilemma are identical with those in *Resurrection,* the full-scale religious novel to which Tolstoy turned forty-six years later.

The "stupendous idea" which was to dominate Tolstoy's inner being after 1870 dates back to March 1855. It was then that Tolstoy conceived the notion that it was his true task to found a new religion: "the religion of Christ, but purged of dogmas and mysticism, promising not a future bliss but giving bliss on earth." Even before producing the novels that brought him immense fame and which, in so many respects, crowded and altered the landscape of Western feeling, Tolstoy had thought of rejecting literature altogether. In the winter of 1865 he expressed abhorrence at the triviality and hollow ambitions of literary life, and of the mundane milieu on which the successful writer or artist had to rely. Two exterior occurrences strengthened Tolstoy's ascetic and anarchist impulses. The spectacle of a public execution, which he witnessed in Paris in 1857, horrified him: "never again under any circumstances will I take service under any form of government whatsoever." In 1860 came the death of his brother, Nikolai Tolstoy. Reflecting on his loss, Tolstoy felt that life without explicit religious action was a lunatic emptiness: "In my search for answers to life's questions I experienced just what is felt by a man lost in a forest." Exactly the *selva oscura* of Dante's Pilgrim. The following year came a bitter quarrel with Turgenev, in whom Tolstoy saw the very incarnation of aesthetic ideals, the pursuit of art for its own sake. Tolstoy resolved to abandon *belles lettres* completely and to devote his time to a systematic study of theology and education.

Instead, he began jotting down rough notes for "a book about the period 1805." By the autumn of 1863 *War and Peace* was in full progress.

That, of course, is the crucial point. Tolstoy's "conversion," the anathema he pronounced on literature and worldly life after 1878, the steps he took to change his whole style of being (and whose specific tactics are already set down in the diaries for 1865), do constitute a logical unfolding of doubts and resolutions which he had felt and expressed from the very start. But an incomparable burst of artistic creation had intervened, challenging to the utmost, perhaps for a time suppressing, moral and religious needs no less central. That challenge, that temporary suppression of the claims of the ideal, crowded on Tolstoy's consciousness with a literally physical, nervous force, during the years in which he completed *Anna Karenina*. When the crisis came, like a torrent ten-years dammed, it had behind it the destructive stress of a mind deeply riven.

It would be merely silly to offer any brief statement of Tolstoy's literary technique. But at its core there is a material, sensuous immediacy, a capacity to make a live presence, a totally unforgettable physical fact of language, that has few rivals outside Homer. A Tolstoyan tree shadows the ground more solidly, with greater feel of dappled light, of leaf-mold, than does any other tree in literature and, very nearly, in common sensation. Tolstoyan horses, frozen before the charge, breasting the wet lash of snow, steam through the page with an indescribable but perfectly obvious directness. Light as it is, Natasha's footfall echoes in the reader's inward ear as do very few private memories. *War and Peace, Anna Karenina, The Cossacks,* hammer to bits the opaque shell which, for most writers and human beings, divides words from objects, abstract symbols from the irreducible, vital "thingness" of things. Sound, smell, the pulse of light, the drag of new earth on one's shoes, the metal taste of spring rain—these reach us through the page of a Tolstoyan novel unblurred, unqualified by the dimming edge of print. As do the specific gravity, the physical and psychological "beingness," "thereness," unmistakable in place and time, of his great host of men and women. Nothing in a Tolstoyan scene but is palpable, warmly resistant to our touch. Live with Pierre, with Levin, with Kitty, but also with the most minor personage—old Prokofy "who was so strong that he could lift the back of the carriage from behind" and whom Nikolai Rostov finds in the hall, plaiting slippers, when he comes home from the wars—and those around you will, by comparison, have a ghostliness.

It was this fantastic at-homeness in the sensual truths and detail of the world, this magic rootedness and immanence (Gorky saw in it something almost daemonic), that Tolstoy strove to annihilate, to tear out of his own genius and out of the social order, in a search for holiness, for God's kingdom on earth.

Tolstoy set down his inner life in voluminous letters and journals. Some of these were meant to be read by the world at large, others by his immediate family or disciples, others yet were marked as entirely secret and hidden. Even these, however, reach out to the imagined reader. Various members of the family also kept diaries, and there is a host of memoirs, personal impressions, interviews recorded by visitors to Yasnaya Polyana from all over the world— conscious that they were in the presence of a titan, whose pronouncements, gestures, and modes of daily life would be of enormous interest to the ages. Thus we can follow, very nearly on a day-to-day basis, the history of Tolstoy's spiritual crises as they deepen from the seventies onward and lead, finally, to the melodrama of flight and of death at Astapovo. In a sense, we know too much. Conflicting voices and details throng the stage, obscuring the essentially simple logic of Tolstoy's attempt to live a life unto God in the midst of the common temptations, needs, and weaknesses of men.

The *Confession,* which Tolstoy probably wrote down in 1879, tells of anguish that had thrust him to the edge of suicide. If there was nothing more to life than a spell of sensory business and nervous striving on a clot of earth full of human folly and misery, why live at all? In the mid-1870s, Tolstoy labored with fierce mental concentration to reconcile revealed religion and the unswerving clarity, the insistent common sense, that characterized his own sensibility. He traveled to celebrated monasteries and spoke, in vain, with revered elders of the Orthodox Church. At some point in 1878–79, the light grew strong within him. Salvation lay not in organized religion, not in the complex edifice of revealed dogma. "To know God and to live is one and the same thing. God is life. Live seeking God and then you will not live without God." The rest was incomprehensible verbiage or the cunning mask under which an official church and state pursued their worldly ends.

There followed an *Examination of Dogmatic Theology* and a *Union and Translation of the Four Gospels,* massive tracts in which Tolstoy refuted the formal teachings of priests and exegetic scholars, setting in their place the compelling simplicity of his own insights. Nonresistance to evil, continence, daily toil of a natural kind, an active love of all living things—these were the meaning of God's message to man. To live according to the precepts of the Sermon on the Mount is a necessary and sufficient cause of happiness. Such existence requires constant self-examination, constant vigilance. Perfection may prove unattainable. But, urged Count Tolstoy, no other course of life is worthy of a genuinely rational, enlightened human being.

During 1882, the domestic conflicts which were to darken the lives of Tolstoy and of his wife and family sprang into the open. Faced with the contrast between his ardent beliefs and the unaltered opulence of an aristocratic manner of daily life, Tolstoy confessed to "horrible spiritual torments." Sonya Tolstoy now understood a good deal of the mechanism and purpose of her husband's conversion, but could not go along with him. "Together with the crowd I see the light of the lantern . . . and I acknowledge it to be *the light,* but I cannot go faster, for I am held back by the crowd, and by my surroundings and my habits." Nor was she alone in her bewilderment and sense of irreparable waste. In a famous appeal, the dying Turgenev adjured Tolstoy to return to literature: "My friend, return to literary activity! . . . My friend, great writer of the Russian land, heed my request!" But to the "great writer of the Russian land," to the creator of Prince Andrei and Anna Karenina, all art was, increasingly, a moral outrage. How could a responsible Christian write novels when the real world was so undeniably full of misery, ignorance, and empty violence? At the close of 1883, Tolstoy completed *What I Believe,* one of the most influential books produced in modern times, a source for many of the current strategies of anarchism and fundamentalist "drop-out," as it was also for Ghandian passive resistance. Sonya devoutly hoped that censorship would suppress the work and that Tolstoy would revert to his true vocation. Instead, he determined to exemplify in his own daily routine the moral precepts which he had now set down with such monumental force.

Even as he completed his ethical manifesto, Tolstoy came into contact with V. G. Chertkov, a former captain of the Guards who had undergone a religious metamorphosis very similar to Tolstoy's own. Endowed with a powerful personality, with fanatical energy and considerable, though partly malign, psychological perception, Chertkov was to become the familiar daemon of Tolstoy's life after 1884. It was he, more than any other individual, who daily confronted Tolstoy with the challenge to live up rigorously to his professed ideals. There is, necessarily, a touch of Judas in such instigation.

The birth of a twelfth child in June 1884 aggravated domestic tensions. Publicly committed to the pursuit of chastity, Tolstoy felt bitter shame over his continued lapses into tireless, torturing sensuality. That he should have made of this wretched conflict, and of the pressures it put on his wife, one of the last of his narrative masterpieces, *The Kreutzer Sonata,* hardly mended matters. Nor did the arrival at the Tolstoy estate, in steadily increasing numbers from 1885 onwards, of a stream of converts or would-be disciples: vegetarians, conscripts seeking to evade military service, young women eager to publicize Tolstoyan principles of continence or of breastfeeding, schoolteachers who saw in Tolstoy's manuals for children and simple folk a great step toward universal literacy, inspired faddists of every species, holy men, impresarios, purveyors of gossip. *What Is to Be Done?*, a titular query famous in Russian life and literature from Chernyshevsky to Lenin, had made of Tolstoy an apostle of anarcho-socialism. To the "dark, dark people" of his own land, and soon of much of the earth, the master of Yasnaya Polyana was a source of abiding hope. He, in turn, seemed to draw almost physically on the dim, tenebrous life-forces of the humble who came to his door. Because Tolstoy was alive, said Gorky, no man or woman anywhere in the world need be wholly an orphan.

Under pressure from Chertkov and caught, as it were, in the dynamic logic of the Tolstoyan movement, Tolstoy strove to relinquish worldly ties. All must be set aside: sex, four courses at dinner, those who prevent a man from emptying his own chamberpot or making his own shoes. Education was a fraud calculated to preserve the existing social order. The only kind worth imparting, and that by practical example alone, was the constant exercise of love and mercy toward one's fellow men and of unstinting service to afflicted humanity. By 1888, Count Tolstoy, who now insisted that even the humblest address him as simply "Lev Nikolayevich," had renounced meat, alcohol and tobacco. Hard physical toil in the fields and the making of shoes for his daughters had replaced the triviality of literary pursuits. Two obvious renunciations remained. In the winter of 1890, Tolstoy divided his estate among his family. This was, in fact, a compromise which he found deeply painful: he had wanted to give all his land to the peasants, who alone, on any principles of justice and common sense, had any right of ownership. In July 1891 Tolstoy divested himself and his family of the copyrights of all his works written since 1881 with the sole exception of *The Death of Ivan Ilyich*. Again, this was a compromise step. It was only Sonya's wild recriminations that prevented Tolstoy from giving up copyrights to the whole of his work and thus depriving his teeming household of its principal source of income.

In the ensuing years, there were many interludes of domestic peace. *Resurrection* and *The Live Corpse* bear witness to the unbroken vitality of Tolstoy's artistic genius even at a time when all but the most didactic, immediately populist of art forms seemed to him reprehensible. At the turn of the century, Sonya looked back with justifiable pride on thirty-eight years of marriage. She could write lucidly to Tolstoy: "I wanted to thank you for the former happiness you gave me and to regret that it did not continue so strongly, fully, and calmly throughout our whole life." Actually, the fiercest turmoil still lay ahead.

Excommunicated in February 1901, Tolstoy riposted by declaring that to consider the man Jesus as God or pray to him "I esteem the greatest blasphemy." In 1906, Tolstoy published his strident yet penetrating attack on Shakespeare (I have tried to shown in my *Tolstoy or Dostoevsky* what may have been the covert psychological roots of this polemic). With merciless consistency, Tolstoy seemed to be assailing, in turn, every idol and convention of established culture, of reason and society, as civilized men had, for a long time, understood them. But even his struggle with the Church seemed to Tolstoy remote and, in certain ways, inconsequential when compared to the conflicts born of his daily life. Tolstoy intimated, provisionally at first but soon with broadening stress, that the very existence of a family such as his was an obstacle to stringent moral conduct and to the discovery of the presence of God within us. Chertkov, Biryukov, the nameless disciples of Tolstoyan pacifism in the punitive battalions of Siberia, the harried Dukhobors—these were his authentic family. It was to them that he owed his remaining strength and the material rewards of his literary genius, now repudiated and almost forgot. "We sit outdoors and eat ten dishes. Ice cream, lackeys, silver service, and beggars pass," noted Tolstoy in the summer of 1905. It was with the beggars that he ardently wished to be, traveling the vastness of Russia, staff in hand, not merely preaching but actually living the Kingdom of God. Sonya's struggles to preserve what she regarded as minimal rights for herself and her children, as minimal ties with the normal way of things, grew more savage and hysterical. The Jubilee year of 1908 saw Tolstoy at the pinnacle of world fame. On July 2nd he wrote in his Secret Diary: "What must I do? Go away from all of this. Where? To God, to die. I criminally desire death." The conflict between Chertkov and Sonya over the future disposal of Tolstoy's royalties took an ever more ferocious turn. Yasnaya Polyana became a hive of intrigue, conspiracy, hysteria, and mutual reproach. On November 1, 1909, in the presence of two devoted disciples, Tolstoy signed a secret will assigning rights in all his works to his daughter Aleksandra. Aleksandra was a passionate Tolstoyan who would, with Chertkov's help, fulfill her father's resolve to make all of his great legacy public property. Sensing that some secret purpose was afoot, Sonya roamed the house and questioned her husband. Tolstoy responded with terrible anger and threatened to shoot himself.

Such was the atmosphere at Yasnaya Polyana when a young student from Moscow, V. F. Bulgakov, joined the household as amanuensis and general factotum to Tolstoy. Like almost everyone else involved in the explosive drama of Tolstoy's struggle with the spirits of darkness and the world, young Bulgakov kept a diary.

First published under the title *Lyov Tolstoi v posledni god yevo zhizni,* Valentin Bulgakov's account of *The Last Year of Leo Tolstoy* is a remarkable document. It comes closer than any other eyewitness testimony to being impartial. Bulgakov had been a convinced Tolstoyan, from at least 1907 on, and owed his position at Yasnaya Polyana to Chertkov's direct recommendation. Indeed, it was under Chertkov's specific direction that he began his daily chronicle of events in the Tolstoy household. But Bulgakov was a person of evident tact and good sense. He came fresh to the eye of the cyclone, unmarked by the long, erosive years of intimate bitterness. He saw things for himself and was quick to observe that all the wrongs were not on Sonya's side. After a while, as he tells us, the diary became truly his own and not a series of communiqués to Chertkov.

That the young disciple worships his master is obvious. The notion of "evaluating his works," of discarding even the most commonplace of Tolstoy's dicta, seemed to him blasphemous. That Leo Tolstoy towered above ordinary humanity, that it was a fantastic privilege to be in his company, to copy his endless spate of correspondence, to sleep on a daybed in order to be near at hand, these were self-evident truths to Bulgakov. His whole book is a record of a profound spiritual infatuation. With Tolstoy's flight and death a new darkness came into the world. But whether consciously or not, Bulgakov noted events as he saw and heard them. And the resulting portrayal is by no means unequivocally in the hero's favor.

Bulgakov conveys the frequent dogmatic banality, the imperious flatness, of the old prophet's beliefs. Refusing to condone inoculation against smallpox, the novelist who had penetrated the inmost death-fears of Prince Andrei or Ivan Ilyich, now proclaimed, "There's no point in trying to escape death, you'll die anyway." Asked for serious guidance on modern literature, Tolstoy declared: "disregard all literature written during the last sixty years—it's all a muddle! And read everything written before that time." To experience genuine philosophic problems was merely a symptom of spiritual weakness. "Whatever is unclear is weak. . . . Only those ethical truths that are clear are firm. And whatever is absolutely clear is firm. We firmly know that two times two is four. . . . Why, why this mysticism?" Inquiries as to the source of faith were met with pellucid triteness: "Reason is not the basis of belief, but there can be no unreasonable belief." Even where Bulgakov concurs, the harsh triviality of many of Tolstoy's primitivist doctrines comes through. Children "need no education whatever . . . it is my sincere conviction that the more learned a man is, the stupider. . . . For me the words *learned* and *stupid* have become synonymous." Faced with the prophetic suggestion that the technology of mass destruction may, one day, make wars impossible, Tolstoy counters with an entirely spurious analogy: "so it follows that to obviate gluttony one must take an emetic, and to preserve men from the sin of lechery they must be united with women who have venereal diseases." Hammer strokes from the old storm king, but many of them hollow and petulant.

Bulgakov dates the beginnings of the final crisis in the Tolstoy ménage as from the 9th and 10th of May 1910. Tolstoy was suffocating. Every day brought missives and visitations from disciples demanding that he break utterly with the remnants of landed ownership and familial life. On May 29th an acrid exchange led to Sonya's departure from the house: "she walked out into a field and lay down in a ditch. They sent someone out with a horse and she was brought back." Away from Yasnaya Polyana, in the spartan home of friends and followers, Tolstoy felt at peace. Countess Tolstoy developed acute symptoms of nervous disturbance and Tolstoy had to return to the scene of incessant battle. On June 28th Bulgakov notes that "Yasnaya Polyana has turned into a sort of fortress, with secret meetings, parleys, and so forth." Chertkov's interference with what she took to be her own sacred interests in Tolstoy's journals and artistic legacy were driving Sonya to a new pitch of frenzy. With the signing of the secret will, and with Sonya's discovery of the most intimate of Tolstoy's diaries, the storm broke. From late July on, possibilities of a violent dénouement were distinctly in the air.

Bulgakov's sympathies for and with Tolstoy in all this wretchedness are undisguised. He found it appalling that so majestic and saintly a figure should be harried by domestic scenes. Often his diary exhibits stupefaction at the fact that neither Countess Tolstoy nor some of Tolstoy's children should admit the blinding truth and purity of Tolstoyan precepts. Nevertheless, just because Bulgakov is a remarkably level-headed witness, the strains of inhumanity, of utter tactlessness, in Tolstoy's behavior are made manifest. An entry for the 5th of August is revealing. Commenting on Sonya's latest hysterical collapse, Tolstoy says: "It's impossible not to feel pity for her, and I rejoice when I succeed in feeling it. I have even made a note concerning this." By mid-September, Bulgakov was in little doubt as to the obsessive, perhaps sinister, motives in Chertkov's strategy. He aims "at the moral destruction of Tolstoy's wife in order to get control of his manuscripts." The conduct of Aleksandra, the most doctrinaire Tolstoyan in the family, struck the young secretary as equally odious. He regarded her as either in conspiracy with Chertkov or, "with typical female antagonism toward the mother," devoting herself to the struggle "as to a kind of sport."

Such was Bulgakov's fairness that he seems, in the end, to have lost something of Tolstoy's absolute trust or, certainly, of the trust of the faithful. I can find no other explanation for Bulgakov's evident unawareness of Tolstoy's flight on the night of October 27th to 28th, or for his absence from Astapovo. Significantly enough, it was Chertkov who requested that he stay behind.

But this is not exclusively a record of bitterness and domestic intrigue. There are memorable snapshots of Tolstoy at his sovereign best. There are fascinating reports of Tolstoy's opinions of Nietzsche, Chekhov, Maupassant and Shaw. The intricate ambivalence of his feelings towards Dostoevsky emerges yet again. Tolstoy rejects Dostoevsky's Christology and speaks slightingly of *The Possessed:* "Nevertheless, of the sixty-four thoughts I had selected from Dostoevsky, he checked thirty-four for inclusion in the book." Bulgakov provides illuminating glimpses into Tolstoy's lifelong relations to music—an art whose spiritual penetration he felt intensely drawn to, yet feared for its irrational, sensuous hold on the human will.

There are touches of delightful contradiction. The apostle of humility is taken aback when two peasants by the roadside do not doff their caps. The great mortifier of all fleshly enchantments and graces rides recklessly through bush and bramble, high in the saddle, as did the hunter and *barin* of the past. Even in the sultry gloom of Tolstoy's last ten months there were moments of sheer summer.

To read this diary today is to be made aware of a striking parallel. Bertrand Russell too turned against many aspects of his aristocratic past in order to become a champion of radicalism, of nonviolence, of anarchic resistance to human follies and cruelties. Like Tolstoy, Russell relinquished the philosophic craft that had brought him great fame and a crowning position among his intellectual and social peers, so that he might reform education, the status of women, men's diets, and the ways in which prisons are built and run. Fanatical disciples sought to appropriate the aging Russell, and in his household too there was, for a time, a Chertkov. Like Count Tolstoy, Earl Russell came to represent the unspoken aspirations, the outraged conscience, of a considerable measure of common humanity. The two men shared the good fortune of a formidable physical resilience. Both found it difficult to love women or any near human beings with full devotion; the abstract weight of human need pressed too sharply upon them. The death of each left a curious stillness.

In his marvelous reminiscences of Tolstoy, Gorky writes: "I, who do not believe in God, looked at him for some reason very cautiously and a little timidly, I looked and thought: 'The man is godlike!'" Bulgakov's scrupulous, engaged narrative allows one to share something of that uncanny impression. It is an awesome business that there should have been a Tolstoy on this small planet. Each one of us is the richer for it.

1970   *George Steiner*

Translator's Note

Bulgakov's diary was written as a personal record and not with an eye for publication. Consequently it has seemed expedient to delete repetitious accounts of his secretarial duties, certain casual references to unknown local persons who played no significant role in the life of Yasnaya Polyana, and the redundant health bulletins inevitable in a large family. The deletions are denoted by diamonds (✦) within the text.

All statements revelatory of Tolstoy's character, his belief, thoughts, and opinions on religious and philosophical questions, art and artists, and the moral and political problems of the day have, of course, been retained.

I am indebted to Professor Bernard Koten of New York University for reading the manuscript and for his invaluable assistance in research.

A. D.

The Tolstoy Family

Lev Nikolayevich Tolstoy (1828–1910)
Sofya Andreyevna ("Sonya") his wife (1844–1919)
Their children:
    Sergei Lvovich (1863–1947)
    Tatyana Lvovna Sukhotina ("Tanya") (1864–1950)
    Ilya Lvovich (1866–1933)
    Lev Lvovich (1869–1945)
    Andrei Lvovich (1877–1916)
    Mikhail Lvovich (1879–1944)
    Aleksandra Lvovna ("Sasha") (1884–   )
Mikhail Sergeyevich Sukhotin (1850–1914) husband of Tatyana
    Lvovna, member of the first Duma, 1906
Tanya ("Tatyana Tatyanovna") their five-year-old daughter
Mikhail Mikhailovich Sukhotin (1884–1921) Sukhotin's son by his
    first wife
Fyodor Mikhailovich Sukhotin ("Dorik") (1895–1920) his second
    son by his first wife

Olga Konstantinovna Tolstaya, née Dieterichs (1872–1951) Andrei's
   first wife, sister of Chertkov's wife
"Sonya" and "Ilyusha," their children
Ekaterina Vasilyevna Tolstaya, Andrei's second wife
Maria Nikolayevna, Sergei Lvovich's wife
"Seryozha," their son
Marya Nikolayevna Tolstaya (1830–1912) Tolstoy's sister, a nun

Associates and Frequent Visitors

To Yasnaya Polyana

Vladimir Grigorevich Chertkov (1854–1936), Tolstoy's leading disciple and closest friend. He was head of the Tolstoy movement,
   organizer, propagandist, editor and publisher of Tolstoyan literature and works by Tolstoy. In 1889 he and his wife and Strakhov
   began working on a compendium of Tolstoy's ideas drawn from
   his unpublished diaries, letters, and manuscripts in rough draft.
   This work was never completed. On his return from England,
   where he had been living in exile, he was not allowed to live
   in the province of Tula. In June 1910 he was finally granted permission to reside at Telyatinki, which became the center of the
   Tolstoy movement
Anna Konstantinovna Chertkova, née Dieterichs, his wife
Vladimir Vladimirovich ("Dima"), their son
Pyotr Alekseyevich Sergeyenko, close friend of Tolstoy and author
   of many articles about him
Aleksei Petrovich Sergeyenko, his son, Chertkov's secretary
Lev Petrovich Sergeyenko, his younger son, who also lived at Telya-
   tinki with the Chertkovs, and later became an actor at the Vakh-
   tangov Theater under the name of Roslanov
Samuil Moiseyevich Belinky, a copyist living at Yasnaya Polyana

Dushan Petrovich Makovitsky, Tolstoy's personal physician

Pavel Aleksandrovich Boulanger, close friend and follower of Tolstoy. Author of *The Life and Teachings of Siddhartha Gautama, Called the Budda,* to which Tolstoy wrote the introduction

Nikolai Nikolayevich Gusev, Tolstoy's secretary from 1907 to 1909, when he was arrested and exiled to the province of Perm for the dissemination of Tolstoy's illegal writings

Pavel Ivanovich Biryukov, close friend and follower of Tolstoy. Author of a four-volume biography of him, and one of the founders of *The Intermediary*

Aleksandr Borisovich Goldenweiser, pianist, professor of music at the Moscow Conservatory

Maria Aleksandrovna Schmidt, a former schoolteacher who, having become acquainted with Tolstoy's works, renounced the Orthodox faith, gave up teaching, and became one of his followers. In 1910 she was occupied in copying his censored works

Varvara Mikhailovna Feokritova, friend of Aleksandra Lvovna, who worked as a copyist for Sofya Andreyevna

Author's Foreword

I met L. N. Tolstoy on August twenty-third, 1907, when I was a student in the historical-philological department at the University of Moscow. I had completed the first year of the course and was about to begin the second. I later visited Lev Nikolayevich in 1908, and again on December twenty-third, 1909, when I took with me to Yasnaya Polyana the manuscript of a work I had compiled, a systematic exposition of Tolstoy's world-view. His position on specific questions had been set forth in certain of his works by Lev Nikolayevich himself—the question of social equality in *What Is to Be Done?*; that of art in *What Is Art?*; that of the worker in *The Slavery of Our Time*; his attitude toward government mainly in

The Kingdom of God Is Within You; and to orthodoxy in his book *A Critique of Dogmatic Theology,* etc., but he had not organized his ideas into a "system" that was expounded in one basic work and he refused to do so. "If that's what people want," he had said, "let them do it themselves."

As a student in a "philosophical group" in the historical-philological department, this was precisely the problem I had become interested in and had developed in a book entitled *The Christian Ethic: Systematic Essays on the World-view of L. N. Tolstoy.* Lev Nikolayevich had given me help in the preparation of this work. When I could not find sufficient material in his published works to enable me to give an account of his views on science and education, he wrote a long, special article, *On Education,* in the form of letters to me, which material I utilized.

In December 1909 Lev Nikolayevich read my work, approved of it, and subsequently supplied a brief foreword to the book. It was published in Moscow (in 1917 and 1919), and later was translated into Bulgarian and French.

At the time of our meeting at Yasnaya Polyana in 1909, Lev Nikolayevich advised me to show my work to V. G. Chertkov, who was then engaged in various publishing activities. With a letter from Lev Nikolayevich introducing me and my work to Chertkov, I visited him at his estate in Krëkshino, near Moscow. After reading Tolstoy's letter and familiarizing himself with my work he felt that he could recommend me for the position of personal secretary to Lev Nikolayevich.

As it happened, not long before this, in August 1909, Tolstoy's secretary, N. N. Gusev, had been arrested at Yasnaya Polyana and exiled to the province of Perm for two years. He was charged with sending through the mails certain of Tolstoy's writings which had been banned by the censor. Lev Nikolayevich was left without an "assistant," as he always called his secretaries. He was helped to some extent by his youngest daughter, Aleksandra Lvovna, but this help was limited for the most part to copying rough drafts, and was not adequate for his needs. Someone was required who was familiar with his world-view and who would be capable of independently answering letters on religious and philosophical questions. In addition to this, Lev Nikolayevich sometimes needed assistance of a more complex nature in connection with his favorite work of recent years, a compilation of thoughts on his conception of life, and for this work he needed a more experienced collaborator. My book had evidently convinced Chertkov that I was capable of fulfilling these requirements. He wrote to Tolstoy, and a few days later informed me that I had been invited to go to Yasnaya Polyana.

"Is this agreeable to you?" he asked.

It was, of course, more than agreeable; I was positively overjoyed to be offered the opportunity of being in constant contact with the man for whom I could feel only the greatest admiration and love.

"In the beginning you will not live at Yasnaya Polyana, but three versts away, at our Telyatinki farm. At the present time our steward, a young peasant, and two or three others are living there. From Telyatinki you can ride over to Yasnaya Polyana every day and get the work from Lev Nikolayevich."

There seemed to be a rather delicate circumstance standing in the way of my immediately taking up residence at Yasnaya Polyana: the jealousy manifested by Tolstoy's youngest daughter toward any new person who appeared in the house, and especially any new "assistant" to her father. It seems that Aleksandra Lvovna had been subject to such feelings even in her relations with N. N. Gusev. Since I had no "aggressive" plans and hoped for nothing but the opportunity of being useful to Lev Nikolayevich, I did not in the least object to living at Telyatinki in the most modest conditions.

I was not particularly surprised at the time by Chertkov's request that I send him copies of the entries in my diary, were I to keep one, and he considered it most desirable that I should do so. Since the administration had banished him from the province of Tula, thus depriving him of personal contact with Tolstoy, it seemed quite natural that he should appreciate having written information on life at Yasnaya Polyana.

Chertkov's secretary, A. P. Sergeyenko, gave me several English notebooks with fine and specially durable interleaves; I was to use an indelible pencil and "transfer paper," tear out the copies along the dotted line, and send them to Krëkshino. I promised to do this and in the beginning scrupulously abided by my promise. In time, however, by the second half of the year 1910, when Chertkov himself appeared on the Yasnaya Polyana scene and the events taking place in the Tolstoy family assumed a dramatic character, I realized how restricted I was by this "censorship" and, on various pretexts, ceased sending Vladimir Grigorevich copies of my diary, his demands notwithstanding.

I was also warned that Tolstoy's wife, both in her character and her views, would be thoroughly unsympathetic, not to say hostile. This I had not expected, especially since, on the occasion of our first meeting, Sofya Andreyevna had made a most favorable, indeed, rather deep impression on me. I liked the direct look of her sparkling brown eyes; I liked her simplicity, affability, and intelligence. And her gracious and hospitable reception of someone she had never seen before but who she instantly felt was in sympathy with her husband's views was very touching. And, naturally, I could feel only the greatest respect for her as Tolstoy's wife, regardless of what her relations with her husband might be.

At last all the preparations were completed. I wound up my affairs in Moscow and departed for the province of Tula.

At the aristocratic estate of Yasnaya Polyana, where Tolstoy's eldest daughter, the charming and clever Tatyana Lvovna, was staying at the time with her husband, M. S. Sukhotin, and their five-year-old daughter Tanya, I was no less warmly received than at the democratic Telyatinki farm. I do not even speak of Lev Nikolayevich, but Sofya Andreyevna welcomed me with her former kindness and, apparently, with complete trust despite my having come "from Chertkov." I was, after all, a "Moscow student," for which one always made allowances.

Aleksandra Lvovna alone treated me rather coldly. Whenever I greeted her or took my leave she politely shook hands with me, but the stern expression of her eyes remained unchanged and her compressed lips made a thin line in her pale face.

I began my work on January seventh, 1910, at first living at Telyatinki, and later either there or at Yasnaya Polyana, until Tolstoy's death on November seventh, 1910.

Throughout the period of my association with Lev Nikolayevich I kept a diary, the entries of which make up this book.

The Last Year of Leo Tolstoy

17 January, 1910

Today, the day of my arrival at Telyatinki, after eating dinner and arranging my room I set out with the farm steward, a young man my own age, for Yasnaya Polyana, the residence of the great man with whom fate has so unexpectedly allied me. I took with me a letter from the Chertkovs to Lev Nikolayevich, and some photographs of him with his grandchildren for their mother, O. K. Tolstaya (Andrei Lvovich's wife), and for their grandmother, Sofya Andreyevna.

But as it happened, Lev Nikolayevich was not at home; from what I could gather from the conversation of those who had lingered in the dining room, he was out walking with some of the family. I had to wait quite a long time for him in the reception room. He came in looking like a sweet old grandfather, brisk and ruddy from the frosty air, and wearing fur-lined Siberian boots.

"I am so glad, so glad you've come!" he said. "Of course, Vladimir Grigorevich wrote to me. And I need your help. *For Every Day* [1] requires so much work. Well, and how is your work coming along?" he asked.

I told him that I had not yet made the revisions, but hoped to do so soon. In the course of the evening, Lev Nikolayevich again asked me about my work. He also expressed an interest in Chertkov's article, "A Double Censorship for Tolstoy," concerning the numerous distortions permitted by *The Russian Herald* when they published Tolstoy's article "On False Science."

Afterward Lev Nikolayevich enjoyed looking at the photographs sent by Chertkov. They showed him telling a story to his grandchildren Sonya and Ilyusha. "Along came a little boy, and what did he see but a cucumber. And such a cucumber!" The children are laughing, their eyes intently fixed on him in anticipation of what is to follow.

"Charming! Charming!" he said. "And how he caught it! I'm going to surprise Sonya and the others with them."

Lev Nikolayevich was going to his room to rest and asked me to wait.

"But what makes your lips so dry? Aren't you well?" he asked me as he was leaving the room.

I replied that I was probably tired, as I had not slept well in the train the night before.

"Well, lie down there," he said, pointing to the sofa. "Rest now, that's fine! And I'll go and sleep too."

"No, thank you. I'm going to read."

I had some interesting material to read: letters from various persons to Lev Nikolayevich, typewritten copies of which Chertkov had sent with me.

In the evening after dinner, at which the Sukhotin family was present, I went to Lev Nikolayevich's study with him.

"Vladimir Grigorevich is spoiling me," he said. "Again he has sent me an assistant. And I think I can use your help, I think I can."

Then we set to work. I had brought him the proofs of the January issue of *For Every Day*. The first thing he gave me to do was to compare the contents of this booklet with the new plan of the collection, which he had worked out after the January issue had been sent to the printer. He proceeded to explain to me the nature of the work. He could not make up his mind, however, whether the latest issue should be printed according to the new plan or the old, that of the four issues which had already appeared. He told me to write and ask Chertkov about this. His latest plan was to bring out a new edition, easier to understand, more popular.

Lev Nikolayevich asked me to come at twelve o'clock tomorrow.

When I left, he accompanied me out to the hall. I was delighted to be with him and, probably to enhance this pleasure, asked him as I was buttoning my coat how he was feeling—though I could see that he was in good health and spirits.

"Fine—for my age!" he replied.

I began telling him how well I felt and how I had enjoyed the week at the Chertkovs'.

"I am so glad, so glad!" said Lev Nikolayevich.

These words were particularly moving coming from him, because one could feel they were obviously spoken with sincerity, that he genuinely rejoiced and was not speaking merely out of politeness. Everything he says is said with sincerity—this I knew both from his writings and from my observation of his personality in the past.

"There is such a wonderful atmosphere there," I went on.

"Won–der–ful!" he exclaimed in a tone of deep conviction.

And when I told him that I felt somehow close to all of them, though I had been staying there only a short time, Lev Nikolayevich remarked:

"That One which is within us, every one, brings us all closer to one another. As all lines converge at the center, so we all come together in the One."

And he brought together the fingers of both hands.

"Well, till tomorrow!" And he raised his hand high and let it drop into mine.

I pressed his hand with love.

18 January

I talked with Lev Nikolayevich after lunch, that is, after he had already worked for about four hours and was more or less tired.

He instructed me to select from his writings the thoughts on inequality for one of the Days of the collection *For Every Day* which had not been composed according to his plan. He also asked me to look over the proofs of the January issue and to correct whatever is stylistically unsatisfactory, that is, to eliminate repetitions, clarify what is obscure, and so forth.

"Boldly!" added Lev Nikolayevich.

I had yet to give him certain of Chertkov's messages, but seeing that he was weary, I inquired:

"You're tired, Lev Nikolayevich—next time, perhaps?"

"No, no, please!" he protested, leaning back in his armchair prepared to listen.

After I took my leave, he was about to go to his room, but turned back.

"Don't mind that I am so gloomy: I'm terribly tired today!" he said, stressing the word "terribly."

How could I not mind? I was not at all happy that I had listened to him and remained so long.

20 January

I rode over to Yasnaya Polyana in the morning for the express purpose of talking to Tolstoy before he had started to work. But no—he was already in his study and asked me to wait.

When I gave him the citations on inequality that I had collected, I remarked that one of them—the idea that man's capacity for devoting himself to the pursuits of art and science by no means shows him to advantage—I had taken from the contemporary philosopher, Lev Shestov.

"A very good thought," he said.

"Lev Shestov has written critically of you, but that probably means nothing to you, does it?"

"Of course not! Why, I frequently introduce into my book the ideas of Nietzsche."

I read him the passage from Shestov, and he agreed to its inclusion in *For Every Day*.*

---

* Later, when looking through the collection, Tolstoy deleted this passage. V.B.

I remarked in passing that the prevalent view today seems to be that artists and scientists are special people, not like other men.

"Yes, yes. Take Chekhov, for instance—have you seen the newspapers? I'm speaking of the articles on the anniversary of his birth. The fact that he didn't know and had never found the meaning of life strikes them all as being somehow special, they see something poetic in it!"

Returning to Shestov's idea, I expressed the opinion that the book itself, the one he had written about Tolstoy, was unsatisfactory, and that in the first place the author could be called to account for his ignorance of Tolstoy.

Lev Nikolayevich acknowledged that he frequently encountered such criticism of his views, but that he was nonetheless interested in Shestov. Unfortunately, I had not brought the book with me.

As for the work, Lev Nikolayevich asked me to collect more thoughts on inequality for all the other months of the year: I had only enough material for January, and the contents of each issue are to conform to an identical plan. Therefore it will be necessary to find at least sixty such passages.

"I'm terribly tired of selecting them myself," said Lev Nikolayevich, knitting his brows and laughing. "It seems to me that this mechanical work is somewhat inhibiting to freedom of thought."

❖

Today Lev Nikolayevich announced that he had decided not to wait for Chertkov's reply, but to publish the remaining issues of *For Every Day* in their present form, according to the old plan. The same material will also come out in a popular version, conforming to the new plan.

We agreed that tomorrow I should come at seven o'clock in the evening.

❖

23 January

. . . Yesterday, as he was about to get up, Lev Nikolayevich felt
weak and lay down again. He is quite well today, however, and
asked his doctor, Dushan Petrovich Makovitsky, to have me come in.
He was in his study looking over the fair-copy sheets of the
simplified version of *For Every Day,* which lay on the little movable
table. They were again covered with corrections. On learning that
I had not yet seen the rough drafts of this version, Lev Nikolayevich
said that it was just as well, as they were undecipherable, and that
now he would give me the fair copy. For the first time, in order to
acquaint himself with the character of my work and also because
he had to look over the rest of it himself, he gave me the material
for about ten days.

✧

I informed Lev Nikolayevich that Chertkov intended to publish
a periodical that would contain information about the activities of
the free-religion movements, and the more interesting letters sent to
Tolstoy.

"Now, why does he start that!" Tolstoy exclaimed. "However,"
he immediately checked himself, "I'm looking at it from my own
point of view; I have so much work just now that I try to avoid
anything superfluous and do only what is most important."

Afterward he attentively and considerately heard me out while
I explained the purpose and significance of the proposed publication.

"I have just now been occupied with letters concerning the
cooperative movement, of which I have received several," he said.
"And in replying to them, I have said that a man cannot be wholly
absorbed in the cooperative movement, that this is only a part of the
religious movement, but that participation in it is compatible with
human dignity, as it is not connected with force, on which absolutely
everything is based today. Even such a lofty occupation as teaching
has been debased! Not long ago one teacher wrote me that he simply
did not know what to do, what to teach his pupils."

25 January

Today I had an unexpected companion on my ride to Lev Nikolayevich—an old acquaintance of his, a follower and former Petersburg student, Mikhail Skipetrov. . . . He took out an extremely warm and moving letter that Tolstoy had written to him and showed it to me. He coughs terribly, and having traveled twelve versts, seemed tired and weak. To my inquiry about his health, Skipetrov candidly replied that he had consumption. It was hard for him to carry on a conversation and he lay down to rest. Even when lying down he continued to cough.

Later he told me about his meetings with Lev Nikolayevich. It seems that there were two in all. The first was characterized by an extraordinary spiritual uplift on the part of both Skipetrov and Lev Nikolayevich. According to Skipetrov, they sat on a park bench weeping, unable to speak for their tears. Skipetrov, who is an exceptionally "spiritual" man, as they say, told Lev Nikolayevich the story of his father's death, and talked about his own joyous sense of the beauty of nature and the power of life, despite his illness, and Lev Nikolayevich wept.

When we arrived at Yasnaya Polyana and I told Lev Nikolayevich that Skipetrov, "to whom you have written," had come and wanted to see him, he did not at once remember him.

"Yes, of course, of course!" he exclaimed. "Now I recall our conversation in the park. Please, ask him to come in."

I first gave Lev Nikolayevich the work I had done. He was surprised that I had found sixty passages on inequality.

❖

Afterward, when Stripetrov came in, he told Lev Nikolayevich about his experiences during the past autumn, when his outlook on free religion had undergone a change. Among other things, Skipetrov said that partly under the influence of his illness—tuberculosis of the lungs—he sometimes suffered spiritual torments. All this he had already told me, so I did not feel that I had to leave the room.

"Well, for that matter," Tolstoy began, "I can tell you that this happens to me even at my age—in my eighty-second year—and it happened when I was younger too. Because of pain in my liver, much that would have passed unnoticed in normal conditions, hinders me, becomes an obstacle. And I think that's how it has been with you; in other words, your spiritual suffering was the result of your severe illness. Generally man's physical side exerts a strong influence on the spiritual.

"Not long ago," Lev Nikolayevich continued, "I received from Kalachev, who is in prison, a long letter that is imbued with a feeling of happiness and spiritual uplift. And they all feel like that there. It's understandable. Within the four walls of a prison, where there is nothing left for them to do, anything else would be impossible—the spiritual consciousness is awakened and it keeps growing and growing. Kalachev writes of the convicts that one of them said: 'It's a greater pity to kill a crow than a man: from a crow you get nothing, but for a man's clothes, however poor, you can get a ruble.' And there are those convicts, foul-mouthed, crawling with lice, yet their spiritual state is positively enviable."

Skipetrov observed that he did not by any means feel himself sufficiently steadfast in his religious views, his faith in God, and had not definitely clarified everything for himself.

"But, my dear," exclaimed Lev Nikolayevich fervently and impetuously, "that is the whole of life!"

Then in answer to Skipetrov's question whether he recognized original theoretical problems in science apart from their practical significance, such as the discoveries in astronomy, and so on, Tolstoy replied:

"I have never denied them. I only say that this interest is impossible in our time. Knowledge ought to develop uniformly, whereas in our day some branches of knowledge are singularly overextended, expanded, while others remain in a rudimentary state. This is an anomaly, it's not normal. But, in another period, I do not deny that both the parallax and the comets of Galileo will have their importance. My correspondence on this subject with the

German anarchist Schmidt—a good man, but unfortunately very devoted to scholarship—will soon appear. I reply to his objections."

Later Lev Nikolayevich told us of his idea about the necessity of composing a manual of self-instruction—just that, not a textbook—on the various branches of science for those people who crave knowledge, education, and cannot find it anywhere except in the schools, which only corrupt. These people, from whom Lev Nikolayevich receives letters every day, are for the most part young peasants, barely literate, who have completed perhaps no more than lower school. A manual of self-instruction is needed first for language and mathematics (arithmetic and geometry), and then for an altogether new subject: "The History of Mankind's Moral Crusades." Lev Nikolayevich is confident not only that they are needed, but that *The Intermediary* [2] would undertake the printing of these manuals and receive an income from them.

Strange as it may seem, this same idea about just such manuals of self-instruction had once occurred to me. Now I am heart and soul in sympathy with Lev Nikolayevich's idea. He has already talked about it to Boulanger. And as the latter happens to be at Yasnaya Polyana just now, Lev Nikolayevich decided to send for him, which he did by vigorously pounding on the wall next to his little table. Aleksandra Lvovna appeared and he asked her to call Boulanger.

"Pavel Aleksandrovich," he said, when Boulanger came in, "these gentlemen here, that is, not gentlemen, but rather brothers, friends, are going to work on the manuals of self-instruction, and you will be editor in chief."

Lev Nikolayevich again enlarged on his idea concerning the manuals.

Later Boulanger began reading to him in our presence the simplified version of his article on the life and teachings of Buddha. Lev Nikolayevich made comments and corrections. Soon he went off to bathe and the reading was interrupted. We all said good-bye to him and left.

26 January

This evening two sledges with bells jingling drove simultaneously into the avenue of the Yasnaya Polyana estate. It turned out that the writer P. A. Sergeyenko, to whom I was introduced in the porch of the house, had arrived from Yasenki. I had already met and become friends with his sons, Aleksei and Lev, while I was staying at Chertkov's in Krëkshino. Sergeyenko brought a gramophone and records of Tolstoy's voice, which were made recently.

Lev Nikolayevich was upstairs in the dining room playing chess with Sukhotin. His son Andrei and his wife were also there. After greeting me, Tolstoy asked me to wait, and I went down to Dushan Petrovich Makovitsky's room. In a little while Lev Nikolayevich came in and dictated corrections for his reply to a letter from Siberia about "life beyond the grave." As there did not happen to be any blank paper on Dushan's table, I was writing on a couple of sheets torn out of my notebook. Seeing me tear out another two sheets, Tolstoy said:

"Ai, ai! You're tearing out so much paper! Come, I'll make you a present of a notebook. I have more than enough. Sofya Andreyevna rewards me with them."

Lev Nikolayevich promised to look over my work in the morning; meanwhile he asked Tatyana Lvovna to give me the next pages of the simplified version of *For Every Day,* and invited me to stay and listen to the gramophone.

Lev Nikolayevich himself listened together with the others. For the most part he remained silent as first his own voice, then those of Kubelik, Patti, and Troyanovsky were reproduced on the gramophone.

An interesting incident occurred while we were listening. The machine stood in the drawing room, the mouth of the horn turned toward the dining room—for greater effectiveness no doubt—where the listeners sat in a semicircle near the drawing-room door. Then for some reason the gramophone was carried into the dining room and placed on the big table close to the wall opposite the door, with the horn turned toward the corner where all the Tolstoys and Sukhotins were cozily seated in the lamplight at the round table. In the interval between two numbers, Lev Nikolayevich said:

"The horn should be turned toward the door, then *they* could hear too."

They were the footmen, a little boy, a woman, and someone else—in other words, some of the servants who had congregated on the staircase and were peering through the balustrade into the dining room in an effort to catch "the Count's words," as I heard them say when I passed them on the stairs.

There was a momentary silence. Then Andrei Lvovich, who was continually fussing with the gramophone, quickly said:

"It's all right, Papa, it can be heard all through the house, even downstairs."

"Even in my room you can hear everything," added Sofya Andreyevna.

Tolstoy said no more. Five minutes later Andrei Lvovich turned the horn as his father had suggested.

"Well, Papa," said Tatyana Lvovna with a laugh, "you're tired of it now, aren't you?"

Lev Nikolayevich made no reply, but seemed to hunch down in his chair.

"I expect it's a little too much, isn't it?" she pursued, still laughing.

And everyone began to laugh.

After about ten minutes Tolstoy got up and left the room.

They put on the Glinka duet, "Do not tempt me," and then, "Fignera," as Tatyana Lvovna called it.

Lev Nikolayevich came back as the piece ended and said that it was "very nice." He liked still more Ballistin's rendering of the serenade from *Don Giovanni*. It had always been a particular favorite of his. Sitting down in the Voltaire chair near the door he talked for a long time with Sergeyenko about the construction of the gramophone.

Tea was served. Sofya Andreyevna invited me to stay. When

we sat down at the table and began drinking tea, Lev Nikolayevich again left the room. An animated conversation sprang up about patriotism, the superiority of western Europe over Russia, and, ultimately, about land, landowners, and peasants. In time I was to learn that conversation in the big dining room of the white house at Yasnaya Polyana often turned on this theme. Much was said and at great length, and they argued passionately and unyieldingly. Sukhotin, his wife, and Sergeyenko spoke of the extreme animosity of the peasantry to landowners and masters in general.

"The Russian muzhik is a coward!" asserted Andrei Lvovich. "I have seen with my own eyes five dragoons thrash in turn everyone in a village of five hundred families."

"The peasants are all drunkards!" said Sofya Andreyevna. "The army is worth no more than is spent on wine—that is something that has been proven statistically. It's certainly not because of having too little land that they are impoverished."

Tolstoy came in. Conversation ceased, but only momentarily. He sat down at the table and his brows contracted as he listened. A yellow knitted jacket was thrown over his shoulders.

"If the peasants had land," he declared quietly but firmly, "we should not have those idiotic flowerbeds," and with a disdainful gesture he indicated a basket of beautiful, fragrant hyacinths on the table.

No one said a word.

"There would be neither such idiotic things as that," he continued, "nor would there be such idiotic people as those who pay footmen ten rubles a month."

"Fifteen," Sofya Andreyevna corrected him.

"Well, fifteen."

"Landowners are the most unfortunate people!" remonstrated Sofya Andreyevna. "Do you think that impoverished landowners buy gramophones and that sort of thing? Certainly not! They are bought by merchants, capitalists, plunderers——"

"What are you trying to say—that we are less villainous than they?" Toystoy rejoined with a laugh.

Everyone began to laugh.

Lev Nikolayevich asked Dushan Petrovich to bring him a letter he had received a few days ago from an exiled revolutionary, and he read it aloud.

In essence what the letter said was the following:

"No, Lev Nikolayevich, I am by no means in agreement with you that human relations are improved by love alone. Only the well-educated and those who have always been well-fed can talk like that. But what is to be said to a hungry man with children, a man who has suffered all his life under the yoke of tyrants? He will combat them and try to liberate himself from bondage. And now, before your own death, I say to you, Lev Nikolayevich, that the world is still battening on blood, that again and again men will fight and kill, not only the masters, men and women alike, but even their children, so that we shall not have to look forward to evil from them too. I regret that you will not live to see it with your own eyes and be convinced of your mistake. I wish you a happy death."

This letter had a powerful effect on everyone. Andrei Lvovich bowed his head over his glass in silence. Sofya Andreyevna decided that since the letter came from Siberia it must be from an exile, and if the man was an exile, then of course he was a criminal.

"Otherwise he would not have been sent there," was her explanation.

They tried in vain to change her opinion.

This whole scene made a deep impression on me. For the first time I clearly saw the discord that Lev Nikolayevich must have had to live through as a result of the incompatibility of his fundamental convictions and inclinations with his environment.

In the solitude of the sledge, which the force of the wind had swept off the road, and feeling somewhat annoyed by the delay, I briefly recounted to my Telyatinki comrade who had accompanied me to Yasnaya Polyana today, the conversation that had taken place in the dining room and Lev Nikolayevich's remark about the hyacinths. This remark, and the whole conversation, seemed to me extraordinarily significant.

A curious conviction arose in my soul that Lev Nikolayevich's personal life, despite his advanced age, *was not yet over,* that he would undoubtedly undertake something more—something of a nature that no one could expect from him now. It seemed to me that with such power and sincerity, and with his agonizing awareness of the anomaly, the falsity of his position, it would be impossible that he should not attempt to extricate himself from it by some means.

My companion was drowsily wheezing and scarcely heard me. And I felt ashamed that after being enthralled by the company of Lev Nikolayevich and his family I had found my driver waiting in the servants' room. There was no way to atone for my guilt toward him.

28 January

I have been going to Yasnaya in the mornings; the road is often snowbound in the evening, and in a snowstorm one can lose the way. The morning is not convenient for Lev Nikolayevich: he prefers to sit down to his own work at once; nevertheless, he has asked me to come in the morning. It was decided that he would prepare whatever was necessary and discuss with me the most important features of the work. I dislike feeling that I might hamper him, but there seems to be no other way. If, however, it proves to be inconvenient for him, then of course the schedule will be changed.

He looked over the corrections I had made on the proofs of the first ten days of the simplified, or "popular," version of the January issue of *For Every Day* and agreed with some of them but not with others. I gave him the work I had done for the remaining days in January.

When we first went into his study after Lev Nikolayevich's walk, he said to me:

"I was just thinking about you. Tell me, doesn't this change in your life frighten you?"

I answered in absolute sincerity that it did not, though at first I had felt something akin to fear, and I described to him in detail my present spiritual state.

"May God help you!" said Lev Nikolayevich, and he gave me several pieces of advice about life, which I shall not quote here as they coincide with what he said earlier and are to be found in his writings.

He also said that he ascribes tremendous importance to "work on oneself" mentally, which is to say that a man should keep watch on his thoughts and catch himself in any feeling of ill-will toward another, or evil thoughts in general, and strive to check and suppress them instantly.

"It is a powerful aid in directing one's steps toward right activity," said Lev Nikolayevich. "I state this as a practical rule, a prescription for mental hygiene, and I consider it very important."

Today, laughing good-naturedly, Lev Nikolayevich gave me the notebook he had promised me the other day. He was, if one may so express it, extremely kind today.

✧

30 January

Went with Grauberger and Tokarev to Yasnaya. In the hall we were cordially welcomed by Tatyana Lvovna.

"Please come upstairs," she said.

I, Grauberger, in his modest gray shirt, and Tokarev, in a jacket and tussah shirt front, went into the large, bright dining room. There we were greeted just as cordially by M. S. Sukhotin, O. K. Tolstaya, and her children. They urged us to join them at lunch, but we refused, as we had just eaten dinner at Telyatinki. An animated, spontaneous conversation began.

"Is Sofya Andreyevna at home?" I asked Dushan Petrovich, who was sitting next to me.

"No, she has gone to Moscow for five days," he replied.

Then it became clear to me why it was possible to invite Grauberger and Tokarev to come upstairs and have lunch, and why there was an atmosphere of such unconstrained simplicity.

"All the inventions of civilization are advantageous and interesting only in the beginning," said Lev Nikolayevich, "and then they become irksome. Take this, for example," he pointed to the gramophone, "it's an absolute horror!"

The conversation turned to the desperate poverty in which the peasants live, and the bitter resentment of the people.

"Yesterday I met a peasant with whom I had talked of this before. He wants to own land, to settle on it, to be a free man. They don't want to work for the landowners at all, because there nothing belongs to them—and that's why they work little and drink. And you don't know what to say in such cases when you yourself are living in these luxurious conditions. Yet you don't give this up because you are entangled in it in all sorts of ways. It's an agonizing experience!"

They began to talk about England, where Miss Shanks, a recent visitor, lives.

"There the worker considers himself fortunate to work for a master, and thinks that's how it should be. This is not true with us, and in this respect Russia is more advanced than England. Apropos, I have received a copy of one of their comedies, published in a luxurious, illustrated edition, but very silly! In it the 'masters' simply cannot understand how a worker could sit down at the same table with them. They feel insulted and walk out. But a bishop recognizes the man who was cleaning latrines as his long-lost brother, and so on. This confidence in their own superiority on the part of the rich is typical."

I reminded Lev Nikolayevich that this is precisely what is depicted in his *Lucerne*.

"And what is that about? To tell you the truth, I've forgotten."

"In it an Englishman and his wife also get up and leave when the author, or narrator, brings a ragged, wandering minstrel with him to the table."

"Of course, of course! and it was I who brought him in. All that really happened."

One of the visitors, Grauberger, talked about how people are like children, and said that in their childish state it is better to ask nothing of them, but to treat them as children.

At first Lev Nikolayevich listened to him very sympathetically and agreed with him: "True, true!" But later he said:

"That's true, only there is one thing I don't like in it: the lack of respect for people. We should not condemn others. One may think this about the human race in general, but one cannot talk that way about Marya, or Ivan, or Petya." And he went on to defend his view.

❖

1 February

In the dining room Tatyana Lvovna was reading a report in *The Russian Word* about the production in Paris of Rostand's play, *Chanticler*. When she read aloud that the costumes for some of the roosters in the ball scene in the poultry yard had cost the theater several thousand francs, and that one of them had delivered a patriotic monologue, Lev Nikolayevich said:

"Grauberger is right—they are children, odious children! That's like the Moscow merchant who gave thousands to the clown Durov for his performing pig, and then had it roasted and ate it."

❖

2 February

"Well, have you had any news, any letters?" asked Lev Nikolayevich as he led me into his study.

"Yes, I've just received a letter from my mother."

"Ah! And what does she write?"

"She upbraids me for leaving Moscow and going to Krëkshino. She simply cannot reconcile herself to the fact that I have left Moscow and the university."

Lev Nikolayevich sympathized with me.

"You must try to appeal to her feelings, make her realize that it's painful for you too."

"But I've already tried, many times, Lev Nikolayevich, and now it's very hard; people just don't understand."

"I know, it's hard. But you must keep on trying."

"She even reproaches me with something like frivolity, saying that I never finish anything I start; that I left the university, began to study singing, and dropped that too."

"You sing—you have a good voice?"

"I sing, yes. But I wasn't thinking of going into opera; I gave all that up."

"And why not go into opera?" asked Tolstoy, cocking his head and looking down at his feet with an ironic yet kindly smile.

"But that's such a useless life, Lev Nikolayevich. And for whom would I be singing in the city? You yourself have written that art provides an opportunity for the rich to pursue a life of idleness. I'd rather sing in the country for the peasants."

"I know, I know," said Lev Nikolayevich, tilting back his head. "I am only taking stock of myself. I ask myself: am I alone in holding such views?"

As for the work, I expressed the opinion that it would be better to publish the thoughts on faith in two booklets; Lev Nikolayevich decided, however, to put them into one, but asked me to combine the homogeneous material and to organize it better.

"These booklets of thoughts on individual questions interest me very much," said Lev Nikolayevich. "Only I keep giving you so much trouble," he added, and in such a guilty tone of voice.

I have noticed this note of guilt in his voice before, at such times as he was either asking me to do some piece of work or praising work I have already done for him.

After leaving him, and having talked to Aleksandra Lvovna

about sending some of Tolstoy's books to certain persons, I encountered him once more on the stairs.

"You're not despondent?" he asked.

"No!"

"Take care that you don't lose heart! 'He that endureth to the end shall be saved.' *He that endureth not* to the end, the same shall be saved!—which could be said about the university and your remaining there."

Lev Nikolayevich went out for his ride and I got into my sledge to drive home.

"Good-bye, Lev Nikolayevich!"

"Good-bye!" he called back as he rode off. "I have great expectations of you!"

What does that mean, I wondered?

"Expectations of what, Lev Nikolayevich?"

Then I recalled what he had said about the work he gave me today for the booklet *On Faith,* and which he again mentioned in the hall, saying that he attached great importance to it.

4 February

Today when I arrived Lev Nikolayevich was at lunch in the dining room.

"You have typhus at Telyatinki," Sofya Andreyevna said to me. "See that you don't infect Lev Nikolayevich. You can infect me, but not him!"

I reassured her by informing her that all intercourse between the inhabitants of the village and the farm where I lived had been broken off.

Lev Nikolayevich at once asked to see what I had done with the work he gave me yesterday. I explained that I had broken down the thoughts on faith into sections, according to their content, and read to him the headings of the various categories.

"1. What does true faith comprise? 2. The law of true faith is clear and simple. 3. The true law of God is love for every living creature. 4. Faith governs men's lives. 5. False faith. 6. Outward worship is not consonant with true faith. 7. The concept of reward for having lived a good life is not in harmony with true faith. 8. Reason confirms the principles of faith. 9. Man's religious consciousness never ceases to move forward."

"Very interesting," said Lev Nikolayevich. "Well, and did you throw out some of the thoughts?"

"No, not one."

"And I thought you would throw out a lot of them."

Lev Nikolayevich positively amazes me by the liberty he grants me—a liberty which I simply cannot bring myself to exercise— as well as the license he allows the other members of his household to evaluate his works. Now how could I "throw out" these or any of the thoughts of Tolstoy in a collection compiled by him? To transpose or reorganize them, this I can—but to "throw them out!"

Quite unlike my attitude is the intrepidity of Mikhail Sergeyevich Sukhotin, who in criticizing Lev Nikolayevich sometimes furiously attacks one or another expression or page of his writings. And I am struck not only by this intrepidity, but by the good humor with which Tolstoy listens to his son-in-law on such occasions. This is undoubtedly one of his most remarkable qualities.

Having listened to my plan for arranging the material in the booklet *On Faith,* Lev Nikolayevich asked me to come into the study. There he gave me the material he himself had arranged for one of the next booklets, and then went back to the dining room.

Returning a few minutes later, he sat down to read my work and then asked me to take to the "Remington room" those letters which he entrusted to me to answer.

When I came back, Lev Nikolayevich said that what he had looked over was very good, and gave me the thoughts for the second booklet, *On the Soul,* for a similar systematic arrangement.

"I should like you to be freer, bolder, in making changes in the text. And in general I should like criticism, more criticism."

I screwed up my courage and, with Lev Nikolayevich's permission, severely criticized his disposition of the thoughts in the booklet he had given me to look over today.

"Your arrangement," I said to him, "is, if I may so express it, *formal:* you divide the thoughts into positive, negative, metaphysical, parables, and so forth. I, on the other hand, have classified them *according to content.* And this, it seems to me, is better."

"Yes, that is true," he agreed, and asked me once again to organize the thoughts for the second booklet in exactly the same way.*

Later I talked to Lev Nikolayevich about my work on *The Christian Ethic,* as I have finished making the revisions he suggested. Regarding its publication, he advised me to write to V. A. Posse in Petersburg, editor of the monthly magazine *Life for Everyone,* adding that he, Tolstoy, was interested in seeing it published and was prepared to send Posse a "covering letter."

I was in the dining room reading the newspaper when Lev Nikolayevich came out of the drawing room.

"Are you going for your ride, Lev Nikolayevich?" I asked.

"No, just for a little airing."

All at once it occurred to me that one day when he was out walking Lev Nikolayevich had suddenly lurched violently, as if propelled by a strong wind, and a look of exhaustion had come over his face. And then I recalled that when I was taking leave of him in the study, and asked: "Are you tired today, Lev Nikolayevich?" he had replied: "Yes, I am completely overworked."

I became alarmed for this dear person, but I could not bring

---

* During the time that Tolstoy was compiling booklets on individual questions (guided in the main by material from his own collection *For Every Day*), I myself, though helping him with it, did not realize what was to come of this work. But toward the end of the year it turned out to be *The Way of Life,* his last big work. In later entries of this diary the reader will have the opportunity to follow the course of Tolstoy's work on the composition of this book. But in the beginning the work was not called *The Way of Life,* but *Thoughts on Life.* The aforementioned booklets, *On Faith* and *On the Soul* formed the first chapters of *The Way of Life.*—V.B.

myself to speak to him about the need for more rest. And besides,
I knew that he would pay no attention to such advice.

✧

7 February

Today one M. V. Shmelkov came from Yasnaya Polyana
bringing me a note from Lev Nikolayevich which said: "Dear Val.
Fyod., look after this new friend of ours, have a talk with him,
and then bring him to see me. L. Tolstoy."

Shmelkov and I arrived at Yasnaya after one o'clock and missed
Lev Nikolayevich, who had already gone out for his ride. We
decided that Shmelkov and M. V. Bulygin, who had come with
us, should wait for Tolstoy, who would return before evening, when
he would rest and have dinner, and that I would go back home.
But just as I had put on my things and was about to leave Lev
Nikolayevich came in, and despite everyone's pleas that he not
trouble himself to talk to the visitors before dinner, he insisted that
I take off my things and stay, saying that he would look over my
work, and he went in to see Shmelkov and Bulygin.

Shmelkov is an assistant railroad mechanic who is in sympathy
with Tolstoy's views. Considering his own work useless, he wants
to give it up and be a farmer, though he has neither land nor
money. He is married and has three children.

Lev Nikolayevich advised him to continue making a living at
his former work, remarking that working on a railroad is still one
of the more acceptable occupations for a Christian.

"He's a fortunate man!" said Lev Nikolayevich to Bulygin,
referring to the fact that Shmelkov had told him that his wife is
in complete sympathy with his views.

A question arose concerning the upbringing of children and
whether they needed what is called "an education."

"They need no education whatever," said Lev Nikolayevich.
"And I am not being paradoxical, as they say of me, but it is my

sincere conviction that the more learned a man is, the stupider.
I was reading an article by N———, who is learned, yet an utter
fool, an absolutely stupid man. One may be learned and still be a
fool. For me the words *learned* and *stupid* have become synonymous.
And what about N———? And that other one who's just as
celebrated?"

"Mechnikov?"

."Yes, yes! Dolgorukov invited me to a meeting of a 'peace
society' which is to be attended by d'Estournelles[3] and other
visitors from France. And he turns out to be an opponent of
antimilitarism. He says that science will so far perfect the
implements of warfare, invent such infallible electrical torpedoes,
that waging war will no longer be possible and will cease. I wanted
to say to him in this connection: so it follows that to obviate
gluttony one must take an emetic, and to preserve men from the
sin of lechery they must be united with women who have venereal
diseases?"

I must add that Lev Nikolayevich said all this in a calm, rather
weary tone of voice, but with complete conviction and not a trace
of bitterness.

✧

As I was saying good-bye to him, he again detained me and
expressed his amazement that Shmelkov (whom he liked very
much, as did I) could be imbued with such lofty aspirations while
living in circumstances and among people that were entirely
unfavorable to them (as Shmelkov himself had said), and how,
on the other hand, some people are absolutely incapable of
understanding the existence in themselves of a high spiritual
principle.

"It calls to mind the Indian proverb about the spoon that knows
not the taste of the food it holds," he added.

10 February

Today, in reference to the collection of thoughts, Lev Nikolayevich said:

"Sometimes I find it interesting and at other times it seems to me that it is too monotonous. What do you think?"

I said that inasmuch as these little booklets are meant for simple people, and as there is no other popular philosophical literature, in my opinion they are very much needed. He said nothing further about it.

Later he informed me that he intended using passages from Dostoyevsky in the collection *For Every Day*. He has read an article about him in *Russian Antiquities* and it suggested to him the idea of how much interesting material there is in the works of Dostoyevsky, and how little he has drawn on them.

Lev Nikolayevich wants to entrust the selecting of these thoughts to me, and to this end will see that I have Dostoyevsky's works tomorrow.

"Gogol, Dostoyevsky, and, strange as it may seem, Pushkin, are the writers I particularly value," said Lev Nikolayevich. "But Pushkin was still a young man, he was only beginning to be formed and had not experienced anything—unlike Chekhov—yet he had written such verses as: 'When for mortal man the tumultuous world falls silent . . .' "

Concerning Chekhov I remarked that, on the contrary, it seemed to me that he had been moving closer to Tolstoy, and I even tried to draw a parallel between them: his views on the intelligentsia in the plays for instance. Lev Nikolayevich took exception to this.

"All that is merely the consequence of a certain tendency to irony. It is not satire, which springs from a specific need, but merely irony—irony based on nothing."

Lev Nikolayevich left me to read the article on Dostoyevsky and went out for his ride.

11 February

When I arrived today I learned that Aleksandra Lvovna, who has been helping with the correspondence, is sick in bed with measles. In view of this, V. M. Feokritova, who types Tolstoy's work and Sofya Andreyevna's memoirs, asked me to stay at Yasnaya Polyana for a while, as she would not be able to cope with the work alone.

"We've been talking about you all morning, and even wanted to send for you," she said.

I replied that of course her proposal was entirely agreeable to me. I went in to see Lev Nikolayevich, gave him the booklets, and was given another one. He too said that he would be glad if I would stay, and, in view of this, gave me all the letters he had received today—more than twenty—to answer. I did not attempt to do any work during the day, as I had to go home to return the horse and to get a few of my things.

There was a doctor here from Tula who was telling Lev Nikolayevich about the "heroism" of one of his patients who, in defending his farm from assault by thieves, had killed one of them. Lev Nikolayevich was silent. He himself had led the doctor into this conversation by asking him about the four death sentences handed down in Tula. But that question seemed to be of no concern to the doctor. He left for Tula before dinner was over.

"These men who are sentenced to death for murder and robbery interest me very much," said Lev Nikolayevich. "I simply cannot comprehend how it is possible to kill a complete stranger for the sake of a hundred, or even a thousand, rubles. Though I do understand the cause of such a state. It arises from a temporary clouding of the mind. Some people simply do not believe in the kingdom of heaven or in miracles, and for those who are convinced of the futility of all that there is temporarily no need for it. And they have nothing."

✧

In the evening, when Sofya Andreyevna was showing me where I was to sleep, wash, etc., I saw a part of the house I had not seen before, where her room is located. Among other things, she showed me her experiments in painting. She was extremely amiable and said she had asked me to live there because she is going to Moscow for four days and is afraid to leave Lev Nikolayevich without constant assistance. I am even to sleep in the room next to his bedroom, to which a bell from his room is connected.

At tea Sofya Andreyevna said to Lev Nikolayevich:

"I am leaving you in Bulgakov's care."

"I don't need any care," protested Lev Nikolayevich.

I worked for a long time. Late in the evening Lev Nikolayevich came into the room.

"That's enough, that's enough. Stop now and go to bed."

I lay down on the same sofa in the "Remington room" where Gusev used to sleep. Lev Nikolayevich was sleeping in the next room and I had to walk on tiptoe so as not to wake him. I heard him coughing from time to time.

12 February

About one o'clock in the morning, when I was just beginning to fall asleep, I heard someone groaning. Not far from my room is the room of Sukhotin's son, who is ill. I had promised Tatyana Lvovna and Mikhail Sergeyevich that in case he began tossing or became delirious during the night and the nurse needed help and called me, I would go in. So I thought it was he moaning and crying out, but the nurse did not come and I continued to lie there. Finally I decided to go and have a look at the sick child. I hurriedly dressed and went down the corridor to his door, half opened it and listened. To my complete surprise, I suddenly realized that the moans and cries were not coming from Dorik's room, but from Lev Nikolayevich's bedroom.

"Is anything wrong?" I wondered, and for some reason immediately recalled Zola's dying in his sleep from charcoal fumes.

I quickly turned the door handle and went into Lev Nikolayevich's room.

He uttered a loud groan. It was dark in the room.

"Who is it? Who's there?" I heard him say.

"It's I, Lev Nikolayevich, Valentin Fyodorovich. Don't you feel well?"

"No—I'm not well—I have a pain in my side and a cough. Did I wake you?"

"No, it's all right. Shall I call Dushan Petrovich?"

"No, no, that's not necessary. Go back to bed."

"Perhaps I ought to call him, Lev Nikolayevich."

"No, it's not necessary. There's nothing he can do."

I continued to ask questions instead of instantly realizing that all I had to do was to go and get Dushan.

"No, it's not necessary! I'm better off alone. Go and sleep."

I left and went for Dushan Petrovich. He did not go in to Lev Nikolayevich at once, but lay down on the sofa in the drawing room, which is the second room from Lev Nikolayevich's bedroom. The moans began again, however, and continued to be heard from time to time, then ceased altogether and the rest of the night passed quietly.

Dushan said that this sometimes happens with Lev Nikolayevich, that he occasionally moans and cries out at night (I had not known this), but that this time, since he is ill, it is "another matter," and I did well to go for him.

Lev Nikolayevich woke up this morning not entirely well. According to Dushan, his liver is making itself felt.

He came out in his dressing gown for a little while and offered me money for expenses, which I refused, telling him that I had some. About eleven o'clock he sent to inquire whether I would be ready to write soon. When I went in he dictated the foreword to Boulanger's article on Buddhism and asked me to improve its rough style.

Sorting Lev Nikolayevich's correspondence today, I was curious to see which letters he would leave unanswered. In the majority of cases they were either bombastic, pathetic, or effusive letters which placed the sincerity of their authors in doubt.

The day was spent in work.

At dinner Lev Nikolayevich was very animated and gay.

"It's terribly revolting when old men champ their food as I do," he said, munching. "I think to myself: how disgusting it must be to watch me!"

"Old men are altogether disgusting," observed M. S. Sukhotin.

"No, I don't agree!" responded Lev Nikolayevich with a laugh.

"Well, at least I am disgusting to myself," pursued M. S.

"Of course, because you're an old man," retorted Lev Nikolayevich, "but I'm not."

"Grandfather," prattled his little granddaughter (the one they call 'Tatyana Tatyanovna'), who was sitting next to him, "did you see my little pigtail?" And she turned her head to show it to him.

"What little picture?"

"Pigtail!"

"Pigtail? Ah, that's nice! But it's so very little, even smaller than a sexton's."

Grandfather and granddaughter again ate their dessert from one plate.

"Besides being pleasant, it's very helpful," he instructed her. "They have to wash only one plate instead of two." And he added: "Some day, in the year 1975, Tatyana Mikhailovna will say: 'You remember Tolstoy, who lived a long time ago? Well, he and I used to eat from the same plate.' "

Lev Nikolayevich recounted a dream he had last night. He dreamed that he had picked up an iron stake and set off somewhere with it. And a man stole up behind him and slandered him to the people who had gathered around him, saying: "Look, there goes Tolstoy! How much harm he has brought to everyone, the heretic!" Then Lev Nikolayevich turned around and killed the man with his iron stake. But a moment later he apparently rose from the dead, because his lips moved and he spoke.

There was also conversation of a more serious nature at dinner. They talked at some length about the constitutions of various countries and of their illusory blessings.

In the evening this dear grandfather came and sat down with me on the sofa in front of my table and read to me the rough drafts of his replies to letters, so that I can more easily decipher them later. As he sat there by my side, I glanced sideways at his serious face and the clean, fluffy gray beard in the lamplight.

Someone has said that every man has his own special smell. Oddly enough, it seems to me that Tolstoy has a kind of very strong church smell compounded of cypress, the sacristy, and communion bread.

When he came in to tea, Lev Nikolayevich exclaimed:

"Heaven only knows what I've done today!"

I enumerated the various pieces of work he had done in the course of the day.

They talked a great deal about literature at tea, especially about Ibsen, the theater, and the Moscow Art Theater in particular. Lev Nikolayevich expressed a desire to see their production of *The Inspector-General*. There was more talk about d'Estournelles.

"The French, in any case, are a most sympathetic people," said Lev Nikolayevich. "They are moving ahead politically, and they gave the first impetus to revolution. Their thinkers are also remarkable: Rousseau, Pascal—brilliant, lucid. Much as I esteem Kant, he is so—not that he isn't deep, but the style is heavy."

I told Lev Nikolayevich this evening that answering the letters he receives gives one a certain satisfaction, because they are, for the most part, serious, urgent, and come from simple workers and peasants.

"Yes, one's conscience tells one that these letters must be answered," he said.

He has a sore throat and a slight fever.

"I shall cry out during the night again," he said.

He thanked me for coming in last night, saying that I was right to have done so.

13 February

Lev Nikolayevich had a peaceful night. In the morning he sent me an apple by Dushan Petrovich.

Apropos his not feeling very well these days, M. S. Sukhotin teases him:

"Mind you don't get sick while Sofya Andreyevna is away! If you do she'll come back and say: 'You see, I have only to leave and Lev Nikolayevich falls ill!' It's the breath of life to her."

"Yes, I'm getting old now!" said Lev Nikolayevich.

Referring to the prolonged hue and cry over the French visitors headed by d'Estournelles, Lev Nikolayevich observed:

"To talk of peace while opposing antimilitarism—that is the most abominable hypocrisy! Somebody wants war. Actually, the entire present-day system is supported by it. The peasant sees this, but not the learned professor."

He expressed surprise at my handwriting today.

"How you write! No, really, it's so precise and elegant, it's a pleasure to look at it! I wish I could write like that."

As he was about to retire, he said:

"I'll try not to disturb you tonight."

He evidently expected and feared some unpleasantness.

✦

A word or two about the character of the correspondence that Lev Nikolayevich receives. I have observed that requests for autographs come mostly from abroad.

... Besides the so-called "good letters," that is, those that are serious, sincere, and more or less original, Lev Nikolayevich receives a number of "begging letters" (appeals for material help), which he leaves unanswered, as well as "proselytizing letters" from those attempting to convert him to Orthodoxy or other accepted views.

14 February

It is worth noting that Lev Nikolayevich often thinks about
V. G. Chertkov. Today at dinner he mentioned him in connection
with letters received from him and the accurate text of his,
Toystoy's, article which appeared in the newspapers under the
title *The Last Stage of My Life.* And Lev Nikolayevich often
inquires whether I get letters from Krëkshino, and asks me to tell
him what they say.

One trait that is characteristic of him: at dinner, when the dessert
was served, he said:

"Even this cake is an expression of insane luxury. In my day
we got along with plain pastry straws, or various kinds of jelly
puddings, or pancakes. Such a cake as this was served only for a
big name-day party."

After dinner today Lev Nikolayevich, M. S. Sukhotin, and I had
an animated conversation about refusing military service, which
came about because of my prospective refusal. Mikhail Sergeyevich
and I had begun the conversation earlier in the day when walking
in the garden; we had argued about whether I ought to postpone
my refusal as long as possible, taking advantage of the right of
deferment granted me when I was at the university, or whether I
ought to leave the university at once, where I am now enrolled only
nominally, and thereby become liable to being called up and to
all the consequences of refusing. I took my stand upon the moral
necessity of the latter position; Sukhotin, however, tried to dissuade
me: "Don't be in a hurry; take your time; don't destroy yourself,
the laws might be changed."

I decided to ask Lev Nikolayevich which of us is right.

We talked for a long time. Lev Nikolayevich categorically
refused to express an opinion or give advice, saying that a man must
decide such questions for himself. He attached no importance to
the consequences of refusing (such as the influence it has on
others, etc.). "I cannot"—therein are all a man's reasons for refusing.

Among other things, he said: "I am unable to imagine the

feelings of a man—like you or Sergei Bulygin—taking such a step. For me, an old man, it would hold no fears; I have only a few more months to live, a year perhaps, but for a young man so much lies ahead!"

He also said that for him prison would be a release from the painful situation in which he now finds himself. It is impossible to convey the entire conversation, but it stirred me deeply. And they both seemed to be in a rather elated mood. At any rate, when I went back to my "Remington room" I still heard the sound of their voices in conversation. During their chess game, however, the usual silence reigned.

At tea they talked of various matters. At one moment Lev Nikolayevich sat staring into a corner, then suddenly came out with:

"How disgusting it is—that gramophone with its horn!"

Everyone was of the same opinion, and the "invention of civilization" again came in for considerable disparagement.

"How do you feel?" he asked me.

"Fine!"

"You are the only one of us who is cheerful—you and Dushan. Well, good night!"

15 February

✧

Lev Nikolayevich said today, speaking of the thoughts chosen for the little booklets of the collection *For Every Day,* that it was very interesting, joyous work for him and that he no longer doubted that it was needed.

During the morning I had to go into his room several times for one reason or another while he was working, and I apologized. With his characteristic tact he protested:

"What do you mean! It is I who should be afraid of disturbing you, not you me!"

Before dinner there was a visitor, an elderly gentleman with a resounding double name, who asked Lev Nikolayevich to read a poem he had written and to satisfy him that it did not have a "morbid tenor." Of course he only tired Lev Nikolayevich. He kept talking of his own affairs and was reluctant to leave.

At dinner Lev Nikolayevich spoke of a story by Leonid Andreyev which was published in *Russia's Morning*.[4]

"It's written in some kind of incomprehensible language that is not Russian—must be Spanish. It's all about a priest who climbs into a locomotive, opens the throttle, and drives off. I consider Kuprin the most talented of today's writers—and that's because his trend is less mad."

They discussed Izmailov's parodies of contemporary writers.

"Izmailov writes well," remarked Lev Nikolayevich.

✧

16 February

✧

When he came into the dining room for dinner, Lev Nikolayevich said that he had been reading Gogol's *Dead Souls* with M. S. Sukhotin's son, Mikhail. Speaking of Gogol he said:

"It's remarkable that when he describes something it comes out badly, but as soon as his characters begin to talk—it's good. We've been reading about Sobakevich. Really!" And Lev Nikolayevich laughed merrily. " 'One procurator is a good man, but that one—a swine! . . . And the governor? A crook! . . .' " And again he broke into genial laughter.

✧

They were talking about dreams. Lev Nikolayevich told about dreaming that he was at a ball, waltzing with a certain lady and feeling embarrassed because he was dancing in an old-fashioned way while everyone else was dancing in a new style.

"Dreams are an amazing phenomenon," said Lev Nikolayevich. "Pascal was absolutely right when he said in one of his maxims that if dreams were coherent we should not know what was the dream and what was reality."

Today Lev Nikolayevich received a long, fervid letter from a

student at the University of Kiev, Boris Mandzhos, imploring him
to leave Yasnaya Polyana and the unnatural conditions in which
he is living here.

"Dear, good Lev Nikolayevich," he wrote in part, "give your
life for man and mankind—perform the last act that remains
to be done in this world, the one that will make you immortal
in the minds of humanity. . . . Renounce your title, distribute your
property among your relations and the poor, leave without a kopeck
and go, making your way from city to city as a beggar. . . . Deny
yourself if you cannot deny those who are close to you in the
family circle."

Lev Nikolayevich sent the following letter of reply to Mandzhos,
asking me not to mention it to anyone.

> Your letter touched me deeply. What you advise me to do
> is exactly what I dream of doing but thus far have been unable
> to do. There are many reasons for this (but sparing myself is
> not one of them), the main one being that such a step should
> in no way affect others. That is not within our power and should
> not guide our actions. One can and should do this only when
> it becomes necessary, and not for some hypothetical, external
> purpose, but to satisfy the requirements of the soul, and when it
> becomes as morally impossible to remain in the old conditions
> as it is physically impossible not to cough when one cannot
> breathe. I am not far from such a position, and drawing nearer
> and nearer to it every day.
>
> What you advise me to do: to renounce my social position
> and property and distribute it to whoever has the right to count
> on it after my death, was done by me twenty-five years ago. But
> the fact that I continue to live in the family with my wife and
> daughter, in shameful, appalling conditions of luxury while
> surrounded by poverty, has been a source of ceaseless and ever-
> increasing torment to me, and there is not a day in which I do
> not think about following your advice.
>
> I thank you very much for your letter. This letter to you

will be known to only one other person. By the same token,
I ask you not to show it to anyone.

With love,

Lev Nikolayevich

Evening was drawing in when I went to Lev Nikolayevich's
study to get something. The letter from the Kiev student happened
to be mentioned. He was standing in front of the big window, one
hand thrust into his belt and his head thrown back, pensively
gazing into the darkening garden.

"If it were not for my daughter, if it were not for Sasha, I would
have left! I would have left!"

I could not restrain myself and told Lev Nikolayevich what
was in my mind regarding these continual demands made on him
to leave Yasnaya Polyana. It seems to me that those who make
such demands lack confidence in him. They ought to learn to trust
him. Personally, having acquainted myself in some detail with his
writings of the past few years, I can only feel that whatever Tolstoy
may do is for the best, that it is all necessary for him, consequently
all is as it should be. If he remains at Yasnaya Polyana, then I believe
that this is as it should be; if he were to leave, then I would
believe that that was as it should be.

Lev Nikolayevich listened very attentively and, it seemed to
me, sympathetically to my tirade. He gave no outward expression
of his attitude toward it, if one discounts the characteristic
exclamations of surprise and sympathy that several times escaped
him: "H-ha! . . . H-ha!"

Contrary to custom, his reply to the student Mandzhos was not
typed on the Remington in several copies. I made a copy by hand,
which Lev Nikolayevich signed, and kept the original myself.

18 February

This is the day of St. Leo, pope of Rome—Lev Nikolayevich's name day. But in the house of a man who has been excommunicated it would be rather strange to expect this day to be different from any other. Nevertheless, there was a cake at dinner—a "name-day cake," according to Sofya Andreyevna. This is probably a survival of former traditions still observed by the family.

Lev Nikolayevich's first words when he came to the table were addressed to Mikhail Sukhotin.

"Well, how are things going with Chichikov?"

And they again talked of Gogol's work, which young Sukhotin is reading.

Lev Nikolayevich was reminded of an "abusive" letter he had received today, and told them about it. I too had read the letter. Its author berated Tolstoy for six pages and then, in a postscript, declared: "But you're a good old man for all that."

It was rather like Sobakevich's expression about the procurator, only in reverse.

Lev Nikolayevich was interested in the question of just why the author of this letter had taken such a malicious attitude toward him. As it turned out, this was not the first letter he had received from him.

Tatyana Lvovna reminded Lev Nikolayevich that his correspondent, who had visited them in the past, was a poet.

"Ah! Now I understand!" exclaimed Lev Nikolayevich. "That bears out the Latin apothegm: *irritabilis gens poetarum.*"

After dinner Lev Nikolayevich read aloud Izmailov's witty parody of a work by Leonid Andreyev.

As he signed the notification for registered letters this evening, he shook his head ruefully.

"So many notifications, and such futile letters!"

In addition to my other duties, I am now responsible for distributing booklets and money to wayfarers and beggars.

19 February

Lev Nikolayevich had three visitors this morning: a young man who, try as he might, could not explain why he had come, a "newspaper employee" asking for money to get to Petersburg, and a teacher banished by the administration—also seeking material aid.

Later there arrived an old acquaintance of the Tolstoys', Prince D. D. Obolensky, a good-natured, talkative old man. Lev Nikolayevich calls him Job because of the numerous crushing blows fate has dealt him: the loss of a large fortune, the premature, and in certain instances tragic, deaths of several of his children, and so on. Obolensky now works as a journalist and, incidentally, writes about his visits to Yasnaya Polyana in *The Russian Word,* which pays him something.

They discussed certain legal cases in which Lev Nikolayevich is interested, and the Tula attorney, B. O. Goldenblat, who is handling the cases. Obolensky read aloud the speech against the Estimate of the Synod, which was given in the Duma by the Constitutional-Democrat Karaulov. It was a strong, sincere speech, which everyone, including Lev Nikolayevich, liked.

Today one of his correspondents wrote to Lev Nikolayevich: "And, in addition, I should like you to send me two books, one on experimental and one on organic chemistry." In another letter, from a woman, we read: "I will tell you my secret, a secret I have cherished for almost three years: I want, want desperately to learn to be a writer."

20 February

This morning Lev Nikolayevich complained that his work on the preface to Boulanger's article on Buddhism was going badly.

"I now have such interesting work to do on the booklets *For Every Day,* and this preface distracts and hinders me dreadfully."

I must note that Lev Nikolayevich has rewritten it six or seven times already.

"I'm an old fogy," he said at dinner, "one of those men who if they don't feel like writing, or aren't in the mood, write worse than a district clerk."

"You mean that you require inspiration, a visitation from your Muse?" asked M. S. Sukhotin.

"Yes, the need to write must be irresistible, like a cough."

Lev Nikolayevich returned from his morning walk accompanied by a Norwegian journalist, Levin, who was formerly a Russian subject.

"Here is a friend of Björnson's!" he said, introducing him.

✦

Besides the Norwegian, the Tula attorney Goldenblat came with his two children to discuss certain legal matters and Lev Nikolayevich's prospective visit to one of the men who has been imprisoned. He left after dinner.

There was a long and interesting conversation this evening between Lev Nikolayevich and the Norwegian journalist.

"You have a real paradise there in Norway!" said Lev Nikolayevich. "I think I'll go there. And, you know, it's good that you have an unfavorable climate—it keeps the parasites away. It's true that you have few tourists, isn't it? Now, if only those parasites don't come!"

Levin enlarged on the superiority of the Norwegian laws, and on the fact that poverty, being prohibited by law, is nonexistent in Norway.

"Well, that's not what attracts me," said Lev Nikolayevich. "From what you were saying, there is nothing in the nature of a religious movement to be found among the people, and everything is controlled by law, in other words, by the police, as in the recent instance of violence. And I don't believe any good can come from the police. No, I won't go to Norway!"

Levin admitted that everything was controlled by the police, including the recent instance of violence, but insisted that the Norwegian police are fine, courteous men.

"Look at the relations of our police with children. Not only are the children not afraid of them, they are very fond of them. If, for instance, a policeman encounters a lost child, he buys him candy and amuses him. I myself saw a policeman taking a little boy to the police station, and the child was hopping after him on one foot."

"No, I won't go there," declared Lev Nikolayevich once more.

"And now I'll tell you something, after which you will hardly entertain any further wish to go there," interjected M. S. Sukhotin. "If, for instance, a thief takes to his heels," he said, turning to Levin, "will the police chase him and drag him off to the police station?"

"They will," replied the Norwegian, somewhat confused and taken aback.

"Well, now will you go to Norway?" asked Sukhotin, again addressing Lev Nikolayevich.

"No, no, I won't go! Here you are boasting about everything there, and in Shanghai, where there is probably a larger population than you have in your entire country, the Chinese quarter of the city gets along very nicely without any police," said Lev Nikolayevich.

At eleven o'clock the visitor departed, pleased with everything and grateful. Lev Nikolayevich remained in the dining room talking with Mikhail Sergeyevich about the dreadful catastrophe at Khodynka at the time of the coronation in 1896.[5]

"I have wanted to write something on this subject, it is very interesting to me. The psychology of the event is so complex. The panic-stricken crowd, the children trying to escape as best they could by pushing with their heads and shoulders, the merchant Morozov crying out that he would pay eighteen thousand rubles to be rescued. Why exactly eighteen thousand? And above all, that abrupt change: first everyone happy, in a festive mood, and then—that tragedy, those crushed bodies—horrible!"

A silence fell.

Lev Nikolayevich was sitting in a chair by one of the windows, his head thrown back, reflecting.

"It's amazing," he said after a while as he stood up to go to bed. "It would appear that the peasants have taken to being rude to me. Today, for instance, three of them failed to bow to me, though I had greeted them. They always used to bow to me. And do you know what they said to one of the men who did not take off his cap when I greeted him? Hm?" he asked Mikhail Sergeyevich as he went to the door. "They said: 'Don't take it off, don't take off your cap or the lice will crawl out!' That's to take their revenge," he added with a laugh and went out.

He looked terribly tired. Visitors invariably exhausted him.

21 February

This morning two men came to see Lev Nikolayevich, one an elderly man, an Old Believer,* and the other a young peasant who came on some personal business. At seven o'clock in the evening, by the fast train, the Molostvovs arrived: he is Marshal of the Nobility for the Tetyushy district of Kazan, and his wife is investigating the Russian sectarian movement. Each of the visitors talked with Lev Nikolayevich of his own interests. . . . Later the Khodynka episode came up. This was a particularly welcome subject, as Molostvov had witnessed the event. With his uncle, General Ber, who was in charge of all the festivities, he had been close to the Tsar's pavilion.

At tea Lev Nikolayevich was dejected and remarked, apropos of what I do not recall, that it was hard to live in the world.

"Why should it be hard for you?" asked Sofya Andreyevna. "Everybody loves you."

"It's still hard!" retorted Lev Nikolayevich. "And why shouldn't it be hard for me? Because of this fine food, perhaps?"

"Of course not! I said because everybody loves you."

---

* A large sect that separated itself from the Russian Orthodox Church in the seventeenth century. They took their name from their refusal to accept the new books of service as edited and corrected by Patriarch Nikon. Translator's Note.

"I suppose," he rejoined, "that everyone is thinking: 'The damned old fool, he says one thing and does another; he lives quite differently. It's time he croaked—and even that will be hypocritical.' And it's absolutely true. I often receive such letters— and those are my friends, the ones who write like that. They are right. Every day when I go out, there stand a half-dozen ragged beggars, and I mount my horse and ride off followed by my coachman!"

Molostvov, a very kind, simple man, tried to comfort Lev Nikolayevich, but then gave up, evidently feeling that it was not a matter for consolation.

In the evening, reading one of the letters I had written in which I had expressed myself in rather sharp, candid terms about the government, church superstitions, and so on, Lev Nikolayevich said:

"Oh, oh! This could be bad for you. How is it you aren't afraid? And it might be unpleasant for your mother."

I pointed out to him that the letter would be sealed.

Today Lev Nikolayevich completed the general plan for all thirty booklets of *For Every Day*. I had prepared for him the booklet *The Temptation of Vanity*.[6]

I sent off a great many letters and five packets of money to the amount of sixty rubles. The money is sent by Lev Nikolayevich to men in prison who share his views. To each of these men he sends five rubles a month. Today the money for two months was sent to six men. Lev Nikolayevich also helps the families of several of them. The money comes from his royalties for performances of his plays *The Power of Darkness* and *The Fruits of Enlightenment* in the Imperial theaters. Originally Lev Nikolayevich wanted to refuse these fees, but when he was informed that in that case the money would be used for the development of the Imperial ballet, he decided to accept the royalties. They amount to two or three thousand rubles a year, and the entire sum goes to help those who are in prison, peasants who have lost everything in a fire, and other needy persons.

22 February

✧

"I have just been thinking," said Lev Nikolayevich, coming in to tea, "how *everything remains*. And this applies to all people equally. Everything that Tanya does remains because it is reflected not only in Tanichka, but even in Verochka."

Verochka is Tatyana Lvovna's maid, who grew up at Yasnaya Polyana.

Later he talked about a letter from a certain teacher.

"He writes that the clergy interferes in his activity. I think that the work of a teacher is so essential that nothing can take its place, and that he can work successfully in spite of the opposition of the clergy."

He spoke again about his article for Boulanger, saying that it was going badly, yet the subject was so important it required that the article be well handled.

They played the gramophone: Mikhailova and Varya Panina singing, and Troyanovsky playing the balalaika.

"Makes you feel like dancing!" exclaimed Lev Nikolayevich, listening to Troyanovsky's playing of a *hopak*.

Everyone liked Panina's singing too. I recalled something that Lev Nikolayevich had said recently:

"It's amazing—gypsy music, and far from being appreciated." They lingered over Panina longer than the others. Listening to her powerful, almost masculine voice, very subtly interpreting song after song, the audience was involuntarily captivated.

✧

When the music was over there was a conversation on the advantages and disadvantages of the gramophone and mechanical musical instruments in general. Lev Nikolayevich praised the *"Mignonne"* player piano, which mechanically reproduces the playing of pianists. He had heard it in Moscow.

"The disadvantages lie in its monotony: the pieces all sound alike. A live artist plays with variety and nuance."

In this connection he said:

"The artist ought to bring more photography to his work."

When Lev Nikolayevich was about to go to bed, I took to his study the letters for him to sign.

"I received a letter from Paris, from Halperin-Kaminsky," he said, "and now I am waiting for the play he has sent me, *La Barricade*, by Paul Bourget, and the reviews of it. It advocates violence. And speaks of your humble servant. Yes, they are still far from nonresistance. It's always like that. When it comes to nonresistance, they always find it . . ."

"A stumbling block?" I suggested.

"A stumbling block!" he agreed.

23 *February*

A merchant from Samara was here, a big, black-bearded man, very serious but childishly naive. He is concerned about the problem of reward and punishment in the next world. After talking to him a little, Lev Nikolayevich turned him over to me.

"He looks after my affairs," he said. "All that I am saying to you he knows too. And he will give you some books."

The merchant departed visibly relieved after his talk with Lev Nikolayevich (he had been tormented by fear of punishment after death), and with a signed photograph of him. He had absolutely insisted on its being autographed: "I bestow on So-and-So." It was the "I bestow" that he particularly wanted on the photograph, and Lev Nikolayevich obliged him.

After lunch I accompanied Lev Nikolayevich on his horseback ride. We rode to the village of Osvannikovo, about six versts from Yasnaya, to visit M. A. Schmidt, who is ill. In the beginning he rode at a walk, and I thought we should continue that way the whole time—but no! Half the time, and especially on the way back, he rode at such a brisk trot on his splendid Délire that I had to gallop to keep up with him. He sits his horse beautifully—erect, his right hand on his hip and his left hand holding the reins. It is a splendid sight to see him flying into the wind, his horse kicking up the powdered snow and his gray beard shining in the sun.

In the evening, when Lev Nikolayevich was still resting in his room, M. S. Sukhotin and Sofya Andreyevna jested about how he liked to ride fast and show off the skill of his horsemanship, and that he had no doubt wanted to impress me. His ride today has tired him, however. He has not been feeling well, besides which, his right knee is giving him pain for some reason. Dushan fears that this is the beginning of an attack of embolism from which Lev Nikolayevich suffers.

After tea he and Mikhail Sergeyevich read the French articles on Bourget's *La Barricade,* which came today.

He also received a beautiful letter from a young girl in Pyatigorsk. She had written to him not long ago saying that she wanted to take poison and had already bought some carbolic acid. Lev Nikolayevich answered her letter and sent her some books. Now she has written to say that three days after receiving his letter she had commenced to vacillate, not knowing what to do, but that in the end she had thrown away the carbolic acid and is now beginning to believe that life is not entirely evil, and that the good toward which man strives is attainable. The letter is very sincere, and gives one no cause to think that there is anything untruthful in it.

24 February

Lev Nikolayevich is not well. Though he took a walk in the morning, he has not gone out again and did not eat lunch.

A ladies' tailor, the author of a manual on tailoring, arrived from Petersburg. He spent the whole day here and wore everyone out. He made himself at home in one of the downstairs rooms, was here for dinner in the evening, and sent postcards to all his acquaintants with greetings from Yasnaya Polyana. He kept trying to induce Sofya Andreyevna to accept as a gift a silk muff he had made, but she categorically refused and, incidentally, let him know that personally she considered only fur muffs suitable. He undertook to teach Tatyana Lvovna to work buttonholes. Finally we did not know what to do with the man, who was reluctant to understand that he had sufficiently imposed on his hosts' time.

In the end Lev Nikolayevich called the tailor into the little drawing room and a brief conversation took place between them. As Lev Nikolayevich related it afterward, he had said to the tailor that every man has his own job—he as well as the tailor—and that there was no particular necessity for them to prevent one another from getting on with it. The tall, foppish figure of the tailor glided out of the drawing room and promptly vanished from Yasnaya Polyana.

A letter came from Moscow from Malakhieva, a contributor to *Russian Thought,* in which she asks Lev Nikolayevich whether he will permit the philosopher Lev Shestov to visit Yasnaya Polyana, if only briefly. After consulting Mikhail Sergeyevich and questioning me as to what I know of Shestov as a writer, Lev Nikolayevich asked me to write and tell Malakhieva that he would be willing to receive him. It must be said that in making this decision he was definitely influenced by the fact that Shestov has taken issue with him in his writings, as Lev Nikolayevich already knew.

At the table, the subject of farm machinery happened to come up. Recalling a worthless article on labor in *Essays on Political Economy* by Professor Zheleznov, who writes, among other things, that Tolstoy seems to advocate a return to the use of primitive farm implements, I asked Lev Nikolayevich whether he is in sympathy with the widespread use of agricultural machines.

"Yes, of course!" he replied. "How could one not be in sympathy with it? I only say that they ought to be introduced gradually."

His idea was understandable to me: what he meant was that before devising expensive agricultural machines it is necessary to take care of the more vital needs of the peasants—mainly to allot land to them.

25 February

Lev Nikolayevich took a walk again this morning, but he neither ate lunch nor went for his customary two-o'clock ride. He remained in his study working even more assiduously than usual.

At tea Sofya Andreyevna began reciting Tyuchev's poetry. Lev Nikolayevich prompted and encouraged her and recited some verses himself.

"If a poem is good," he said, "every word is in the right place."

They reminisced about Tyuchev, whom they had known, as had M. S. Sukhotin.

"Today," Lev Nikolayevich went on to say, "after reading the newspaper from beginning to end, I am forced to conclude that the two most important events in the entire world are the death of Komissarzhevskaya and the anniversary of Savinaya. Great actresses, both of them—but how awful! To think that language, which ought to serve for the transmission of ideas, should be so perverted!"

These so-called "begging letters" that Lev Nikolayevich receives are amazing. One young girl writes to ask for a hundred rubles for her wedding, because "being the daughter of an officer, tradition requires" thus and so. Then some young man asks for a hundred rubles to prepare for the examinations to qualify as a volunteer noncommissioned officer, and so on.

There was not much for the post today. Lev Nikolayevich finished the introduction to Boulanger's article, and I have already sent it to Posse.

26 February

Lev Nikolayevich is not well. He neither ate lunch nor went out for his walk. As yesterday, he did an unusual amount of work.

Three people came this morning to have a look at Tolstoy, but after waiting in vain near the porch, they went away.

Sofya Andreyevna put on a puppet show for her grandchildren after dinner. A booth was set up in the hall, playbills were typed on the Remington, and the gramophone served as the orchestra. The play, composed by Sofya Andreyevna herself, was called *The Lost Girl*. Concealed behind a curtain, she operated the puppets and spoke all the lines of the female characters. M. S. Sukhotin spoke those of the male characters.

As soon as they put on the gramophone, even before the play had begun, Lev Nikolayevich started to leave, but then he stayed to watch the little spectators decorously enter to the festive strains of a march and take their seats in front of the miniature stage.

The curtain went up and the play began. "Papa" and "Mamma" were cautioning their daughter Liza against going into the woods, where she might meet with harm from "bandits." Lev Nikolayevich went up close to the stage, and screwing up his eyes peered at the moving figures of the performers. Then he went to his room, only to return a moment later carrying a rather large box. He sat down at some distance, hastily opened the box, and took out binoculars, which he trained on the stage. When I glanced back at him again he was slapping his knee and laughing merrily. A few minutes later he went out, taking the binoculars with him.

Sofya Andreyevna was extremely tired after the performance and lay down on the couch in the hall during tea.

"Now I begin to appreciate Komissarzhevskaya," said Lev Nikolayevich, pointing to his wife.

Everyone laughed and began talking about the performance. They mentioned that the actors had jumped over walls to get onto the stage (they could hardly have done otherwise, as the wires were attached to their heads).

"Now at the Moscow Art Theater the actors are confined to the set," observed Lev Nikolayevich jestingly, "but here the play is so fascinating that they can leap over walls without distracting the audience's attention or spoiling the impression."

Lev Nikolayevich received a letter from N. N. Gusev containing an extract from a letter written by the peasant Kalachev. This

passage, which was about life and God, so delighted Lev
Nikolayevich that he asked me to bring the letter and read it aloud.

"There you are—that's what peasants talk about now!
Professors don't talk like that, let alone bishops."

They were discussing education, and Lev Nikolayevich said:

"All that is given to a man by education is insignificant compared
with his character—it's only a thousandth part. Of course, I am
judging by myself—a man always interprets everything subjectively."

I have prepared and submitted to Lev Nikolayevich the fourth
booklet of thoughts: *The Superstition of Inequality*.[7]

27 February

Some Kuban Cossacks have come from the Caucasus to consult
Lev Nikolayevich about what attitude to take toward military
service. They are fine men, and Lev Nikolayevich liked them very
much. About one of them, a remarkably capable preacher, Lev
Nikolayevich later said to me:

"In him the religious feeling is combined with a desire for fame
and the superstition that it is possible to arrange other people's
lives."

There arrived by post the de luxe edition—outwardly at least—
of a biography of L. N. Tolstoy by Sergeyenko and Molostvo,
containing unsuitable illustrations and many errors, such as a
beautifully executed drawing of the Tolstoy house in Moscow on
the cover, with the inscription: "View of the park at Yasnaya
Polyana." In the section describing Tolstoy's youth there is a
vignette depicting naked women floating in the clouds that encircle
the head of the twenty-year-old Tolstoy!

The book was shown to Lev Nikolayevich. He was quite
indifferent to its defects.

"Never mind, let it go," he said. "It's handsome, that's what
most people want."

Later, when he had examined it more closely, he said:

"It's incredibly bad! They've excluded everything spiritual, and what is left is materialistic, tasteless, and vulgar."

✧

A former sailor, a revolutionary who took part in the uprising in the south, came to see Lev Nikolayevich the other day. He asked for fifteen rubles in order to reach the Rumanian or Bulgarian border and get out of Russia. I was not very much impressed with the man, but Lev Nikolayevich, who walked in the park with him, was drawn to him and took a lively interest in helping him. He sent him to the Chertkovs' farm to rest and collected from members of the household the necessary sum, for which the man is to come tomorrow. I mention this incident to show the absence of any dogmatism in Tolstoy.

✧

28 February

The Cossacks came again in the morning to say good-bye, also the revolutionary, who was delighted with the help Lev Nikolayevich had given him. Besides these people, a man and wife, Ukrainian landowners, came to see Lev Nikolayevich. They are very nice people from the steppes and arrived all dressed up and quite excited. Lev Nikolayevich received them in the drawing room. As far as I was able to judge, the discussion was a serious and important one for the couple. They came out of the drawing room looking very moved and in tears.[8]

Lev Nikolayevich's health is somewhat improved today. He went for a sleigh ride after lunch, and that is a good sign.

Today some poetry was received which was sent to him from Tobolsk. At first he thought it was from the penal-servitude warden, and he was about to write him that he was not engaged in reviewing and publishing verse. But the letter proved to be from a convict, and one who was in need of money, so he decided to send the poems to a magazine. At my suggestion he sent them to Yakubovich-Melshin at *Russian Wealth*.[9]

Incidentally, Lev Nikolayevich had to send off three parcels of the banned publication *Reprints*.[10] He asked me to get the books together, but wanted to write the addresses himself so as not to involve me. However, I did not want him to get into difficulties.

Shrovetide is reflected in the letters Lev Nikolayevich has been receiving. Today one of his correspondents writes: "A joyous Shrovetide to you, and best wishes for a merry mood and the best of health. Eat fish and little hot pancakes in good health!"

Then there was this touching letter:

"I beseech you most humbly, Lev Nikolayevich, I am a poor man, an orphan, and since I have no means at all, I beseech you, please, Lev Nikolayevich, to take me on as a pupil at least. I have heard so much about your very wise teachings and your great kindness. Therefore I beseech you, Lev Nikolayevich, will you not remove the blindfold from my eyes, for I am now in such darkness it would seem that I cannot see the light."

I wrote to this man that Lev Nikolayevich takes no pupils, that people who share his views learn about them from his works, and that I was sending him some books.

Lev Nikolayevich approved of my letter. Often, when giving me letters to answer, he does not note even briefly what the answer should be, but just writes on the envelope: "V.F." or "V.F. answer this." Later, of course, he reads my answers.

1 March

"I have received a letter with some verses," Lev Nikolayevich said to me in the morning, as we were going through the day's correspondence, "and I wanted to leave it unanswered, but it is weighing on my conscience. It's from a young man, an eighteen-year-old peasant. So please write something to him."

Today more poems turned up and Lev Nikolayevich himself wrote a long letter on "the pernicious epidemic of verse-making."

In the evening, perhaps in connection with Yarotsky's book, Lev Nikolayevich said:

"Most people get into such a rut in life, and they find it terribly difficult to get out of it. Even when it is necessary they generally don't care to do it—and so they remain in the rut. It is the same in the sphere of religion, and also in science. Dushan Petrovich got into just such a rut in his attitude toward Jews, and he and I were talking about this today," he added with a smile.

I have not yet mentioned this sad defect in Dushan Petrovich—his anti-Semitism. For some incomprehensible reason, this man, whose views and personal life might serve as an example to every one of us, harbors feelings of ill-will toward a whole people. They say that this is a result of impressions formed during a childhood spent in a Jewish district in Hungary. In any case, I have never been able to understand this strange weakness of his, and neither has Lev Nikolayevich nor any of his associates. More than once Lev Nikolayevich has told Dushan that his dislike of Jews is the material God gave him for working on himself and overcoming this defect in himself. "If it were not for this, Dushan would be a saint," he has often said of his friend.

Dushan Petrovich did not let Lev Nikolayevich's remark about his being in a rut go unanswered. He argued with great obstinacy.

"How is it possible to hate, or to dislike, a whole people?" Lev Nikolayevich said. "I understand that it is possible instinctively to feel a dislike for certain shortcomings of Jews, but it is impossible to condemn all of them: on the contrary, you should try to rid yourself of this feeling of ill-will as of a fault in yourself. Otherwise you will be showing sympathy and support for such misanthropic societies as the Union of the Russian People, which organizes Jewish pogroms and that sort of thing. The Jews are oppressed, they are discriminated against, and you should not blame them for participating in every protest against the government, for taking part in a revolution. If I myself have seen special traits in the Russian people, have singled out Russian peasants as having especially attractive characteristics, I am sorry. I am sorry and I am ready to repudiate this. You can find sympathetic traits in any people. The Jews have outstanding qualities, their talent for music, for instance. You say that their bad characteristics predominate, that they are more dissolute than other people, as proved by statistics, but I believe that these statistics are false; statistics on greater or less morality are at variance with religious feeling. What does the word 'Jew' mean? For me it is absolutely meaningless. I know only that there are *people*. I know what the map shows— that Jews live here, Germans here, Frenchmen here, but dividing people into different nations seems to me fantastic. I can no more be conscious of this than I can be conscious of the fourth dimension in geometry. Ill-feeling can exist only toward an individual. If you do not like Jews, the only way to make them better, the only expedient against them, is to give them equal rights, make them equal with everyone else, since, I repeat, they are discriminated against. But it is not even a matter of the consequences, but of the requirements of religious ideology. For me to agree with you would be exactly like repudiating everything I believe in, renouncing what is my principal conviction, which is that all men are equal. And I cannot understand how you, with your views, with your life, can take such an attitude to an entire people. I think that you have only to want to rid yourself of such a feeling as a defect."

Dushan Petrovich continued to argue, disagreed with Lev Nikolayevich, and evidently held to his own opinion.

2 *March*

✧

I have received a letter from V. A. Posse in which he writes that Bitner, the editor of *The Herald of Knowledge,* is prepared to publish my work, *The Christian Ethic.* I read the letter to Lev Nikolayevich and he advised me to send the work to Bitner, which I shall do in a few days.

Lev Nikolayevich is very weak today. After breakfast he lay down and slept. He went around in his sleeveless black peasant coat all day, as he felt chilly.

After dinner the philosopher Lev Shestov arrived from Moscow and stayed till ten o'clock. He was alone with Lev Nikolayevich in his study for a long time, perhaps an hour and a half.

"We talked as you can talk only when you are two—three would have been a crowd," said Lev Nikolayevich, citing the English proverb.

His guest apparently failed to impress him, however. Later he said of him:

"He is not a philosopher, but a man of letters."

Nor did I observe any special satisfaction or spiritual uplift in Shestov as a result of his conversation with Tolstoy.

"Is it really possible to discuss everything in such a short time?" he said in answer to my question as to what impression Lev Nikolayevich had made on him.

In a word, it was a case of what is called "incompatible natures."

3 March

✧

When he came into the "Remington room" this morning, Lev Nikolayevich said of Shestov:

"Some people think for themselves, others for the public. He thinks for the public."

To my mind this is extraordinarily apt.

✧

After lunch Lev Nikolayevich went out on horseback. I accompanied him. This time he rode at a walk and only on the way back, as we approached Yasnaya Polyana, did he ride at a trot for a while, and this had unfortunate consequences: afterward he was ill again. "One is tempted," he said later.

✧

There was a new face at dinner. Sergei Lvovich, Lev Nikalayevich's son, has come from Moscow for only one day. In the evening Lev Nikolayevich played cards with him and his two daughters.

At tea they talked at length about the trial of the revolutionist Chaikovsky,[11] with whom several of those present are acquainted.

4 March

The pianist A. B. Goldenweiser has arrived. And from the Tambov province, the religious peasant, Andrei Tarasov, whom Lev Nikolayevich liked so much, has come to visit him. The peasant has gone off to Telyatinki to stay for a short time.

There was a letter this morning from the Bulgarian Shopov. He had refused to accept military service because of his religious convictions and has been committed to "the worst prison in Bulgaria." Lev Nikolayevich wrote to him himself immediately.

"How I would like to join up with such people!" said the Tambov peasant to Lev Nikolayevich, after I had told him about Shopov.

"I would myself," Lev Nikolayevich said to him, "but, you see, you and I have not been found worthy!"

When I first saw Lev Nikolayevich this morning, he was lying on the couch in the drawing room sorting his correspondence. When I asked him how he felt, he said:

"Quite poorly; my leg hurts and I feel weak. It is all due to our ride yesterday. Do you remember how I put my horse to a trot going up the hill? It is because of that—it was then that I felt I was getting tired, because of having to rise up in the stirrups."

He said the same thing to Goldenweiser when he saw him later, adding (as he has said before) that physical indisposition has a bad effect on one's spiritual mood.

"If my stomach is upset," he said with a laugh, "I keep running into dog excrement everywhere when I'm out walking, so that even a walk is spoiled for me, but if, on the other hand, I am in good health, I see the clouds, the forest, beautiful places."

When he was telling Goldenweiser about Lev Shestov's visit, Lev Nikolayevich pursued his discussion of philosophers who think for themselves and those who think for the public. In the first group he put Schopenhauer and Kant, and in the second, Vladimir Solovyov[12] and Khomyakov.[13]

Lev Nikolayevich came in to see me before breakfast. I was sitting on the sofa in front of the desk and the granddaughter of the "great writer of the land of Russia," the charming little "Tatyana Tatyanovna," or "the treasure," as her parents still call her, stood on the sofa behind me tickling my neck. When Lev Nikolayevich came in, she began to coax him in her high little voice and cunning way.

"Grandfather, sit down on the little sofa! Sit down on the sofa, Grandfather!"

She evidently wanted very much to slip her hands under his collar and tickle his neck. But Grandfather begged off because he had not yet had breakfast.

After breakfast, in spite of not feeling well, he went out for a drive with Goldenweiser.

✧

In the evening Lev Nikolayevich came into the "Remington room."

"I have been reading the Strakhov[14] book which you brought," he said to Goldenweiser. "I have only read 'Spirit and Matter.' It is really a wonderful book. It will be one of the most remarkable works. People just don't know about him yet. He is a philosopher indeed, and a philosopher who thinks and writes for himself. And he touches on the most profound philosophical questions. Oh, what a splendid book! Meekness, humility, and seriousness— these are Strakhov's distinctive features."

Lev Nikolayevich received a letter from Nazhivin asking him to send a recent photograph for one of his books. When he was going through the letters to be sent off today (most of them written by himself), Lev Nikolayevich asked me to fetch from his study a folder of portraits of himself so he could select one for Nazhivin. When I had brought in the folder, Goldenweiser and I began going through it together.

All at once Lev Nikolayevich smiled broadly and said:

"I look at these portraits and think—especially now, after reading Strakhov—and I am being absolutely sincere—that all this fame of mine is like a puff of smoke! The work of Strakhov, and men such as he, is serious, but nobody needs writing like mine, or Leonid Andreyev's, or Andrei Biely's, and it will disappear. Otherwise there would not be all this fanfare over us, all these portraits."

After tea Goldenweiser sat down at the piano. He played two pieces by Scriabin, two by Arensky, and two by Liszt, and then only Chopin. They were all beautifully played.

"Splendid, wonderful!" said Lev Nikolayevich after hearing one of the Scriabin preludes.

He liked the Arensky too. The composer had visited Yasnaya Polyana and he remembered him as being a very likable man.

"Rubbish, rub-bish!" he exclaimed after hearing the Liszt. "There is no inspiration in that. All of these," and he demonstrated with his fingers how certain passages were played, "are not worth playing or composing when set beside the simplicity, the elegance, of the piece you played before."

He was referring to the Arensky composition.

✧

After listening to Chopin for a long time, he remarked:

"I must say that all of civilization could vanish, go to the devil, except for music—that would be a shame!"

A discussion arose concerning Chopin's relations with George Sand.

"Why do you repeat such filth?" Lev Nikolayevich said to Tatyana Lvovna, breaking his silence, then, turning to the others, added with a laugh: "Just let your sister get involved and you will always hear that sort of muck!"

"I'll get even with you, just you wait!" said Tatyana Lvovna, shaking a finger at him.

"People confuse trashy love affairs with creativity," Tolstoy continued. "Creativity is spiritual, divine, and sexual love is animal. They infer one from the other! Chopin did not compose because that woman was leading a loose life" (he smiled wryly), "but because of those transports, that urge to create.

"Why is it," he asked a little later, "that painting and poetry are understandable to everyone, just as religion is, but that music is the exception? Would any simple, untrained fellow—even one inclined to aesthetic 'feelings'—understand such music?* Would he experience the same pleasure we have just had? This interests me very much! I think that he would not understand it. Therefore I would like music to be more simple, to be universal."

Incidentally, Lev Nikolayevich wrote in his letter to Nazhivin: "I am living well, moving gradually toward what is always a blessing: the weakening of the body and the liberation of the spirit."

I have prepared the booklet *The Superstition of the State*.[15] Aleksandra Lvovna, who has almost completely recovered, has been helping me with the work, checking off the "mild" letters, collecting and making parcels of books, and so on. Although the worm of jealousy makes its appearance from time to time and is still crawling around in her soul, she seems to have realized since knowing me better that I am not such a monster after all and am no threat to her, and she is now a little more indulgent toward me. She has admitted to me that she is jealous, and this may be a sign that her jealousy has lessened. . . .

✧

5 March

"Lev Nikolayevich, may I ask you a question that has nothing to do with the work?" I inquired.

"Please do, please do! I am only too glad! When there is work, communication seems to be suspended, and I am happy in such instances to be asked a question, if I can answer it."

I asked him whether only physical labor can be considered

---

* Lev Nikolayevich very much disliked the word "feelings." V.B.

entirely moral, or whether work that is not physical but that is unquestionably useful and necessary, such as the work of a good schoolteacher, or Dushan's work as a doctor (which Lev Nikolayevich sometimes refers to as "holy") is also free from extraneous, harmful influence.

Lev Nikolayevich expressed himself to the effect that work can be moral without being physical.

"But if he can breathe fresh air, what man would want to breathe foul air?" he said. "So it is with physical labor. Man must always strive for perfection, though he may never achieve it. And in his present state it may be better, and more essential, to be a prison warden! Perhaps just that. They tell of a woman whose job it was to make up the actors in a theater, and whose earnings were spent on sick, crippled dogs she gathered up and cared for. Now it would be the greatest bigotry to say that she was acting immorally because of taking money from people and spending it on dogs. Absolute bigotry! In such a case it is necessary to liberate yourself from the temptation of human approbation, and not think of what people say about you. This is harder to combat than personal lust, especially for you young people—but for us old people too. I have rid myself of this temptation only in the last year and a half. I'm still striving, and rejoice when I succeed."

This afternoon Lev Nikolayevich rode over to Telyatinki with the Tambov peasant Andrei Tarasov, who had come from there to see him. Lev Nikolayevich continues to be very much interested in him.

"He takes up every moral question in turn," he said of him today. "He is married and has two children, and now he thinks it might be better for him and his wife to live together as brother and sister. He has saved some money—five hundred rubles—and asks what he should do with it, whether it is good to have this money."

Today Lev Nikolayevich organized his ideas for the booklet *The Deception of False Faith,*[16] that is, arranged the thoughts in several sections, and, as in the preceding booklets, in a definite, consecutive order.

6 March

Today is a field day for all the newspapers: Khomyakov has resigned his chairmanship of the Duma. This is now the foremost news of the day.

"Didn't I tell you, Lev Nikolayevich, that the row raised by Purishkevich would have very serious consequences?" was M. S. Sukhotin's greeting to Lev Nikolayevich this morning. "Khomyakov has resigned!"

"Is that really important?" asked Lev Nikolayevich.

"Come now—the chairman of the Duma——"

"What difference does it make? Khomyakov goes and some Tolbakyov will take his place. They are all alike. Just as the divine spirit dwells in all, so does the spirit of stupidity," said Lev Nikolayevich with a smile. "The spirit of the devil is in everyone."

A very interesting letter on the sex question came today. ("Don't show it to Sasha, it's very dirty!" was Lev Nikolayevich's first comment.) The letter gave evidence of his good influence. He was extremely agitated by it, and wrote an answer, but his correspondent had put no address on the letter, not wishing to trouble him to reply, and consequently the letter was not sent.

I am leaving Yasnaya Polyana today to go to Moscow and set my affairs in order at the university, where I am still enrolled as a student.

❖

10 March

Returned to Yasnaya only today after my trip to Moscow; also went to Krëkshino to see the Chertkovs.

While still at the station I heard the welcome news that Lev Nikolayevich was in good health. I saw him and managed to get some work done: organized the ideas for the booklet *Liberation from Sin, Temptation, Superstition, and Deception in Striving for Continence.*

◆

12 *March*

On arriving at Yasnaya this morning, I learned to my amazement that Lev Nikolayevich had not yet gone for his walk, was not even up, in fact, though it was past nine o'clock. The whole household was worried. About eleven o'clock he got up feeling perfectly well. He himself was surprised that he had slept so long. It was probably only because he had gone to bed late after an evening spent in reading letters he had written long ago to a distant relative, Countess A. A. Tolstaya.[17] The letters were very interesting, they say. Lev Nikolayevich had listened with great attention as they were read aloud, and in the end was very much stirred by them. I recall that one day before I went away he said of these letters:

"I do not remember them; I only remember that I was conducting an intellectual flirtation in them."

The artist Meshkov has come from Moscow to paint a portrait of Lev Nikolayevich.

On his way out for his walk after lunch, Lev Nikolayevich said to his son-in-law:

"You think how pleasant it is to die, and yet how much unpleasantness you cause by your death!"

"Yes, yes, you are causing a great deal of unpleasantness," affirmed M. S. Sukhotin.

Lev Nikolayevich was very kind to me today; his eyes, his whole face, glowed with kindness. I note this because I cannot help being moved by it.

13 March

In *Discourses* there is an excerpt from one of Tolstoy's letters to Gusev. Referring to Halley's comet, he wrote:

"The idea that a comet could collide with the earth and destroy it was very pleasant to me. Why not admit the possibility? And having accepted it, it becomes quite clear that all the material consequences, the visible, tangible results of activity in the material world are—nothing. Spiritual life can be as little disturbed by the destruction of the world as the life of the world by the death of a fly. Less so, in fact. We do not believe this simply because we ascribe such inordinate significance to the life of the material world."

Someone remarked, rather unfortunately, that anything Tolstoy might write would be published.

"Yes, that's the trouble," said Lev Nikolayevich. "I so often write my characteristic nonsense, and it inevitably finds its way into print."

Today I brought him the booklet *The Effort to Control Our Thinking,*[18] and three letters written according to his instructions, which he immediately read. To one he added a note indicating his agreement with what I had written, and concerning the other he said:

"It happens to be just what I wanted to say: that whether to serve as a village elder or a tax collector, whether to get married in church—these are things a man must decide for himself and carry out to the degree that his strength permits. I have realized with particular clarity that it is necessary to strive toward the attainment of one's ideal with all one's powers, but there is no need to minimize it. Marriage and sexual life with one's wife is admissible, but one can rise above it and live as brother and sister. It is admissible that one may have property and protect it, but a man can also renounce it completely. I say this in the sense that this is easier—I say it to refute the objection that it is difficult."

Later, when I was about to take my leave, he said:

"You don't spend much time with us. Stay for dinner. Did you walk here today? It's wonderful now—there will be a moon tonight."

A young man came to see Lev Nikolayevich; he found him rather vague and sent him to me. It seems that he is a clerk in a hat shop, and having read Tolstoy's works no longer wants to do such work, for in selling one must practice deception. He has come all the way from Ekaterinburg to ask advice on what sort of work he might do that would be freer and more honest. I sent him with a note to Telyatinki, where he can spend the night. When I told Lev Nikolayevich about him at dinner, he was pleased and said that he seemed "quite nice."

Tatyana Lvovna remembered that in the morning she had seen a boy "with such a bad face" standing near the porch.

"Worse than yours?" asked Lev Nikolayevich.

"Worse than mine!" she replied with a laugh.

When any member of the household calls someone stupid or bad, Lev Nikolayevich has a habit of saying: "More stupid than you?" or "Worse than you?" and it usually disconcerts them. That is what he was doing at the moment.

"It's not that his face was homely," Tatyana Lvovna continued, "but it was downright bad, like a man who drinks, smokes——"

"Or doesn't get enough to eat," added Lev Nikolayevich.

When he sat down to his game of chess with M. S. Sukhotin, Meshkov and Tatyana Lvovna settled down to sketch them. "Tatyana Tatyanovna" asked me for a pencil and also sat down at the table to "draw Grandfather." Her older brother Dorik was copying a picture from a postcard. I too sat down in a corner and began sketching Meshkov at work and Lev Nikolayevich and Sukhotin. . . .

✧

15 March

I took Lev Nikolayevich the booklet *Liberation from Sin through Self-Abnegation*,[19] and a letter he had instructed me to write. He gave me another letter to answer—the exposition of a particular philosophical theory; but after reading it, it seemed to me hardly necessary to reply (such a muddle in the mind of the philosopher) and Lev Nikolayevich agreed with me.

I received a letter from V. V. Bitner in Petersburg concerning his agreement to publish my book. I told Lev Nikolayevich and he was very pleased.

"I should look it over again: there was too systematic a classification of sins. However, I rely on your sensitivity."

P. A. Sergeyenko has sent Lev Nikolayevich Leskov's thoughts on life and religion, which have much in common with Tolstoy's views. He was very much moved by them.

"Listen," he said, bringing this material into the "Remington room" where both Tatyana Lvovna and I were working.

" 'It is better to be not doing than to be doing nothing,' " he read. " 'If Christ had lived today and published the Gospels, the ladies would have requested his autograph, and that would have been the end of the whole affair.' "

After reading another passage he suddenly turned around and went out. It seems he had begun to weep.

"He has always been prone to tears," whispered Tatyana Lvovna. "When he was a little boy they used to call him 'Lev the Howler.' And in this respect I am just like him."

A moment later he returned, the sheets of paper still in his hand, and read:

" 'They never would have made a religion of Christ but for the invention of the Resurrection—and Paul was the prime inventor.' Why, that is so true, and so profound!"

Later, in the drawing room, he read Leskov to the members of the household and the guests, Aleksandr Aleksandrovich Stakhovich and his sister, Sofya Aleksandrovna, who is a maid of honor at Court. They recalled that in a spiritual sense Tolstoy had had a great influence on Leskov.

"Leskov himself said that he was going along with a candle when he saw ahead of him a man carrying a torch, and he joined him and walked with him. He considered Tolstoy the man with the torch," said Tatyana Lvovna.

16 March

The magazine *Life for Everyone* has come with Boulanger's article and Tolstoy's foreword to it. Lev Nikolayevich was worried that the editor might have to pay dearly for the harsh criticism of the church in the foreword.

"As Posse said," he remarked later, "the magazine is good in that it does not omit a single word from the articles it prints."

Lev Nikolayevich also received a letter from the Novgorod metalworker V. A. Molochnikov, who is in prison. Molochnikov has a family to support, and Lev Nikolayevich feels great sympathy for him.

"It would be all right for you and me to be in prison," he said to me, "you have no family and I have left all that behind me."

He gave me two letters to answer, one from the revolutionary in Siberia whose first letter in January he had read aloud to a large company, among whom were Andrei Lvovich and Sergeyenko. The revolutionary wrote in the same implacable spirit against the teachings of love and nonresistance.

"This is evidently one of the deaf ones, one of those who do not wish to hear," Lev Nikolayevich said to me, "but I should like to answer him. Read it and perhaps you will write to him."

As he was going through the correspondence he came upon a proselytizing letter.

"It's amazing," he said, "I have always noticed that if a man is firm in his belief, he never tries to convert anyone; but if he is uncertain, vacillating in his faith, he invariably finds it necessary to convert everyone to it—like Aleksandra Andreyevna Tolstaya (whose correspondence with Lev Nikolayevich they recently read aloud at Yasnaya Polyana).

Fyodor Perevoznikov, a nice young man who has come from Krëkshino and is staying with us at Telyatinki, was in the hall when we were putting on our things to go out (Lev Nikolayevich to go for his ride), and he announced that V. G. Chertkov was planning to spend the summer in Serpukhov, on the border of the Moscow and Tula provinces. He is prohibited from entering the Tula province.

"So it will be easier for me to ride over there?" said Lev Nikolayevich with a laugh.

"Why are you laughing?"

"It seems so funny to me that a man can live in Serpukhov, but no nearer. And all because someone took it into his head to draw an imaginary line and create a province. How stupid it is!"

19 March

I learned from Lev Nikolayevich that N. N. Gusev's home in exile has been searched. They found an article by Tolstoy and threaten to make him answerable for it and to add to his punishment. . . .

Lev Nikolayevich is not feeling well today; he has caught cold and speaks through his nose and in a bass voice.

I gave him the twenty-seventh and twenty-first booklets of thoughts: *Liberation from False Doctrine in Freedom of Thought,* and *True Life in the Present,*[20] as well as a long letter, written according to his instruction, in which he speaks of science and art. He approved of the letter.

"Only yesterday I was thinking and making notes in my diary about science," he said. "This is what I wrote: suppose a man from Mars, who knows nothing about life on earth, were to come here.

He is told that one percent of the people have instituted religion, art, and science for themselves, and that the remaining ninety-nine percent do not share in all this. I think that it would be clear to him that life on earth is not good, and that its religion and science can be neither good nor true."

Laughing, Lev Nikolayevich showed me the last issue of *New Russia,* in which out of ten thoughts from *For Every Day* only one had been printed: the rest had been deleted by the censor and replaced by ellipses, leaving only the numbers of the thoughts and the names of the authors.

From time to time I have noted here that Lev Nikolayevich recites verse or speaks of it, and that it is always Pushkin, Tyuchev, or Fet. In this connection I quote a very interesting excerpt from one of his letters today (to Ozerova):

"I do not like poetry in general. It moves me, I believe, primarily as a recollection of certain youthful impressions, and then only the most perfect verses of Pushkin and Tyuchev."

21 March

The Ernfelts [21] have arrived at Telyatinki—father, daughter, and son. We all set out for Yasnaya together with Dima Chertkov. Lev Nikolayevich is not well and goes around in his dressing gown. He is still quite hoarse, but came out to greet them and then went back to his room.

I gave him my letter to the revolutionary who "does not wish to hear." It turns out that he has received another letter from him to which he has already written a reply, though he has not sent it. I was about to suggest that my letter not be sent, but he would not hear of it.

"They probably have some sort of circle where they share their thoughts," he said. "If the letter has no influence on him, it may influence others. And, in general, one should not think about results. We do this for our own satisfaction, though it may mean nothing to him. He does not even want to read my books, and yet, who knows—he may change. If one does this with all one's heart, as I do, and as I am sure you do, then it probably will prove to be useful, if not at the moment at some future time. Now, today, I was reading about a sex questionnaire that was circulated among students. It seems that the number of male virgins has increased: it was formerly twenty percent and is now twenty-seven. And one of the main reasons for continence is moral considerations. Evidently they are being influenced by moral teachings. Recently there was a letter from a young man who writes that he had been in doubt about how to act in this problem of his sex life, but after reading *The Kreutzer Sonata* he decided to remain virgin. So, there you are, these things are never in vain, they always have results. It's not like building seven hundred palaces and distributing billions: that, like a flowing river, passes and is no more."

He read my letter and approved of it.

"Yes," he observed, "one gets the impression that he will not understand such views. But it is hard to argue with the conclusions: you see, he is unable to change his fundamental outlook."

The revolutionary had written: "Socialism is my faith, my God."

"But it is always comforting to think," Lev Nikolayevich added, "that others may understand."

"Ask Ernfelt and the children to come in here," he said, as I was about to leave the study. "I want to talk to them, but, I'm sorry to say, I can't talk out there."

He had in mind the constant hubbub in the drawing room, where, as today, he is unceremoniously interrupted, or the general conversation sometimes takes an objectionable, shallow turn.

After talking with Lev Nikolayevich in his study, the Ernfelts went out to have a look at the park and the environs of Yasnaya Polyana. Later they kept exclaiming rapturously over how picturesque everything was.

In their absence Lev Nikolayevich came into the drawing room, sat down in the Voltaire armchair, and listened to Dima Chertkov's stories about the loose morals of the Krëkshino peasants.

"Religion is needed," said Lev Nikolayevich. "I will go on

singing the same tune. Without it there will always be debauchery, frippery, vodka."

Sofya Andreyevna happened to suggest that I read aloud a newly discovered poem written by Lermontov in his youth, which has just been published in *The Russian Word*.

"It's boring!" Lev Nikolayevich objected.

He took the newspaper.

"What inferior verse this is," he said, and read aloud several lines, which, in fact, were not of great artistic merit.

And the rest of the poem was left unread.

After dinner Lev Nikolayevich played chess with Ernfelt. They each won a game. Later, while still at the chess table, a discussion arose. Gradually everyone gathered around them: Tatyana Lvovna, Olga Konstantinovna, Dushan Petrovich, the Ernfelt children, Dima Chertkov, and I.

Mostly they talked about Henry George.[22] It seems that nowhere has he been recognized or understood: neither in Finland, according to Ernfelt, nor by the Russian peasants, as witnessed by Lev Nikolayevich, not to speak of the governments of all the European states.

"It's amazing," said Lev Nikolayevich while on the subject, "people think not in terms of the requirements of the spirit, but in terms of the advantages of the situation in which they find themselves. And that is true of the majority of the privileged classes. The situation as regards the land question is the same today as it was under serfdom, before the emancipation of the peasants. I always cite this comparison. Progressive people then as now felt the injustice of slavery in relation to landed property, but, like the Decembrists if for different reasons, they could not abolish it, though they tried. And just as there were those who defended serfdom then, so there are those who defend landed property now."

Later Lev Nikolayevich questioned Ernfelt about Finland.

"True justice should apply not to one people but to all mankind," he said in connection with Ernfelt's statement about the patriotism of the majority of Finns.

"What is the level of literacy?" he asked Ernfelt.

"Very high," was the answer.

Lev Nikolayevich told us about a plan he has for a reference dictionary for the people.

"You see, here we have an encyclopedia standing on the shelf and we can use it at any time," he said, "but there is nothing like that for simple people. Of course, it has to be a reference book that has been worked out for them. We have got to take our dictionary, throw out one thing, rewrite another. Take, for instance, some little known writer. Obviously such an entry should be eliminated. But then words like 'Holland,' or 'electricity' are, of course, necessary, but must be defined for people who, at best, have learned to read and write. I have been thinking about this, and recently received a letter from Kharkov in which I was told that someone unknown to me has expressed a desire to contribute fifteen thousand rubles for a good cause, and asks me to suggest what it should be. I think the money could be used for compiling such a dictionary. I have written a letter about it, but have not yet received a reply."

⬦

23 March

When I arrived at Yasnaya Polyana today I found a letter addressed to me from Dima Chertkov, who had left with the Finns. He wrote that Lev Nikolayevich has agreed to write a play for the peasants to perform, which we are to put on at Telyatinki. This was confirmed by Lev Nikolayevich.

Today he read to me a letter he had written on suicides. Its basic idea is the need for religion. The beginning is very witty and amusing and is written in a form that approximates literature. Listening to it I could not control my laughter. Lev Nikolayevich laughed too, then he said:

"I have just read in the newspaper a professor's opinion on the subject of suicide. He mentions various causes, psychological and others, but not a word about the absence of religion."

They kept me at Yasnaya Polyana until evening so that I could hear the music of a young man, A. P. Voitichenko from Nezhin, who has come to play the dulcimer for Lev Nikolayevich. He played very well. At his request, Lev Nikolayevich gave him an inscribed photograph, remarking, however, that his playing lacked rhythm and that his transitions from *piano* to *forte* were too abrupt.

"I consider it my duty to tell you this," he said, "because I see that you have real talent."

The musician fully agreed with his observations. Afterward Sofya Andreyevna put on the gramophone to give the young man an opportunity to hear Troyanovsky play the balalaika.

"*Bis, bis!*" exclaimed Lev Nikolayevich, after listening to Troyanovsky's performance of *Scène de Ballet*. Yesterday too when they played this piece he had asked that it be repeated.

When the rollicking music of the *hopak* was heard, Lev Nikolayevich, who was playing chess with Sukhotin, without ceasing to follow the moves of the game, began tapping his feet and clapping his hands so vigorously that it could be heard in the dining room.

24 *March*

I brought Lev Nikolayevich the last, the thirty-first, booklet of thoughts: *Life Is a Blessing*.

As he took it from me he said:

"You know, I have started crossing out your section headings. You won't be angry with me, will you? They were very helpful to me, but the reader will confuse them with the text."

"You are not offended, are you?" he asked me again later, and I assured him that I had no such thought that the important thing was that whatever was done should be for his convenience and as he thought best.

He received "an appalling letter" today from Molochnikov describing his prison.

✧

28 March

I set out for Yasnaya Polyana with Chertkov's eighteen-year-old son shortly after six o'clock. Everywhere there was either thick mud or water holes in the snow. Just outside of the village we saw a troika stuck in a hollow. Dima, who was wearing high boots, went to help the coachman. A gentleman and lady got out of the droshky and stood in the snow. At first we took the man for the Czech professor, Masaryk, whom the Tolstoys are expecting today, but it turned out to be Mikhail Aleksandrovich Stakhovich and his sister. The horses got out of the snow somehow, and the Stakhoviches drove on.

There was particular animation and merriment at Yasnaya. Masaryk has not arrived but will come tomorrow.

A letter addressed to me came from the poet Yakubovich-Melshin of *Russian Wealth,* informing us that of the six poems written by the Tobolsk exile, which Lev Nikolayevich had asked me to send to him, four would be published. I told Lev Nikolayevich.

"Now, that's wonderful!" he said.

I was in the "Remington room" sorting Lev Nikolayevich's latest articles and letters when I heard his bell. Aleksandra Lvovna dashed out of the drawing room and into his study, but immediately came out again.

"Mr. Ober-secretary, you are wanted!" she announced.

I hastily went to Lev Nikolayevich. Dima was with him.

"We're just having a talk. No secrets—but two is company, three's a crowd, as the English say. I like that enormously," said Lev Nikolayevich. . . .

He told me he had received an abusive letter today, filled with the most outspoken, cynical invective. It made him feel sad. He had also received a letter from a priest asking to be told, without recourse to philosophy or literature, whether or not Lev Nikolayevich thought that Christ had been resurrected in the flesh.

"It's a very kind letter," he said. "As unpleasant as it was for me, I had to answer him. I wrote that if Christ knew about this invention of the Resurrection, he would be very much distressed."

He then told us that he felt "really sorry for" an old beggar woman in the village who, as a result of having deceived everyone, was now deprived of the help she had formerly received from people.

"If she came to you, she would be refused help, and if she comes here, she will be refused too," he said.

✧

When he came into the "Remington room" later, Lev Nikolayevich discussed the play to be performed at Telyatinki. He had already told Dima that he had a drama all worked out in his mind and had only to sit down and write it. He has an idea for a comedy as well.

"But I have to give thought to the writing," he said to Dima. "You have an audience that is not exacting, but when it gets to the newspapers, when it becomes known—— But I should like to write plays only for the people of Yasenki, Telyatinki, and Yasnaya Polyana."

Aleksandra Lvovna also wants to take part in the Telyatinki performance.

"Give me the role of some old woman," she said to her father.

"Don't you want to play the village policeman?" he suggested with a smile.

"No!" she replied in horror.

We went into the drawing room, where general animation reigned at the tea table.

After tea Lev Nikolayevich read my letters and repeatedly advised me not to send one of them, which spoke of the criminal nature of military service. He was afraid the letter would be opened and I would have to "answer for" my opinions. Moreover, my correspondent aroused his suspicions.

"Pray that I get the play written," he said to us in farewell.

29 March

Lev Nikolayevich had already left to go riding when I arrived today. I became acquainted with the philosopher F. A. Strakhov, who has come from Moscow. Lev Nikolayevich included many of his ideas in *The Circle of Reading,* and recently praised very highly his book *The Search for Truth.* Besides Stakhovich and his sister, Masaryk is visiting the Tolstoys. Unfortunately he was sleeping while I was at Yasnaya Polyana and I only saw the outline of his figure on Dushan's bed, his head covered with a blanket.

When Lev Nikolayevich returned from his ride, he changed his wet socks for dry ones, and, not putting on his boots but carrying them in his hand, appeared in the drawing room where they were having tea. Spreading out his arms he humorously made a slight bow and sat down at the tea table.

He was given a telegram that had been sent to him from a student in the Petersburg Forestry Institute, asking to be "supported by telegram" until he could find work giving lessons.

"That's a new device!" Sukhotin remarked.

Stakhovich calculated that the telegram had cost the student a ruble and a half. He took the telegram from Lev Nikolayevich saying that he would make inquiries about the student in Petersburg and perhaps help him.

✧

31 March

Belinky has brought me two letters to answer. One, very interesting, from the same exiled revolutionary from Siberia who had written Lev Nikolayevich in such an implacable spirit, and to whom I wrote recently. My letter has not yet reached him. Now he writes that he is standing at the crossroads: Tolstoy's letter has evidently made him think, and he has been particularly influenced by V. G. Chertkov's little book, *Our Revolution,*[23] which Lev Nikolayevich sent to him. "I had no sooner read it than I was brought up short," he writes. The only thing he could not accept was the idea of God—"some kind of bugbear." On the envelope Lev Nikolayevich had made a note that I should write to him about God.

Belinky informed me that Lev Nikolayevich has decided to restore my section headings in the booklets of thoughts. . . .

He also brought the third issue of *Russian Wealth* for this year, with Korolenko's article on the death penalty (*An Everyday Occurrence*. Part I). Lev Nikolayevich cried when he read it and has written the author about his impressions. We read it aloud here.

✧

3 April

Lev Nikolayevich is very weak again. He has neither been working nor going out for his walk.

"I am inexpressibly weak. I cannot tell you how weak!" he said to me.

"Vladimir Grigorevich's (Chertkov's) case is now being settled in Petersburg," I told him. "Fedya Perevoznikov has arrived from Krëkshino and told us about it."

"Oh, now that is welcome news!" he exclaimed, and added, referring to Chertkov's exile: "The whole thing is stupid!"

He dressed while I was with him and, as the weather was fine, went out for a short walk.

When he came in, he went to Dushan's room to ask him about some young man who had come to see him this morning and whom he had not received because of not feeling well.

"He is on my conscience," said Lev Nikolayevich.

He was, in Dushan's words, "the usual petitioner." Dushan appeased him.

✧

Lev Nikolayevich gave me a ruble to change and told me to give a twenty-kopeck piece to one of the perennial beggars—one who receives much more than any of the others and is always terribly irate and demanding.

"He will curse me," said Lev Nikolayevich.

"Is that from the count himself?" the beggar asked me, holding the twenty kopeck piece on his outstretched palm.

"Yes."

And the complaints began. . . .

5 April

Lev Nikolayevich has recovered. He began to feel better yesterday.

✧

He changes amazingly according to the state of his health: when he is ill he is gloomy, taciturn, and writes in his diary, but even at such times struggles with "evil feelings"—though I have never seen any manifestation of them; when he is well, on the other hand, he is very animated, his talk is cheerful, his gait brisk, and he has a great capacity for work. That is how he was today. Just from the expression of his face and the tone of his voice one could see that he had recovered.

✧

6 April

I left Yasnaya Polyana early this morning. It was a beautiful morning. Spring is delightful here. It is lovely generally at this time of year, but in such a picturesque spot as Yasnaya Polyana the beauty of spring is enhanced a hundredfold.

I had to go back again in the evening, however, with Lev Sergeyenko and Dima. I took to Lev Nikolayevich the booklets on drunkenness he had asked me to bring from Telyatinki. They are to be sent to a factory for distribution among the workers.

An Ekaterinoslav peasant, Ipatov, was here to see Lev Nikolayevich today. He is a former Old Believer and Lev Nikolayevich liked him very much.

"These Old Believers are always so steadfast," he said.

✧

7 April

In the evening Lev Nikolayevich looked over the letters I had written, and to one of them (a letter to Ruban on the changes in the external conditions of life) added a long postscript enlarging on the idea I had expressed.

This was in the study. He bent over the table and it was as if he had forgotten I was there. I stood near him without disturbing the silence. A squat little kerosene lamp with a white shade stood on the movable shelf of the work table shedding its light on Lev Nikolayevich. He knit his brows as he wrote. Having covered one page, he turned it over without blotting it and continued writing. All of a sudden he would utter a cry: "Oh!" Something was not right—he corrected it, made an insertion, and wrote on. This crying out is something he often does when playing chess.

"That's nothing; it's not necessary to copy it over. Send it as it is," he said when he had finished.

He took out his notebook and, as always, read the reminder he had written concerning whatever work he might have entrusted to me.

"Yes," he recalled. "Get the Leskov material from Tanya. I want you to select from it those thoughts which are particularly clear and fresh to add to my book. And take others, too, which we have not come across, and insert them in the other booklets." [24]

I obtained the Leskov material from Tatyana Lvovna.

At tea Lev Nikolayevich asked about Lev Sergeyenko.

"Is he digging in the earth?"

"Yes."

They began talking about this boy, whose parents want to send him out to Irkutsk and enroll him in a middle school there. He, however, wants to remain with us at Telyatinki, as V. G. Chertkov has proposed to him, and not go to school at all.

Sofya Andreyevna and Tatyana Lvovna said that he had something to live on now, but wondered what would happen to him later, what would he do? I remonstrated that a man could always find work and that if the worse came to the worst, he could take anything whatsoever—he had only to curtail his needs.

Lev Nikolayevich listened, nodded his head, and remarked:

"Yes, of course, of course, how can you not find something?"

And then he told us about a shelter for elderly writers and their wives and children that is being set up in some remote spot several versts from a railroad, in a little village that belonged to Pushkin. A manager is needed for it, probably an intelligent young man, and one of the organizers has told Lev Nikolayevich that only someone who had no place to go would take the position.

So here was one position for someone like Sergeyenko. Besides, he is accustomed to physical work.

After telling us about the Pushkin shelter for writers, Lev Nikolayevich proceeded to recount the story *The Good Life* by S. T. Semyonov. It is about a peasant who becomes a doorkeeper in a wealthy home, grows unused to physical toil, then loses his job and gradually drinks himself to death.

Lev Nikolayevich told the whole story wonderfully. He speaks very fluently, with never any confusion or hesitancy in his choice of words, often highlighting artistic details and even conveying the distinctive speech of individual characters.

I do not know in what connection he happened to mention an unknown young lady who visited him today.

"Such a young girl, and so gay! She was well dressed, wore a

chain around her neck and some sort of little chain on her arm—
obviously costly. She says she wants to help people, to open a school,
something entirely new, with a new program, but that she lacks
only the money and the education. She intends to get the
education, and asks me, of course, for the money. I said to her:
'What sort of program do you have?' She started rummaging about,
took out some kind of notebook, and a mass of little papers spilled
out of it! She gathered them up and began to read from them. I
was sure she would go on reading for a long time. Well, I thought,
I'll hear her out. She pointed to one bit of paper; I looked at it
and saw written in blue pencil: 'Religion, History, Geography,' and
so on and so forth," and he began to laugh. "I told her that I could
not help her. She was not particularly disconcerted by this and
replied: 'Then give me one of your hairs.' "

"What? What is that? A hair?!" everyone interrupted him with
exclamations at this point.

"Yes, yes! A hair—one of my hairs!" Lev Nikolayevich laughed
merrily along with the others. "So I said to her that I did not wish
to give her a hair."

Today the vice-president of the Petersburg branch of the Society
for Peace was here to see Lev Nikolayevich. This man, as Lev
Nikolayevich expressed it, turned out to be less capable of
understanding his reasoning than the young lady he described.

"Well, we have had a nice little evening today," said dear
Dushan Petrovich in his impossible Slovak accent, after everyone
had dispersed.

9 April

Having looked through "Leskov's thoughts" yesterday, I came
to a rather unexpected conclusion: these thoughts which had so
moved Lev Nikolayevich turn out to be, not Leskov's, but, from
various indisputable indications, Tolstoy's own ideas. Apparently
they had been taken from a notebook of Leskov's in which he had
simply jotted down the ideas of Tolstoy that appealed to him. I was

even able to indicate the specific works from which they had been taken.

When I told Lev Nikolayevich about it he took this revelation quite calmly and asked me nonetheless to include in the various notebooks the ideas from the Leskov notebook that were not to be found in *Thoughts on Life*.

Only later, when he was leafing through the notebook, did Lev Nikolayevich remark:

"I am delighted: I recognize my own ideas!"

✧

10 April

I brought Lev Nikolayevich the thoughts I had selected from Dostoyevsky, two books on death with some additional material, and what I had selected from the Leskov notebook for inclusion in sections of *Thoughts on Life*.

"I want Dostoyevsky in the booklets," Lev Nikolayevich said again.

He looked through the Dostoyevsky thoughts, but did not care very much for them.

"They are not strong; they're diffuse," he said. "And then there is a certain mystical attitude—Christ, Christ!"

Later he said:

"Dostoyevsky's attacks on the revolutionaries are not good: he judges them superficially, without penetrating their state of mind."

Nevertheless, of the sixty-four thoughts I had selected from Dostoyevsky, he checked thirty-four for inclusion in the book.

✧

There is great distress at Yasnaya today. It has been discovered, only just discovered, that Aleksandra Lvovna has tuberculosis of the lungs. In two days she will leave for the Crimea accompanied by V. M. Feokritova.

Lev Nikolayevich walks about in silence. They say that he has cried several times. He has not asked Aleksandra Lvovna any questions whatever, does not talk to her in fact.

"We have not looked each other in the eye since my illness was diagnosed," said Aleksandra Lvovna, speaking of her father.

She herself is quite calm.

✧

Incidentally, I learned by chance only today that Lev Nikolayevich borrowed the title and general idea of *The Circle of Reading* from an old Russian Orthodox collection that we have here.

In view of the approaching departure for the Crimea of several members of the household, I am once again moving from Telyatinki to Yasnaya Polyana and shall sleep here tonight.

11 April

✧

Dima Chertkov came to ask me to go to a rehearsal of the play at Telyatinki. I was about to refuse, but Lev Nikolayevich asked me to go. I am the director and play the principal role, that of the Imp, in Toystoy's play, *The First Distiller*.[25] I came back in time for evening tea.

✧

There were several people here this evening, Dima among them. Lev Nikolayevich was reminded of his new, unfinished play.

"It's like the two peasants," he said. "One calls to the other to come in bathing. 'I've already been in,' he replies. That's how it is with me—I've already been in. I've taken everything off, I'm all undressed, but I just can't get into the water!"

12 April

An amazing coincidence. Lev Nikolayevich received a letter from Petrazhitsky, one of his close friends in the Caucasus, who wrote that he felt the approach of death and would like to hear from

him. Lev Nikolayevich intended to write, but today received a
letter informing him that Petrazhitsky had died. In reference to
this Tolstoy said:

"I do not believe in premonitions, but a premonition of death—
that I believe."

After lunch I went riding with Lev Nikolayevich; again we
rode in a new direction, along the Tula highway and then back
through the forest by various paths and little roads. The weather
was fine. Coming out on the highway, we overtook a passer-by. Lev
Nikolayevich greeted him. I was riding somewhat behind.

"What forest is this?" the man asked, as I came abreast of him.

"I do not know, except that it is not ours."

"I see. I wanted to cut a walking stick for myself without having
to worry about it. What estate would you be from?

"Yasnaya Polyana."

"Who is that up ahead—His Excellency?"

"Yes, that is Count Tolstoy."

"Ah! . . . You know, I've been walking around here for seven
years without ever seeing him, but now I've seen him! And here
we've had a talk about him too. . . . Well, well!"

We encountered some men from Tula with their loaded carts,
townsfolk in boots and jackets. They took off their hats and bowed
low to Lev Nikolayevich. I looked back after we had passed and
they were all standing in the road in a little group following us
with their eyes.

Lev Nikolayevich's horse Délire shied at every bush today, and
he had difficulty controlling her. He believes that it is because the
horse's vision is impaired, though she has always been skittish
according to him.

"I'll have to train her," said Lev Nikolayevich.

Train her—and he is over eighty-two!

We have often ridden through the forest at random as we did
today. Lev Nikolayevich will say: "I'll try this," and let his horse
go along some path. We may see what appears to be a gully that is
impossible to cross and turn back, or it may be an impassable
thicket. In the latter case Lev Nikolayevich does not retreat: parting

the branches with his hands and continually bending low, he
boldly rides forward. It seems to me that he enjoys overcoming
these little obstacles on his rides: if the path curves, he will invariably
take a short cut, turning and going straight into dense trees and
bushes; if there is a knoll, he goes over it; if a bridge has been
thrown over a ditch, he avoids it and crosses right over the
precipice.

As soon as the forest path became straight and the trees were
more sparse, Lev Nikolayevich put his horse to a trot. I had to
gallop to catch up with him.

✦

Sofya Andreyevna read a chapter that was not included in the
published edition of *Childhood* which described the charms of the
hunt.[26]

"And a good thing it was omitted," remarked Lev Nikolayevich.

He spoke again of the revolution that has taken place in public
opinion within his memory. This is evident in the attitude toward
hunting: formerly it was unthinkable not to be keen on it, whereas
now many people regard it as an evil. The same is true of the
attitude of the peasants to stealing: in the past it would never have
entered anyone's head that the poor were victimized by the rich,
and as a consequence forced to steal, whereas now everyone
realizes it.

In connection with *Childhood* I recalled that on one of my
former visits to Yasnaya Polyna Lev Nikolayevich had said to me:

"I have never denied art. On the contrary, I have advanced it as
the necessary condition of a rational human life, but only insofar
as it contributes to human understanding. You too are occupied
with art, are you not? What appeals to you, prose or verse?
Prose. . . . You see, there are so many writers today—everyone wants
to be a writer! I am certain, for instance, that in the post that was
just brought there are several letters from budding authors. They
ask to be read, to be published. But in literature one must observe
a kind of chastity and speak out only when it becomes necessary.
In my opinion a writer should undertake only what has not been

written or conceived before. After all, anyone can write: 'The sun shone, the grass . . .' and so on. Now you ask how I began writing. Well, it was with *Childhood*. When I wrote that, it seemed to me that no one before me had felt and depicted all the charm and poetry of childhood in just that way. I repeat: in literature too chastity is necessary. Here I am working on a collection of my thoughts, and I write and rewrite the same thing twelve times over. The writer should have this circumspect, chaste attitude toward his work." And then he added: "This will probably be my last work."

13 April

In the morning, for the first time, Lev Nikolayevich called me into the study to help him open and read his mail.

"This is very distracting," he complained, apparently wanting to get to his own work as quickly as possible.

There were visitors today: A. B. Goldenweiser and his wife, I. I. Gorbunov-Posadov,[27] and M. A. Schmidt.

At dinner M. A. Schmidt told us about how a peasant of her acquaintance spoke of the landed gentry dissipating the money of the toiling peasants, "and then extracting their blood," as she expressed it. To this Lev Nikolayevich replied:

"Just as there is magic in nature—it was winter, and now in a couple of days it will be spring—so there is magic in the people. Not long ago there was not a single peasant who would have uttered the sort of thing you have just related, and now they all think in that way."

He spoke of having read a book of Akhsharumov's poems.

"I decided that I would make every effort to find some poetry I could praise. And I succeeded. There is nothing new in these poems, but they are certainly better than the decadents."

He wrote a letter to Akhsharumov about his poetry.

In a discussion about magazines for the general public—*Life for Everyone* and *The Magazine for Everyone*—Goldenweiser remarked that it was the fine literature published in the latter that attracted readers.

"Is it really possible that literature can attract people?" asked Lev Nikolayevich in surprise. "In my old age I am unable to understand this."

He mentioned the fact that there was no one as old as he in the whole village of Yasnaya. The others began talking about how the peasants age earlier that "we" do. I saw Lev Nikolayevich frown.

"Of course. That's because we take care of our bodies, and they are all worn out," he said quietly, exploring his own thoughts, it seemed to me, rather than wishing to share them with others.

Goldenweiser played beautifully, but, unfortunately, very little. We felt hesitant about asking him to play, but Lev Nikolayevich was the first to speak. Again the music made a powerful impression on him.

"When a good musical composition pleases you, you feel as though you had written it yourself," he observed, after listening to Chopin's Etude in E major, Opus 10.

Goldenweiser told us that Chopin himself had considered the lyric theme of this étude one of his finest melodies.

"Beautiful! Beautiful!" exclaimed Lev Nikolayevich when the music was over, and he recalled the things that had pleased him most.

"If a man from Mars were to come and say of this that it is worthless, I would dispute him. But there is just one thing—it is not comprehensible to the people. In this I am so spoiled—more than in anything else. I love music above all other arts; with the feelings it evokes in me, it would be the hardest for me to part with."

Later he said:

"I have not heard any of the decadents in music. I know the decadents in literature. This is my third psychological misunderstanding" (no one ventured to ask him what the other two were). "What goes on in their heads—the Balmonts, Bryusovs, and Bielys!"

Goldenweiser promised to come for Easter and acquaint
him with the decadents in music. Lev Nikolayevich urged him to
come.

Saying good night to everyone, Lev Nikolayevich remarked:

"My powers for work are in inverse proportion to my desire.
Sometimes I lack the desire to work, but now I have to restrain it."

✧

Today he wrote a letter that I believe must be the shortest one
ever written. It consisted of one word: "Rostóv" and his signature.
It was sent to a third-grade pupil who had asked him whether
the family name in *War and Peace* was pronounced Róstov or
Rostóv.

14 April

In the morning a woman by the name of Bodyanskaya arrived.
Her husband was sentenced to death for his participation in the
movement of 1905; later the sentence was commuted to six years
of penal servitude. According to her he was not guilty. She came
to Lev Nikolayevich with a letter from his acquaintance Yushko
and asked him to arrange a meeting for her with the tsarina or with
Stolypin. Lev Nikolayevich and Tatyana Lvovna gave her letters to
Count Olsufyev and S. A. Stakhovich.

Besides Bodyanskaya, the photographers "Sherin and Nabgolts"
were here. Sofya Andreyevna had sent for them to make a new
photograph of Lev Nikolayevich for the twelfth edition of his
collected works, which she is now preparing. They photographed
him on the terrace, where he posed most reluctantly.

A letter came from the Englishman Istam, secretary of some
"peace society," one of those organizations that have, it seems, only
the remotest relation to peace. Mr. Istam asks Lev Nikolayevich
to participate in the activities of the society. Lev Nikolayevich
summoned me and dictated a reply, sharply critical of associations
that term themselves "peace societies" while at the same time
maintaining a negative attitude to antimilitarism.

After lunch I accompanied Lev Nikolayevich on his ride. As we rode out of the estate we encountered a young man, a "seaman," as he said introducing himself, who happened to be on his way to see Lev Nikolayevich to ask him for material assistance. Lev Nikolayevich very gently refused his request.

"Please don't have any ill-feeling toward me," he added.

"Excuse me!" said the young "seaman." "Excuse me!" he repeated, and gallantly lifted his little cap.

We rode to Osvyannikovo. Lev Nikolayevich sat for a while on the terrace of the little house occupied by I. I. Gorbunov-Posadov. Ivan Ivanovich, his wife and children, P. A. Boulanger, and M. A. Schmidt all gathered to sit and talk with the beloved guest.

Out of this conversation I shall note only something that Lev Nikolayevich said:

"Christ was premature. His teaching was so contrary to the established views that it was necessary to distort it in order to cram it into those——" he did not complete the sentence. "And only here and there does it shine through."

In Osvyannikovo we got the proofs of several of the booklets of *Thoughts on Life*, which Ivan Ivanovich had brought from Moscow.

S. D. Nikolayev who, with his family, has settled in Yasnaya Polyana for the summer, came in the evening, and consequently there was talk of Henry George. Nikolayevich is an assiduous propagandist and translator of George.

✥

For some reason we began talking about theosophy.

"Everything about it is good," observed Lev Nikolayevich, "except that the theosophists know what is to be in the next world and what there was prior to this one."

Before going to his room Lev Nikolayevich turned to me and said:

"I do not know what title to use for the booklet: *The Sin of Intemperance*, or *The Sin of Serving the Body*, or *The Sin of Serving the Lusts of the Body*. They are all poor."

I advised using *The Sin of Satisfying the Body*.[28]

"That is better," he said.

I will quote an excerpt from a letter he wrote today to a peasant who shares his views.

"You ask whether I like the life I am now leading. No, I do not. I do not like it because I am living with my family in luxury, while around me there is poverty and need, and I can neither extricate myself from the luxury nor remedy the poverty and need. This I do not like. But what I do like about my life is that I do what is within my power, and to the extent of my power, to follow Christ's precept and love God and my neighbor. To love God means to love the perfection of good and to draw as close as you can to it. To love your neighbor means to love all men equally as your brothers and sisters. It is to this, and this alone, that I aspire. And since I am approaching it little by little, though imperfectly, I do not despair but rejoice.

"You ask too whether I rejoice, and if so over what—what joy I expect. I rejoice that I can fulfill to the extent of my powers the lesson given me by the Master: to work for the establishment of that Kingdom of God toward which we all strive."

15 April

Lev Nikolayevich received a letter from the famous English playwright Bernard Shaw, and after reading it made a note on the envelope: "clever-foolish." In his letter Shaw makes witty remarks about God, the soul, etc. Lev Nikolayevich could not help reacting adversely to this frivolous tone in a discussion of such important questions, and in the letter he dictated to me on the terrace this morning declared himself sharply and categorically opposed to the English writer on these matters.

I asked Lev Nikolayevich's permission to write a few lines myself in answer to a letter he had left unanswered, a naive but good letter in which there was a request for money to buy a camera.

"Do a kind deed," he replied. "It is a good letter, but as soon as it is a question of money, my ardor is dampened and I become disheartened."

In the evening at the table it was said of someone, I. I. Gorbunov I believe, that he was being tried for some political matter.

"Nowadays every decent man is being tried," said Lev Nikolayevich. "It is as Khiryakov [29] writes: 'I am unworthy of that honor, but I accept it in advance.' "

16 April

A village schoolteacher, Vasily Petrovich Mazurin, who is in sympathy with Tolstoy's views, was here today. Lev Nikolayevich liked him very much.

"Always the same moral questions," he said to me in speaking of him later. "The bringing up of children, chastity. As soon as one question arises, all the others follow in its wake. . . ."

Lev Nikolayevich is not in good health today. He did not eat lunch and did not want to ride his horse. But later he called me and said:

"I am going to pretend that I want to give you pleasure," and he smiled, for he could not have failed to notice that I gladly accompany him on his ride.

Various medications have been proposed, but it seems that his illness (liver, stomach) is of such long standing that the usual treatment is no longer efficacious.

"It's nothing, nearer to death," he said, and added: "You see how ineffectual all these external measures are."

We rode to Telyatinki. As we were leaving the village of Yasnaya Polyana, Lev Nikolayevich stopped at one of the huts.

"Where do the Kurnosenkovs live?"

"Here, benefactor," answered a peasant woman.

"Is it you that Aleksandra Lvovna has been helping?"

"Indeed it is."

"Then here you are. She asked me to give this to you." And Lev Nikolayevich gave the woman some money.

Bows and expressions of gratitude.

"Is your husband still ailing?"

"He is."

"Well, good-bye!"

"Good-bye, Your Excellency. We humbly thank you."

We approached the next hut, where a dejected-looking woman was sitting in the doorway. She stood up and walked over to Lev Nikolayevich. She too asked for help.

"Who are you?"

"Kurnosenkova."

"What do you mean, Kurnosenkova! I just gave something to Kurnosenkova."

"No, she is not Kurnosenkova, she is so-and-so," and the woman mentioned some other name.

Lev Nikolayevich turned his horse and rode back to the first hut. Though the woman who had been given the money insisted that she too was Kurnosenkova, she admitted that Aleksandra Lvovna had been helping her neighbor, and not her.

Lev Nikolayevich asked her to return the money, which she did quite willingly, smiling cheerfully as if amused at herself. The money was then given to the "real" Kurnosenkova.

Lev Nikolayevich rode on, saddened by the whole episode, and by having had to ask the woman to return the money.

Two other peasant women were walking behind us, talking about the two with whom we had just had dealings.

"What is this all about, women?" asked Lev Nikolayevich, turning his horse toward them.

They began to rail against both the "real" Kurnosenkova and the "impostor." And they were on their way to church in the village of Kochaki, because they were observing the fast.

"That is wrong," said Lev Nikolayevich after riding a little farther. "Here we have envy, and that other woman wanted to deceive us. It's understandable. On the one hand there is need, and on the other the corruptness of the Church," and he pointed in the direction of Kochaki, where there is a parish church.

I remarked that in any case there are more positive than

negative qualities to be found in the people, and cited as proof the letters he receives from simple men. It was from these letters that I first learned clearly what the people are, and especially the Russian people: the kind of men that exist among them, and what great spiritual powers are concealed within them.

"Of course, of course!" Lev Nikolayevich agreed, recalling the teacher who had come to see him today, a man from the laboring class. "Where do they come from!"

"Now, you say," he said later, "that there are those who independently emancipate themselves from the deception of the Church. But among them are those who deny everything, yet whose basic principles remain those of the Church. I had a letter today from one such materialist—Bernard Shaw belongs in this category. In denying God, he argues against the conception of a personal God, God the Creator. Such people reason thus: if God created everything, then he created evil, and so on. The formulation of the question is a Church formulation. Here the influence of the Church is beyond question. You know, in the religion of Buddhists or Confucianists, the concepts of God the Creator, of paradise, of a future life of bliss, are not found; these questions do not exist for them. But they do for us."

At Telyatinki Lev Nikolayevich dropped in at the Chertkov house and sat for a little while with his friends. On the way back we intended to ride through a beautiful little spruce forest, but were unable to cross the Kochaki ditch and the trench that had been dug around the local manor house, so we turned back to the road.

As I rode I read a letter I had received at Telyatinki from the student Skipetrov, an acquaintance of Lev Nikolayevich's whom I have mentioned before in this diary. The letter touched on a question that interests me: the interrelation of the spiritual and physical elements in man and the possibility of their harmonious union in his life and activity. I had never intended to put this question directly to Lev Nikolayevich, though of course it would have interested me to know his opinion. Now the occasion presented itself and it seemed an opportune moment to ask him.

" 'They live only for God,' " wrote Skipetrov about Seryozha Bulygin and another friend of ours. " 'I neither envy this nor do I aspire to it. My life must be a resultant of the animal and the divine. Man must be one beautiful harmony.' "

"As I have always said, and I say it again, the chief aim of human life, its incentive, is a striving for good. And this is not achieved through the life of the body; the life of the body causes suffering. Happiness is achieved through the life of the spirit," said Lev Nikolayevich, after listening to the letter.

I pointed out, by the way, that throughout his letter Skipetrov sought to substitute the word "reason" for "God."

"That comes of learning," replied Lev Nikolayevich. "But those who have not yet liberated themselves from its influence can, once they have emancipated themselves, stand on a normal path. And it seems to me that he does stand on a normal path. I read somewhere," he continued, "that after renouncing a personal God it is difficult to believe in an impersonal God. And this is true. The former can reward you, you can pray to Him, plead with Him; but in order to believe in an impersonal God it is necessary to make yourself his worthy receptacle. But what is good is that people are seeking. Pitiful are those who do not seek, or who think that they have found."

In an apple orchard Lev Nikolayevich explained how to distinguish the leaf bud from that of the blossom.

"In what connection did Shaw write to you, Lev Nikolayevich?" I asked.

"He sent me a play."

"A good play?"

"A poor one. He writes that he was inspired by my work— *The Power of Darkness*, I believe—in which there is a drunken peasant who is in effect better than all the other characters. I think it was *The Power of Darkness*, I don't remember. I have completely forgotten my earlier works. Shaw depicts a peasant who has stolen a horse and is brought to trial for it. He had taken the horse in order to fetch a doctor for a sick man. But the flaw here is that the feeling he ascribes to the peasant is very vague. He went for a

doctor, but a doctor might not have helped. It would have been
another matter if, for instance, he had rushed into a burning
building. Then there would have been a definite feeling of sacri-
ficing himself for another."

In the evening when we were all sitting around the table,
Lev Nikolayevich spoke about the origin of everything according
to scientific theories, about the impossibility of God the Creator,
about spatial and temporal conditions of perception, repeating in
part what he had said to me in the morning.

"You babble so much, Lev Nikolayevich," he said, laughing
as he rose from the table. "No, no, I am joking," he added, "I
enjoyed talking to you."

"Now, here is a field for abstention," he said later. "To abstain
from judging the government. This is something I have not
abstained from, but now I shall."

They began talking about the Russian budget. Tatyana Lvovna
mentioned that she had Professor Ozerov's famous diagrams with
the statistical data on the items of income and expenditure of the
Russian budget.

"Bring them, bring them, I like those figures," Lev Nikolayevich
urged her, as she hesitantly rose from her chair.

They examined the diagram.

"The first thing that strikes you about the introduction of these
airplanes and flying projectiles is that new taxes are being levied
on the people. This is an illustration of the fact that in a certain
moral state of society no material improvement can be beneficial,
but only harmful."

When they had finished looking at the diagrams, Lev Nikolayevich leaned back in his chair, sunk in thought.

"Yes," he said, "when you consider that there are people who
do not understand and do not want to understand what is so clear
and necessary, then you want to die."

There was a silence. Tatyana Lvovna smiled guardedly.

"I would not want to die because of that," she said.

"You would not want to, but I do," he rejoined. "We should

not think of consequences. When you live for external aims there are so many disillusionments and sorrows in life, but when you live for the inner work of perfection, you attain happiness. But there is this inclination to think of consequences."

Incidentally, for the *gens poetarum* a form letter has been devised and printed by hectograph on postcards: "Lev Nikolayevich has read your poetry and found it to be very poor. In short, he advises you not to devote yourself to such pursuits."

17 April

"I am in a gloomy state today," said Lev Nikolayevich, "and I feel terribly weak."

There was an interesting sort of letter in the morning post. A certain Selevin from Elisavetgrad asked to have pointed out to him passages in the Gospel that might be suitable for printing in copybooks which they are bringing out for students. At Lev Nikolayevich's request, I looked through the Gospel published by the Synod and copied out everything that corresponded to genuinely Christian convictions. Lev Nikolayevich looked over the letter and asked me to read two examples of passages I had selected, approved of them, and wrote a postscript calling attention to the Epistle of John. He remarked in passing that he prefers the Gospel of Matthew (because of its detailed account of the Sermon on the Mount) and John.

An issue of a progressive youth magazine published in English was received today.[30] Lev Nikolayevich was very much interested in it and said that if he were young he would go to China.

"The Chinese interest me," he said. "Four hundred million people in whom they want to inculcate European civilization!"

About two o'clock, that is, after Lev Nikolayevich's lunch, a handsome Polish youth in the uniform of a high-school student presented himself at the house. He informed me that he wished to speak to Lev Nikolayevich himself on a very important matter.

When I asked him whether he could tell me what it concerned, he said that he could not. To my surprise he then questioned me as to Lev Nikolayevich's attitude toward revolutionists. I concluded that I had one standing before me and explained briefly, trying not to offend the young man unwittingly by any harsh expressions, that although Lev Nikolayevich took a negative view of the actions of the government, he nevertheless regarded those of the revolutionists negatively too. The young man seemed to be entirely satisfied with this answer, and again expressed a desire to see Tolstoy.

I told Lev Nikolayevich about him and he went down to the terrace where the young man was waiting.

And what happened? Lev Nikolayevich returned with an expression of horror on his face and said that the youth had confessed to being a spy in the service of the government, and that he reported to the authorities the actions of a revolutionary group to which he was closely connected. And what was most absurd was that this young man had expected Lev Nikolayevich to approve of his actions, and that was why he had come to see him. Lev Nikolayevich told this singular visitor that he considered informing on his comrades a dreadful, reprehensible act.

In the evening when he saw that a game which utilized photographs of famous paintings was being played at the round table, Lev Nikolayevich sat down and began to examine the pictures. He liked many of the portraits of old men. The Raphael *Madonna* turned up.

"I do not know why people like the *Sistine Madonna* so much," he said. "There's nothing good about it. I remember that I once went into raptures over it, but that was only because Turgenev and Botkin admired it, and in imitation of them I pretended to like it too. But I don't know how to pretend."

He likes Raphael's *Madonna della Sedia*, and also the following: Titian's *Lavinia's Daughter* ("It is not beautiful, but is obviously such a likeness!"); the same artist's *Mary Magdalen Repenting* ("Superb! I am not speaking of beauty, but of truthfulness, as compared with Raphael's artificiality"); *Girl Counting Money* by

Murillo ("It is exquisite! What an expression! What truthfulness! That is not decadent painting!"); *The Franciscan* by Rubens ("Typical"); and Leonardo de Vinci's *Mona Lisa.*

A word about the letters Lev Nikolayevich receives. Almost all of them begin with a certain formula: "Dear Lev Nikolayevich, since a great many people trouble you, and you receive so many letters, I too will trouble you with a letter." (From the way they begin the exact opposite is expected: since so many people trouble you, I will refrain from doing so.) One would think from these letters that he had many disciples, as this is the word that often accompanies the signature. However, the "disciple" often confines himself to no more than a request for ten to one hundred rubles. The best letters, and by far the greatest number, are from peasants and, for the most part, simple people.

18 April

Easter. Lev Nikolayevich spent the day as usual: he was busy until two o'clock, went for a walk, and worked again in the evening.

In the morning I asked him:

"Lev Nikolayevich, doesn't this day arouse any particular feelings in you?"

"No, none. Only that it is a pity there is such a superstition: they ascribe special significance to this day, the bells are ringing . . ."

Sofya Andreyevna and the other members of the household are celebrating the holiday: everyone is smartly dressed, there are flowers on the table, and Easter cakes.

✧

"I have done some good work," said Lev Nikolayevich, coming into the dining room, where there was no one but me at two o'clock. "I have cut out everything about God in the booklets *Faith, The Soul,* and *Unity.* How can I talk about God when I haven't defined Him?" (The booklet *God* comes after those mentioned.) "It's important for people such as your kind of intellectual who, as a consequence of seeing the word God, will then find everything that follows dull and uninteresting. I can imagine their reaction because of my own attitude to Skovorod when I read him in my youth; everything seemed so boring to me. I don't know why. It was just that those questions didn't interest me. That was the period of my enthusiasm for aesthetic and artistic movements."

I told Lev Nikolayevich how in my early youth, after the loss of my naive, childlike faith, I had been agonizingly concerned with questions about the existence of God and the immortality of the soul. Lev Nikolayevich listened to me with interest and in his turn shared with me the following reminiscences of his own early spiritual life.

"In my youth questions about God and the immortality of the soul preoccupied me intermittently. What especially interested me was freedom of conscience and the problem of time and space. Here I stand talking to Bulgakov; I am cognizant of all this; but what is it that this is cognizant of? This is cognizant of what is cognizant that it is cognizant, and so on to infinity. This touching on infinity led—and here it is particularly clear and definite—to God, to a spiritual beginning. The question of time and space also occupied me for a long time. But even then I did not believe in the Russian Orthodox religion. I remember vaguely reading Kant and Schopenhauer, and it is to them that I owe my views on time and space as forms of perception. But, you know, an idea becomes close to you only when you are aware of it in your soul, when in reading about it it seems to you that it had already occurred to you, that you knew it and are simply recalling it. That's how it was with me when I read the Gospel. In the Gospel I discovered a new world: I had not supposed that there was such depth of thought in it, and it seemed to me strange that it was all compounded with those miracles, the Church, and with this Easter! It all seemed so familiar; it seemed that I had known it all long ago, that I had only forgotten it."

He went outside and watched the children with their grand-mother, Sofya Andreyevna, and their mothers, Olga Konstantinovna and Tatyana Lvovna, rolling eggs on the carpeted terrace.

In the evening at tea he told us about his meeting with the German emperor, Wilhelm I.

"It was at Baden-Baden. I was a young man, a dandy. One day I had been very lucky at roulette and left with a whole bag of gold. Going merrily on my way, I met Count Olsufyev, grandfather of the present count. As we walked on together everyone we encountered bowed low to him. I found it very pleasant to be walking with him. All at once I saw a gentleman coming toward us in a tightly buttoned frock coat, and Olsufyev bowed low to him! They greeted one another, exchanged a few words, and we continued on our way. I asked who this was. It turned out to have been the Crown Prince."

There was a conversation about love, and Lev Nikolayevich said:

"If there is a spiritual life, then love is a degradation. Love for everyone absorbs the feeling of exclusive love. The feeling of exclusive love begins unconsciously, but later a different attitude toward it is possible. It is all a question of your thinking: you can either stop yourself or urge yourself on. And such urging on is what is described by all the Turgenevs and the Tyuchevs who portray love as some sort of lofty, poetic feeling. But when, as the sands are running out, old Tyuchev falls in love and describes it in verse, it is merely revolting! It's like a visitor I had today: he talked about God, religion, but I could see that what he really wanted was a drink of vodka!"

Sofya Andreyevna took exception to this. She said afterward that Lev Nikolayevich had never experienced real love.

It was late in the evening when Lev Nikolayevich retired to his room. After a while he returned and called everyone out to the balcony to enjoy the mild, starry night, the dark trees, already in leaf, the fragrance, and the stars—the stars! We stood so long in admiration that Lev Nikolayevich, who was sleepy, humorously took leave of us, saying:

"I will not detain you, ladies and gentlemen!"

Everyone said good night once more and left him.

19 April

"Good morning, my friend!" said Lev Nikolayevich, extending his hand and greeting me cheerfully as I entered the study this morning. "Well, and how are you?"

"Very well."

"Really well?" he smiled.

Today in the "Remington room," in the presence of O. K. Tolstaya, M. A. Schmidt, and myself, Sofya Andreyevna, coming from her own room, said:

"Lev Nikolayevich has grown far more handsome. Before, he had a nose like a shoe, but now it has gone down and become straight. His expression used to be impassioned, irritable, disturbed, but now it is gracious, kind, and gentle. He never loved me as I loved him. When I encounter him now, or when he comes into my room, I feel: 'Oh, what happiness!' Lev Nikolayevich says that love is a degradation. And for him love was always just that. But he didn't feel the poetry of love. He says that we do not need exclusive love, yet he was still jealous of me when I was fifty. And what would he have done if I had felt this exclusive love for someone else? I think he would have killed himself! Twice he wrote in his diary that if I refused him he would shoot himself. But of course he never would have done it: he would have consoled himself with someone else."

At about eleven o'clock this morning two Japanese arrived from Moscow bringing letters to Lev Nikolayevich and me from our common acquaintance, their compatriot Konisi. One of them is the director of an institute of higher learning in Kyoto, Harada by name, and the other, Koji Mizutaki, is a clerk in the Ministry of Communications, who has been sent here to study Russian.

Lev Nikolayevich received them at once and talked to them for a long time. He devoted most of the day to them, in fact, and they did not leave till late in the evening.

Harada, the elder of the two, was the more dignified and self-assured. Mizutaki, quite young and naive, is inclined to laughter.

Harada is a Christian, Mizutaki a Buddhist with Christian leanings. But they are rather special Christians: rationalists and at the same time public servants. Harada did most of the talking, speaking English with Lev Nikolayevich. Mizutaki spoke Russian quite well, but for the most part listened respectfully. Lev Nikolayevich asked a great many questions about Japan and expressed a negative view both of Japan's striving to incorporate forms of European civilization and of the Japanese enthusiasm for militarism. He also talked about nonresistance and passive resistance.

When at lunch I. I. Gorbunov remarked that it was to be regretted that the Japanese have a mania for imitating European states, Harada rejoined with dignity to the effect that their mikado borrowed from certain states only what was best in them.

There were other visitors: an engineer and a student with their wives came from Petersburg to have a look at Tolstoy and to get his autograph. There was also a student from an ecclesiastical academy and a revolutionary. The former had come to reproach Tolstoy for giving the rights to his works written before 1881 to his family, and the latter to exhort him to "preach the truth with a revolver" (as he told me himself later). Lev Nikolayevich thanked them both for their advice "without which he had managed to live so long," and gave his autograph to the engineer and student and their wives.

After lunch Ivan Ivanovich, O. K. Tolstaya, and I went to show the visitors the park. I saw the theological student and the revolutionary sitting on a bench. I joined them—they readily made room for me—and we had a long talk. As a result they were reconciled to Lev Nikolayevich and almost friends with me by the time they left. They even took some of Tolstoy's books with them.

For me this was a day filled with happiness. I was reminded of the saying: "To be reconciled with an enemy is a twofold gain: you lose an enemy and win a friend."

Before dinner Lev Nikolayevich went out to the terrace where the table had been set for the first time.

"Well, is it all right?" Sofya Andreyevna asked him.

"No, it is not. Why make a shameful spectacle of us? People pass by here and will see all this."

I saw how chagrined Sofya Andreyevna was.

"And I thought you would say: 'Oh, how lovely!' " she said to him quietly at dinner. "The landscape is so . . ."

Before sitting down at the table, I told Lev Nikolayevich about my conversation with two of his visitors. He said that he was sorry he had thanked them ironically for their advice, and glad that I had succeeded in having a little talk with them, though he doubted whether this would have any effect on them. "But, may God grant it," he added.

"Genuine progress comes very slowly," he said to me later in this connection, "because it depends on a change in men's outlook. It moves by generations. The present generation consists of two lines: first the landowners, some of whom you would be ashamed to sit down to dinner with, then of revolutionaries, who despise them and want to do away with them by violence. Both generations must die out and be replaced by new ones. Therefore, everything depends on the children—on how they are brought up."

After dinner we all walked to the village to show the peasants the gramophone, something Lev Nikolayevich had long thought of doing. I carried the case, Ivan Ivanovich the horn, and Lev Nikolayevich and Harada the parcels of records. The gramophone was set up in the square near the hut where the library is housed, all the inhabitants of the village of Yasnaya Polyana were called together, and the machine was started.

We played vocal, orchestra, and balalaika records. They especially liked the balalaika music. There was dancing to the *hopak*, which Lev Nikolayevich watched with lively interest. In general he was very animated and jovial. He walked about among the listeners, talked to the peasants, introduced them to the Japanese and told them about one another, explained the construction of the gramophone, read the librettos of the songs to them, and encouraged the dancers. . . .

✧

21 April

Mikhail Lvovich, Lev Nikolayevich's youngest son, arrived early this morning.

At about two o'clock another guest arrived. I happened to go downstairs for some reason just as Olga Konstantinovna was coming up, and she announced:

"Andreyev has arrived!"

"Which Andreyev? The writer?"

"Yes."

The long-awaited meeting of Tolstoy and Andreyev had been delayed because Andreyev had not been able to visit Yasnaya Polyana before.

I rushed downstairs to the entrance. Andreyev had just got out of the cab. I was immediately struck by his handsome, dark-complexioned face with its somewhat uneasy expression, his white hat and black cape. I believe that Lev Nikolayevich was already there; I do not quite remember. There was a certain bustling about and then I saw that he was introducing everyone to the guest.

"This is my wife . . . my son . . . this is Chertkov's son . . ."

Andreyev's hand, in which he held his hat, was trembling.

Everyone went out to the terrace. Andreyev refused lunch and tea was ordered for him.

A trivial conversation began. Andreyev told us where he had come from, where he was going. It seems that he had been in the south and was on his way to Finland, where he has a summer home. He told us about Gorky, whom he had seen in Capri.

"He has a tremendous love for Russia, and wants to return, but he pretends that it's all the same to him."

He spoke about his interest in painting and color photography. Sofya Andreyevna told him about working on her memoirs and the publication of Tolstoy's works.

Andreyev was very gentle and shy. He agreed with everything Lev Nikolayevich and Sofya Andreyevna said.

A lady arrived with her two daughters. She had appealed to

Lev Nikolayevich earlier with a request that he permit her to talk to him. The little girls, her daughters, are said to have bad characters, and she hoped that Tolstoy might have an influence on them. Lev Nikolayevich talked with them while walking in the garden, and gave them some books.

Afterward he came to the terrace with his hat and walking stick. Andreyev was in conversation with Sofya Andreyevna.

"Aren't you going riding, Lev Nikolayevich?" I asked.

"No, I won't ride," he replied in a rather decisive tone. "In fact, I am not going to ride horseback at all anymore," he added.

I recalled his ride yesterday and my heart contracted. I thought he perhaps felt he had grown too old and that horseback riding was too strenuous for him.

"It arouses feelings of ill-will in people. That's what I am told. The peasants have no horses, and here I go riding on a fine horse. That officer said the same thing yesterday."

Then he suggested a walk to Andreyev, who instantly prepared to accompany him, even refusing the tea that had been served to him.

When Lev Nikolayevich went to the entrance hall for some reason, I followed him and said:

"Lev Nikolayevich, I wanted to say something about your giving up riding. You know, you might think of it this way: if your friends had got together the money and made you a present of the horse, then would you have had to refuse to ride?"

"But that's exactly the situation," he rejoined. "Nevertheless, I shall not ride." *

This evening I told him that Dima Chertkov's advice in this regard was that he should ride a poor horse.

"But, you see, this is a poor horse," he replied. "Her legs are weak, and so are her eyes—she just looks good."

Lev Nikolayevich's walk with Andreyev was not particularly happy. In the meadow they were caught in a heavy rainstorm with

* Only later did I learn that Délire was a gift from the Sukhotins. V.B.

hail, though the morning had been fine and the past few days warm and sunny. I rallied Leonid Andreyev on being such a pessimist that he would ascribe this to fate: as soon as he arrived the weather changed and they had been soaked to the skin. We intended to send a little cart for them and raincoats, but they returned before the horses could be harnessed.

Leonid Andreyev went to change his clothes, and Lev Nikolayevich to take a nap. I set off for Telyatinki to attend a rehearsal of the play and did not come back till after dinner.

When I returned Leonid Andreyev was sitting in the drawing room with the ladies. He was wearing a cream-colored knit sweater which, as he was quite obviously aware, was very becoming to him with his dark complexion, jet-black curls, and thickset figure.

"Is it permitted here? I always go around like this at home," he had said earlier, with an ingenuous air.

We began talking about his works. He himself likes best *Eleazar* and *The Life of Man*, and is beginning to like *Judas Iscariot*. Apropos *The Chasm* and *In the Fog* he said that he no longer writes such stories. He told us how in the beginning he had studied the styles of various writers—Chekhov, Garshin, Tolstoy—had analyzed their works and then tried to imitate them, and had succeeded in every case except the last.

"At first it worked," he said, "but later something happened—all at once it came to a standstill and I could not understand why."

Lev Nikolayevich came in. He suggested to Andreyev that he write for the cheap, kopeck publications of *The Intermediary*. But Andreyev explained that unfortunately he could not do this because, like Chekhov, he had sold to some firm not only what he had already written, but whatever he might write in the future.

At tea he told Lev Nikolayevich about the critic K. Chukovsky, who had raised the question of special dramatic literature for the cinema. Andreyev himself is very enthusiastic about this. Lev Nikolayevich listened rather skeptically at first, but gradually seemed to become more interested.

"I shall certainly write for the cinema!" he announced at the end of the discussion.

In general the conversation around the table was not especially significant.

When Lev Nikolayevich came into my room to look over the letters and sign them, I asked him what impression Andreyev had made on him.

"A good impression. He is clever, and he has good ideas. He's a very tactful man. But I feel that I ought to tell him the whole truth candidly: he writes too much."

"He is very young and enjoys such popularity! It would be interesting to know whether he attaches any importance to his personal life, or is simply content with his fame as a writer."

"Oh, no!" Lev Nikolayevich protested. "We talked about that. On the contrary, he says that he is not writing anything just now, but is thinking about moral questions."

Lev Nikolayevich went to bed and I showed Leonid Andreyev to the room that had been prepared for him—the one that is referred to as "under the vaults," which was formerly Lev Nikolayevich's study and is depicted in Repin's painting.

22 April

I went out to the terrace at the same time as Leonid Andreyev and Lev Nikolayevich, who was just setting out for his morning walk. Andreyev wanted to accompany him, but Lev Nikolayevich did not make an exception even for him and went alone as usual.

"He cannot make any exceptions," said Andreyev fervently, as if justifying Lev Nikolayevich. "His customary routine would be upset—and how many exceptions would he then have to make? I fully understand him."

Just then a young man appeared who shares Tolstoy's views and has come from Archangel province to see him. Lev Nikolaye-

vich met him on the road and told him he would talk to him
later, as he was at that moment going to pray.

On the terrace, which was flooded with sunshine, Leonid
Andreyev sprawled attractively in a wicker armchair and talked
about "the changes in the realm of philosophy which the perfection
of the cinema is bound to produce." I had already read something
about these ideas in an article by Andreyev's critic, A. Izmailov,
who visited us. These changes are to be brought about by the cinema
because in seeing himself on the screen man's consciousness will be
divided: one "I" he feels within himself, the other "I" will be
on the screen.

I was sorry that Andreyev's early departure at ten o'clock this
morning made it impossible for Sofya Andreyevna, who gets up
late, to take his picture with Lev Nikolayevich, as she had planned
to do. But as it happened, Andreyev had a camera loaded with
film in his luggage and so I took his picture, first alone and later
with Lev Nikolayevich. Pictures of the other members of the household, as well as the Goldenweisers, who had come from the station,
and several Telyatinki friends, were taken with Andreyev under
the "tree of the poor."

On returning from his solitary walk, Lev Nikolayevich took
a long walk with Andreyev. Then he went to his room to work
and Andreyev sat with us on the terrace to wait for his cab. When
it arrived he made his farewells to everyone and went upstairs
to say good-bye to Lev Nikolayevich. I preceded him to the study
and heard Lev Nikolayevich say:

"Ah! That must be Leonid Nikolayevich leaving!"

We heard his footsteps and he met Andreyev in the doorway
to the drawing room.

Andreyev thanked him with emotion. Lev Nikolayevich asked
him to come again.

"We shall be closer," he said. "Let me kiss you!" and he leaned
forward to his young fellow writer.

Having stopped in the drawing room I was an involuntary
witness to this scene.

When I accompanied Andreyev out to the cab I saw how deeply moved he was by the parting with Lev Nikolayevich. As we went downstairs he scarcely glanced at the steps, and turning his agitated face toward me said in a broken voice:

"Tell Lev Nikolayevich—tell him that I—that I was happy, that he is—so kind——"

He got into the cab, took hold of his little suitcase and his camera, and drove off followed by our parting words.

Andreyev made a very good impression on everyone at Yasnaya. He was in the highest degree modest, in fact shy, and spoke of Lev Nikolayevich with reverence. His speech was simple, even somewhat coarse in comparison with Lev Nikolayevich's way of speaking, which is comprehensible to everyone and beautifully precise and refined. Also, it seemed to me that he posed a bit, or as O. K. Tolstaya so aptly expressed it, "made himself charming." He dressed "simply but elegantly," as they say, in a picturesque cape, a lounge suit and sweater, and a black necktie tied in a bow, all of which created an effect. He probably finds that his good looks require all these accessories, and seems to attach great importance to public opinion. He spoke of his acquaintance with Gorky ("but, of course, I know him well") with noticeable satisfaction and a trace of pride. There was something I did not like about his enthusiasm for the cinema, color photography, and painting: it reminded me of a certain type of the idle rich who do not know where to apply their energies, or how to employ their time.

For all this, I was completely under his spell as a writer. *The Life of Man* and *Judas Iscariot* are among my favorite works. But such is the peculiarity of Yasnaya Polyana that one involuntarily compares everyone who comes here with Tolstoy and as a rule forms too severe a judgment of the person being observed and is probably unduly critical.

When the guest had departed, Lev Nikolayevich went back to work as usual. He did not go horseback riding after lunch but took a walk with Goldenweiser and Sofya Andreyevna.

Some peasants came from a distant village with a complaint about their landowner, who has deprived them of their common pasture. Lev Nikolayevich gave them a note to the Tula lawyer, Count Tolstoy.

I went to Telyatinki for a rehearsal of *The First Distiller*, and when I returned in the evening found a large gathering in the dining room. Besides Lev Nikolayevich, Sofya Andreyevna, and Olga Konstantinovna, there were the Gorbunovs, the Nikolayevs, the Boulangers, and the Goldenweisers. They began asking me about the play. Lev Nikolayevich will not be able to attend the performance as the Moscow violinist, Boris Sibor, is coming tomorrow for only one evening. Lev Nikolayevich wanted so much to see the play that he tried to think of some way to come either before or after Sibor's playing. But this seems to be impossible. We cannot postpone the performance as several of those taking part in it are leaving as soon as it is over.

"Oh, my writer's pride is wounded!" Lev Nikolayevich exclaimed with a gesture of vexation.

At the table he said that he had been thinking all night about what should be written for the cinema.

"You see, this can be understood by great masses of people, and by all nations. And so you could be writing not four, five, or ten pictures, but as many as fifteen."

I repeated what Andreyev had said about his being the best one to begin writing for the cinema: if he makes a start, all the other writers who would not "stoop" to writing for the screen would follow. Andreyev also said that if Lev Nikolayevich would write something he would tell Drankov, who owns the film company, and he would bring a company of actors and a good director to Yasnaya Polyana to rehearse and film the play right here.

Goldenweiser played.

"Wonderful, wonderful!" said Lev Nikolayevich after hearing Beethoven's first sonata *Quasi una Fantasia*.

Goldenweiser played Chopin mostly. They talked about music.

"I like Haydn's style," said Lev Nikolayevich. "Such simplicity and clarity! Everything is so simple and clear—and completely without artificiality."

He asked about Schumann and Schubert.

"He was a libertine, wasn't he?" he said about the latter.

Olga Konstantinovna mentioned a letter that came today from V. A. Posse, giving his impressions of his trip to the south of Russia, where he had been lecturing on Tolstoy.

"What interesting letters you receive, Papa!"

"I don't deserve it," replied Lev Nikolayevich. "You live in the country and receive information from the four corners of the earth as if you were at a focal point, and the information you value most, that is, about the movement—both positive and negative."

✧

23 April

This morning Lev Nikolayevich returned from his walk carrying an oak branch in leaf. He showed it to us as one more manifestation of an unusually early spring.

I went to Telyatinki this morning and spent the whole day there. The performance of *The First Distiller* took place in the evening in the Chertkov's big barn. . . . It was apparently successful. There was an audience of about two hundred peasants and they left well satisfied. None of the Tolstoys came, as B. Sibor was playing at Yasnaya Polyana. The village policeman was present, however, in civilian dress, and furtively moved about among the spectators during the performance, on guard to see whether "the Tolstoyans" would stir up the peasants with any "unlawful" speeches. But this time his efforts were in vain.

✧

26 April

Today Lev Nikolayevich got up very early, at seven o'clock. This is a sure sign that his health is improving; he is feeling much better.

We had dinner on the terrace and he joined the others in admiring the exceptionally fine weather and the landscape.

The cry of the cuckoo was heard.

"I don't like the cuckoo," said Lev Nikolayevich all of a sudden. "It's tiresome! You don't notice other birds as you do the cuckoo. It's the same as the way you notice a dog barking. You don't notice frogs either."

A rather elaborate-looking dish was served. Someone at the table said that it must be hard on the cook always working in the heat. He was told that Semyon the cook loves his work.

"How could he not love it!" Lev Nikolayevich remarked with irony. "You can only do your work when you love it. I'm sure that the people who do the cleaning love their work too. When you work, the consciousness of the objective toward which you are striving is always present. And they have an objective, of course—to clean."

He frowned: the masters were justifying their position.

In the evening they talked about the writers' congress in Petersburg having arbitrarily published Tolstoy's letter in an abbreviated form. While agreeing that this should not have been done, Lev Nikolayevich dismissed the matter with a wave of the hand saying:

"Well, never mind, they're welcome to it!"

Aleksei Sergeyenko, who had just come from Krëkshino, said that Chertkov intended to see that the letter was published in full in the newspapers.

Lev Nikolayevich smiled and after a moment's silence said:

"If I tried to think of the kind of friend I need, I could think of no one but Chertkov."

In the evening he dictated a letter to Korolenko concerning the second part of his article. Later when I took the letters to his room, he gave me today's letter from Chertkov to send back to him, as is their custom.

"He begs me to resume horseback riding," he said. "That's funny!"

"Why funny?"

"He's really such a nice person."

I said good night. Lev Nikolayevich rose and started to go to his room.

"And what are you doing?" he asked.

"I'm sealing some of the letters."

"Is everything all right with you?"

"Fine. Very fine."

"Thank God for that. Thank God," he repeated. "Here I have all these illnesses," he continued, "but that's all right too. I keep getting closer to death."

"Isn't that frightening, Lev Nikolayevich?"

"Oh, no! You just try to do one thing: to refrain from wanting it. It's important to remember that you must do the work that has been entrusted to you. And just as the workman looks after his spade to see that it's sharp, so you should look after yourself. And that is always possible. Even when decay sets in, you can still live in the decay."

27 April

✦

This evening Lev Nikolayevich shared with me his impressions of a conversation he had had with a Siberian who visited him today.

"It's amazing," he said, "those people live so far away that you have to travel sixteen days to reach them, yet from what he says they do the same, exactly the same stupid things there that they do here: they have the same kind of governors-general and police, the same prostitution, the same drunkenness, the same ragamuffins. Now the Chinese live well, only they work slowly, he says, not like the Russians. That's good. It's not necessary to overwork. Besides spiritual dignity there is the human dignity of the body, and though it's corporeal, there's no need to violate it."

Then he said:

"Still, I look at our peasants who get up at four o'clock in the morning to work. The mornings are so beautiful now—what could take their place? Not the champagne and truffles of those people who sit up till three o'clock in the morning in a tavern and then lie in bed till noon."

Late in the evening he brought me a letter for Aleksandra Lvovna. Looking out of the open window he exclaimed:

"Ah, how lovely! A holiday!"

29 April

✧

I shall note some of the very interesting things that Lev Nikolayevich said in a conversation about religion.

"If a man who sincerely believes is so undeveloped that his belief in the miraculous does not seem unreasonable to him, then we can only admire his faith."

"Reason is not the basis of belief, but there can be no unreasonable belief."

He mentioned a letter in which the writer asked his help in disseminating his own world-view.

"I have a reputation that leads people to think: 'Let Tolstoy say it and everyone will believe it.' If I were to confirm every piece of nonsense men would soon stop believing me."

We talked about a book on science in India, which was sent to Lev Nikolayevich by a native of that country.

"Is science developing in India?" someone asked.

"Thank God, it is not!" answered Lev Nikolayevich with a laugh. "And the way it develops here is that we have a lot of professors."

In the evening at tea, when censorship was being discussed, he said:

"Censorship temporarily suppresses expression and confines men within certain limits, but ultimately the accumulated force breaks through. The government achieves its aim, however; for them it's *après nous le déluge.* As a matter of fact, banning a writer increases his importance. You can see this in Herzen. If he had lived in Russia he would probably have become a scribbler like Andreyev. He'd be writing from morning to night."

In the evening Lev Nikolayevich read the letters I had written.

"Tell me, Lev Nikolayevich, is my language clear and comprehensible? Lev Sergeyenko says that in my letters it's pretentious, and perhaps not understandable to simple people."

"It's precise," said Lev Nikolayevich, "and I approve of that. Nevertheless, it is literary. But then we're all like that. Semyonov writes in absolutely simple, folk language. Sometimes one comes across such apt words. I always underline them."

And he brought a book by S. T. Semyonov and showed me certain examples in it.

30 April

A young man arrived in a troika with bells ringing, a gouty ex-military man called Durnovo,[31] who is evidently related to the former minister. He expounded a theory of interpreting the Gospels which in essence seems to be that they teach that every man should live according to his own understanding. Lev Nikolayevich took issue with this, saying that human understanding varies. But Durnovo argued zealously. He was supported by his wife, who accompanied him and who, as Lev Nikolayevich said, regards her husband as an extraordinary and saintly man. Lev Nikolayevich also became excited in the course of the argument and, naturally, refused to validate this interpretation of the Gospels by lending his name to it, which is what Durnovo had come for.

This conversation took place on the terrace. When I heard the jingling of bells, I knew that the visitors had gone. Lev Nikolayevich came into the "Remington room" and told us the whole story.

The mail was brought and he rang for me.

"I have received a letter from Tanya," he said joyfully. "She wants me to come to Kochety."

Kochety is the estate of Tatyana Lvovna's husband, M. S. Sukhotin, in the Novosil district of Tula. Lev Nikolayevich has long been contemplating this visit and was only waiting for her letter to confirm it.

"When do you think you will go?"

"The sooner the better. Sonya will return from Moscow tomorrow, and I can leave the next day. I want so much to get away from here!" he said laughing. "Sometimes even to the next world."

He gave me the letters to answer. A picture postcard remained on the table.

"What about this?" I asked, starting to take it.

"No, leave it. I always give them to the children in the village," he said, putting it in his wallet, where there was already another one.

While we were at dinner an elderly man with a serious face arrived and said that he had to talk to Tolstoy. When Lev Nikolayevich finished his dinner, he went out to the terrace to see him. I was sitting in my room when, a quarter of an hour later, I heard Lev Nikolayevich shouting to me from downstairs. I ran down and found him at the foot of the stairs, laughing and excited.

"Bring the phonograph here—we must record this. God only knows what he is talking about—that he will save all men, and the apocalypse, and the law of inertia, and electricity—we must record it!"

It appears that Lev Nikolayevich has a phonograph that was a gift from Edison. Belinky, who was here at the time, carried it downstairs and set it up. The visitor turned out to be a completely abnormal person, but an extraordinary orator. He readily agreed to speak into the phonograph and talked ceaselessly and fluently for at least half an hour. Plyusin, Zbaikov, Seryozha Popov, and some others arrived from Telyatinki and they too listened to this speech.

At first Lev Nikolayevich laughed, but later he tried to stop the orator. This was not so easy, however. When he had finished talking into the phonograph, the visitor remained on the terrace and would not let anyone else say a word. Finally Dushan thought of a way to induce him to leave: he suggested that he have something to eat, and the orator gladly accompanied him to the kitchen. Afterward Dushan saw to it that he left the estate.

"Do you know, Lev Nikolayevich," remarked Plyusin, when the

orator had left the terrace, "we were all laughing at him, only
Seryozha Popov did not laugh."

"Yes, I noticed that," said Lev Nikolayevich.

Seryozha Popov continued to sit in silence.

I have said nothing about this youth up to now. He is a follower
of Tolstoy's and strives to embody his views to the utmost degree
in his own life. He is about twenty-three years old and left Petersburg while still in high school to become a wanderer. Since that
time he has roamed all over Russia, stopping for the most part in
various Tolstoyan communities and colonies. This quiet, gentle
creature is kind to everyone, calls everyone his brother, and always
uses the familiar "thou." He even calls the Solov dog his brother.
He is fair-haired, has mild blue eyes, and his outward aspect reflects
his inner nature. He never accepts money from anyone for his
work. Seryozha loves Lev Nikolayevich very much and is always
glad of an opportunity to see him again.

When the orator had departed, Lev Nikolayevich said of him:

"His thoughts are scattered. When an idea is strong it can be
focused, but when it is weak it is diffuse, scattered. One sees this
in oneself."

We talked on the terrace until late in the evening.

Plyusin asked Lev Nikolayevich what was the essential difference
between Christianity and Buddhism.

"True Christianity?"

"Yes."

"None. As in one so in the other, a God of love is propounded
and a personal God denied."

Plyusin reminded him that in his article *Religion and Morals*
he calls Buddhism a negative paganism. But this was said in
reference to official Buddhism.

"I especially like the First Epistle of John, which is never cited
by the clergy, and in which it says: '. . . for he that loveth not his
brother whom he hath seen, how can he love God whom he hath
not seen?' In the words 'God whom he hath not seen' there is a
denial of a personal God, it seems to me. And here it is clearly stated
that 'God is love.'"

We all went upstairs for tea. The dining room was filled with rather unusual visitors for Yasnaya Polyana: Seryozha Popov with his dirty bare feet, the passerby Pyotr Nikitich Lepekhin, a young man who came to Tolstoy late in April of this year with a request that he be given some sort of employment. Incidentally, he gave Tolstoy a little notebook of his "aphorisms," many of which struck Lev Nikolayevich as being very serious and pithy. He sent the youth to Telyatinki, where he has remained as a worker.

Someone reminded Lev Nikolayevich that he has said he loves drunkards.

"I do love them!" he acknowledged. "How can one not love them? They come to me, and I look at them—why, drunkards are of a far better type than usurers, say, and who reviles them? Or robbers, or the rich . . ."

1 May

Sofya Andreyevna returned from Moscow this morning.

After lunch Lev Nikolayevich went alone and on foot to watch the Moscow-Orel automobile race. The drivers recognized him and hailed him, waving their hands and their hats. One of the automobiles stopped near him, and Lev Nikolayevich wished the driver luck as he set off.

❖

Today Dushan, Lev Nikolayevich, and I made preparations to go to Kochety, which Lev Nikolayevich has definitely decided to do tomorrow. He gathered up his papers and packed them himself.

2 May

We left at half-past seven this morning. It was a fine day. We waited at Zaseka for about a quarter of an hour for the train. P. A. Boulanger, E. E. Gorbunova and her children, and Pyotr Nikitich came from Telyatinki to see Lev Nikolayevich off. Mr.

Tapsel, the photographer who came yesterday, and his English friend also appeared. Mr. Tapsel kept walking around and clicking his camera.

✧

When the train from Moscow arrived, it brought I. I. Gorbunov-Posadov. He and Lev Nikolayevich kissed each other joyously. Among the passengers pouring out of the train was a group of high-school boys who crowded around the carriage that Tolstoy entered.

"Tolstoy! Tolstoy!" was heard in the crowd.

At last the train started. Lev Nikolayevich blew kisses to Ivan Ivanovich and the others who were seeing him off, and went into the carriage. Because there were no seats in the third class, for which we had tickets, we sat in the second-class carriage.

"This is unlawful," said Lev Nikolayevich.

He suspected a "plot," if not on the part of Sofya Andreyevna or of us, then on the part of the railway authorities. But there was no plot; the third-class carriage really was full. At about the fourth stop, however, seats became available in the third class, and Lev Nikolayevich insisted that we move to the next car.

When we were seated, he asked us to move the wicker traveling case close to the window and he climbed up on it so that he would have a more extensive view. He was delighted that he could see so far from where he sat, and found it "amusing."

Sitting on the bench opposite him, I attentively observed his face as he gazed out the window. I felt that I was seeing and experiencing something unusual. His head, the expression of his face, his eyes and lips, were all remarkable and beautiful! The whole depth of his soul was reflected in them. . . .

While we were in the second-class carriage, Lev Nikolayevich went through today's correspondence, which we had picked up in Zaseka, then turned to the newspapers and read the latest issues of *New Russia* and *The Russian Word*.

"Here, this is very good, read it," he said, pointing to an apothegm which *New Russia* had taken from the collection *For Every Day*.

"Suffering and torment are experienced only by him who has separated himself from the life of the world and, not seeing his own sins which have brought suffering into the world, considers himself guiltless; consequently he rebels against the sufferings he bears for the sins of the world and for his own spiritual well-being."

"This is what I feel so keenly about myself," said Lev Nikolayevich. "It is especially true of a long life like mine."

✧

He got out of the train and walked about at almost every stop. Once he talked with a lady who was a vegetarian. At the second stop he came over to me and said:

"Look—a typical policeman's face!"

"In what way?"

"Just take a look."

I walked by him. A policeman like any other policeman: fat, well-fed, with a rather good-natured look.

I stopped not far from the station entrance, where a crowd had gathered.

"Is that *he*?" people were asking one another.

"It is, of course it is," the policeman said, walking over to them. "Last year," he said with a broad smile, "he sent a telegram from here saying: 'Send a cart for me.'" And he laughed soundlessly, his whole body rocking. "'Send a cart!'"

In general people were very interested in Lev Nikolayevich. At every stop the conductor immediately let it be known that Tolstoy was in the train, and the stationmasters and telegraph operators strolled by and peered in at the window of our section. If Lev Nikolayevich took a walk, everyone followed him. Not all greeted him, but those who did seemed to do so with special pleasure: they waited for him to pass and when he drew near broke into a loud, cheerful chorus:

"How are you, Lev Nikolayevich?"

Tolstoy took off his hat in response.

Once when the train was already in motion, we heard voices outside the window:

"Tolstoy!"

"Not really?"

"Not really," Lev Nikolayevich repeated.

Just then the train pulled out, and whoever had uttered that ecstatic exclamation missed seeing him.

The conductors were extremely considerate. They tried to keep people from coming into our section, and when anyone managed to get in tried to move him to another seat. But since Tolstoy had no objection to other passengers sitting with us, they were not obliged to move.

✧

"Is Chertkov coming to the Sukhotins?" asked Lev Nikolayevich. "That will be pleasant for me."

A telegram had been sent to Chertkov on Lev Nikolayevich's departure. He is trying to get permission, if not to return to Telyatinki, at least to come to Kochety while Tolstoy is there. During Lev Nikolayevich's last visit to Kochety, Chertkov stayed four versts away in Suvorovo, which is not in the province of Tula but in Orel. Lev Nikolayevich said that this reminded him of Voltaire's exile when he had his castle at Ferney built so that his drawing room was in France and his bedroom in Switzerland.

✧

We had to change trains at Orel and there was an hour's wait. Our baggage was taken into the station, where in a little room off the first- and second-class buffet Dushan heated up some oatmeal porridge for Lev Nikolayevich. The only vegetable available in the buffet was asparagus, which was prepared so late that the attendant let Lev Nikolayevich take the dishes into the train provided he sent them back with a fellow traveler. But Lev Nikolayevich managed to finish eating before the train left.

The attitude of the public to Tolstoy changed radically in Orel. Two traits were conspicuous: intrusiveness and impoliteness. Why I do not know; perhaps because of their great "civilization." While Lev Nikolayevich was eating in the buffet, people crowded around the windows and doors, gaping with curiosity. When we walked down the long platform to the train with our baggage, a line of silent people followed us, scrutinizing Tolstoy intently. No one greeted him—after all, they had not been introduced. When we finally managed to find places in the carriage, people crowded into our section and the neighboring ones, which were already jammed, and continued to stare at him, silently and impassively. A little place had been made free for him next to a window outside of which stood a crowd of curious people. Since the platform of the Orel station is elevated, the whole interior of the car was exposed to their view and they could peer in at him. This complete absence of tact made a very disagreeable impression.

It soon became unbearably stuffy, but the train did not move. I was only glad that Lev Nikolayevich treated these gapers as they deserved, that is, with the utmost imperturbability. Though people were staring at him on all sides, he simply went on with whatever he happened to be doing: he ate the asparagus (because of the overcrowding it was almost impossible to raise the folding table attached to the wall), nibbled a few rusks, offering some to the children who were there, and read the newspaper.

Swarms of curious people began passing through the car: ladies, young girls, functionaries. One gentleman came up to Lev Nikolayevich, introduced himself as the director of a technical high school, and thanked him for the portrait that had once been sent to the pupils of his school, and then left.

From the platform of the car I heard a man on the station platform sneeringly remark to a policeman:

"The count has to treat himself to asparagus!"

Later, when the train pulled out, the man came and sat next to Lev Nikolayevich and talked to him continuously. He was either a police detective or one of those know-it-all traveling salesmen that are usually encountered on trains. In any case, he had nothing in common with Tolstoy. Others who were eager for conversation gathered around and made trivial conversation.

✧

At last we arrived at the Blagodatnoye station, and from there had to travel fifteen versts by cab to reach Kochety. The train noisily sped toward the platform. Dushan and I put our heads out the window. Oh, how lovely! Tatyana Lvovna was standing in the doorway of the station, gayly waving her parasol. Thank God we had arrived!

✧

And so our journey came to an end. The droshky drawn by four horses rapidly brought us to Kochety.

Lev Nikolayevich became animated at the sight of the cool green fields and the handsome old-fashioned dresses of the village women we passed on the way. Because it was Sunday, everyone was in the streets in holiday garb, and smiles of delight kept flitting over his face.

When we reached the house, he said he would not be in haste to leave and jokingly threatened his hosts with a long visit. They responded with joyous invitations to remain for a long time.

"There will be no passersby asking for five-kopeck pieces, no one at odds with the law, no mothers to be reconciled to their daughters," said Lev Nikolayevich. "But many agreeable visitors— which can also be tiring."

We arrived at half-past six in the evening. Dinner was kept waiting and Lev Nikolayevich went to take a rest.

We spoke little at the table, but after dinner coffee was served on the open veranda and, thanks to Mikhail Sergeyevich, there began an interesting conversation about the loquacity of women.

"Since there is only one lady present," said Lev Nikolayevich, meaning his daughter, "I will say that in my opinion, this would be a much better world if women were less talkative. Now, Mikhail Sergeyevich says that they render a great service in freeing us from the obligation of entertaining our guests. That's fine, let them talk then, but in serious affairs—it's disastrous! It is a kind of naive egoism, a desire to put themselves forward."

No wonder Lev Nikolayevich has formed such an opinion of society women! They recalled how on meeting him last year one of the local ladies, the wife of the Marshal of Nobility, had said in a drawling, simpering voice:

"Lev Nikolayevich, do try to be nice to my son: he can't bear you! Talk to him about horses, and then he will forgive you for everything!"

Lev Nikolayevich's stay at Kochety began with his going out alone after dark to take a walk in the park and losing his way. It must be remarked that the park at Kochety is immense: three versts around, and the total length of the many intricate paths is twelve versts. It was not without cause that Tatyana Lvovna feared that walking alone there Lev Nikolayevich might suddenly feel faint, fall down on one of the paths, and not be found.

Several people hurried off in search of him. Bells were rung, a hunting horn blown, and finally Dushan found him walking on one of the paths. It turned out that he had crossed the park and come out on a meadow, then, on turning back, missed the path. When he heard the bells he had walked in the direction of the sound.

"I won't do it again, I won't do it again!" he reiterated in answer to Tatyana Lvovna's reproaches.

She begged him not to go out alone in the evening.

"All right, all right," he replied. "And I shall try to walk on my feet and not on my head."

"Don't joke," was all the dispirited Tatyana Lvovna could say.

We had tea and soon retired to our respective rooms.

❖

3 May

During the day Lev Nikolayevich sat in the park reading. After dinner he took us to see a flowering chestnut tree. On the way he said:

"How lovely! All of this is somehow new for me. Just as if I were seeing it for the first or last time. And there are so many birds—turtledoves, nightingales . . . Oh, how beautifully the nightingales sing! And a little while ago there were eagles flying high in the air, and two kites."

❖

In the evening we listened to some Varya Panina records, which Lev Nikolayevich enjoyed very much.

4 May

This morning Lev Nikolayevich looked into Tatyana Lvovna's room where I was typing the preface to *Thoughts on Life*. He had started writing this a long time ago but has not yet put it into final form.

"God help us!" he said, thrusting his head in at the door. "Still clicking away?"

Referring to this preface, he said:

"It will probably be as Belinky has said, that I shall work on it right up to my death, and then it will not be finished." [32]

✧

"How did you sleep?" someone asked him.

"Well. So many dreams! All of them good, amazing. I even wanted to write down certain complete thoughts. Dreams are interesting in that they reflect the psychology of the individual; the expression of a man's character is psychologically correct in them."

One of the neighboring landowners was here for dinner.

Speaking of his impressions of his walk today, Lev Nikolayevich said:

"If Napoleon had fought in the Novosil district he would certainly have stayed at Kochety: it is the highest point and has a view on all sides."

The play about Napoleon which Bernard Shaw recently sent to Lev Nikolayevich was mentioned. He said he had found it poorly written and artificial.

"There is no end to the wit, but it is devoid of meaning. The characters do not say what they might have said, but what Shaw wants to say through them."

In the evening Lev Nikolayevich read aloud a fragment of

Semyonov's story *At the Abyss*. Then he began and Tatyana Lvovna finished reading another Semyonov story, *Aleksei the Mill-owner*. Both stories delighted him.

"That's the way all peasant life is rising," he said, "from below. We see it from above, but it is rising from below."

He observed that he had found in the bookshelf of Sukhotin's son stereotyped Paris editions of the French classics, La Boétie, Rousseau, etc., which he could not resist reading.

"It's interesting to think what my grandchildren will read," he said. "In our time there was a definite range of classics, and one knew what one had to read to be an educated man. But now such masses of books are being published! One of my visitors asked me to tell him who Knut Hamsun was. Novelists like Hamsun are legion today, and in the politico-economic field, that is, in the field of social questions, there is a host of writers!"

♦

5 May

Today I learned that Lev Nikolayevich has been carrying out the slop pail and waste from his room and emptying it into the refuse pit. He walked rapidly past the window of the room I share with Dushan, in his hat and coat, erect and with his thoughtful gaze directed downward, carrying the large, full pail. Dushan says that he does this summer and winter.

It is characteristic of Lev Nikolayevich that he likes to meet new people. He asked Sukhotin to introduce him to a neighboring landowner, Prince Golitsyn, a strange, rich old man who leads a secluded, solitary life in his huge house. He has also said he would like to get acquainted with the Kochety peasants.

♦

In the evening he read aloud some of the thoughts of La Rochefoucauld.

"Excellent!" he said. " 'It is possible to meet a woman who has never had a lover, but it is hard to find a woman who has had only one.' That is very true."

✧

Before going to bed he told Mikhail Sergeyevich, Dushan, and me, sitting in our room, about having received Ivanov-Razumnik's book *On the Meaning of Life (in F. Sologub, L. Andreyev, L. Shestov).*

"How can you look for the meaning of life in Sologub, or in Chekhov, to whom he also refers? The greatest, most brilliant men have studied the meaning of life for thousands of years, from the Brahmans and Confucius to Kant and Schopenhauer, but all this you are supposed to strike out and search for the meaning of life in Sologub or Shestov. Yet one cannot call the book stupid. But those thinkers were essentially teaching the meaning of life, while with these others one has to make a real effort to discover something about it. They describe how some young girl fell in love, and in this you're supposed to discover it."

6 May

A telegram has been received from Chertkov, as well as a letter, saying that he has received permission to come to Kochety. In the letter he urges Lev Nikolayevich to resume horseback riding. And he cautions him against acceding to those who tell him he should write accusatory articles. Lev Nikolayevich noted on the letter: "A dear person and a precious friend."

Giving me the letters to be answered, he asked me to take one of them to Tatyana Lvovna.

"It's an interesting letter, about the futurist school of art and poetry, in Italy chiefly. It's—it's a complete madhouse!"

This letter, a very amusing one, was read aloud in the evening.

Tatyana Lvovna showed Lev Nikolayevich a pamphlet by Shtil, *The Duties of a Mother* (on sex education) and Chuiko's *To Our Children* (a discussion of the origin of man). Lev Nikolayevich was indignant over the contents of the brochures, in which there were examples of talks with children on man's sex life that were clumsily composed and entirely too frank.

"These are important questions," he said, "which I can say nothing about, and therefore I will not say just anything. Where did man come from? That is something the greatest sages didn't know! And I don't know it either."

7 May

Vladimir Grigorevich Chertkov has arrived. Although Lev Nikolayevich has asked that no one come to his room in the morning, I did not hesitate to knock on his door and tell him of the guest's arrival. He quickly got up and came out to the entry to greet him. They kissed each other affectionately. As often happens when welcoming or seeing someone off, people are moved, somewhat confused, and consequently there is a sudden embarrassment.

Vladimir Grigorevich paid the cabman and Lev Nikolayevich went back into the house. He took out his handkerchief and blew his nose, and I saw that his face was covered with tears.

Vladimir Grigorevich went to his room, where Lev Nikolayevich remained with him.

✧

9 May

✧

They were talking about the sect of Jehovah's Witnesses, one of whose members is being prosecuted by the state, and in connection with the fact that there is a great deal of mysticism and superstition in their beliefs, Lev Nikolayevich said:

"I have been thinking, and have made a note of it, that metaphysics—questions about the soul, about God—which constitutes an essential part of religious teaching, is so abstract and incomprehensible that the less said about it in words the better. It is apprehended by some higher spiritual faculty rather than by reason."

✧

Sofya Andreyevna and Andrei Lvovich have arrived.

It was rather noisy at dinner and at tea this evening. Lev Nikolayevich left the table quite early.

"What, Papa, going to bed so early?" asked Tatyana Lvovna.

"I still have a lot of things to do, and I want to lay out a game of patience," he said, adding when he reached the corridor: "Come to my room, Vladimir Grigorevich."

I took some letters to him. In one of them, following his instructions, I had advised a young man who wrote him a high-flown, flattering letter, "to be simpler and more sincere in his relations with people."

"But perhaps the young man's letter was sincere," remarked Vladimir Grigorevich.

"No," Lev Nikolayevich protested. "There I know I have not erred. But where I did err was with Andrei."

"In what way?" asked Vladimir Grigorevich. "Everything seemed to be all right."

"No, I was not good with him. He began talking about Molochnikov, saying what everyone in Petersburg says, that he is in prison not just because of my books, but because of some kind of propaganda. And I said that those who say that are not worthy of a fraction of the respect that Molochnikov is. In a word, it was not good. I did better with Sofya Andreyevna. Today I told her clearly for the first time how difficult the conditions of our life are for me, downright physically difficult! I spoke fervently, but calmly. She seemed to understand. However, I don't know whether it will be for long."

Vladimir Grigorevich had just invited Lev Nikolayevich to come to Kochety, his place in Stolbovaya near Tula, and Lev Nikolayevich accepted with alacrity. Speaking of the proposed visit, Chertkov had said: "If it is not too unpleasant for you to be so long away from Yasnaya Polyana." At these words Lev Nikolayevich smiled ironically.

I retyped for the third time since we have been here the preface to *Thoughts on Life*, which Lev Nikolayevich has again revised. This is a short, condensed statement of Tolstoy's entire world-view. It is for this reason that he is so interested in it and works so hard on it.

10 May

This morning when I went to Lev Nikolayevich's room in connection with some work, he said:

"I am in extraordinarily poor physical condition today, but my spiritual condition is amazingly good—I feel so well, and I've written so much!"

"But is that really possible?" I asked.

"Of course! That's exactly as it should be! And how do you feel?"

"Well—in body and in spirit."

"And that's how it should be with you. All you have to do is to endeavor always to have the spirit rule over the flesh, to keep it under control."

Today for the first time after such a long interval, Lev Nikolayevich went horseback riding, evidently as a result of Chertkov's influence.

After lunch, together with Chertkov, I went to the study to take him his letters.

Lev Nikolayevich was the first to mention the letters in the newspaper by Stakhovich and Gradovsky attacking Chertkov, who recently came out in the press against the arbitrary abridgment of Tolstoy's letter to the Writers' Congress which was read at their meeting. Lev Nikolayevich acknowledged the justice of Chertkov's rebuke to the presidium of the Congress, and expressed his regret that he is now being subjected to unjust attacks.

"It requires great selflessness on your part," he said to Chertkov. "And brings you no honor whatsoever! But above all, these people fail to understand that you are not speaking for Tolstoy, but are independent, acting on your own."

11 May

✧

Lev Nikolayevich sat down in an armchair.

"I want to go and rest. I believe that one should work only when it pleases God. You keep trying to stop thinking that you have to say something, that someone may need it. One should live according to God's will and not think of the consequences. You remember, I said that if you are thinking of consequences you are probably occupied with personal matters, but if not, you are working for the common cause. That's how one should live, working for the common cause. It's the way birds live, and blades of grass. Theirs is unquestionably the common cause."

At evening tea they talked about the Moscow Art Theater and its new productions. Lev Nikolayevich expressed the opinion that Turgenev's *A Month in the Country* is "trivia." Of Ostrovsky's *For Every Man Enough Simplicity* he said:

"You know, that is not typical of Ostrovsky! Some of his early works are delightful—drawn from the everyday life that he knew and loved and condemned. But he loved, which is necessary for the artist."

✧

12 May

✧

We went horseback riding together, riding more than seven versts to Prince Golitsyn's park. . . . On the way back Lev Nikolayevich took a detour around the estate.

It began to rain, lightly at first, then harder and harder. We took refuge in a shed and later in a little village shop. There, besides the shopkeeper and his son, we found the village policeman and a youth of about eighteen, also escaping from the rain. The young man, who wore a dark jacket and a clean cap, had a rather bad face. We had seen him earlier on the road riding a fine horse.

"Where are you from?" asked Lev Nikolayevich, sitting down on a stool at the counter.

"The Golitsyn estate."

"And what do you do there?"

The young man was embarrassed.

"Natural son," the shopkeeper obligingly informed us in a loud voice.

A conversation started about land, the peasants' needs, large families, and chastity.

"I met a peasant woman who complained that life was hard with six children," said Lev Nikolayevich. "And I said to her: 'Where did they come from—out of the forest, perhaps?' Why shouldn't people have two or three children and stop—and then live like brother and sister? Why, in fact, are there so many children? Because of carnal lust."

"That's how it is," concurred the shopkeeper.

And the "natural son" gave a loud snort, probably thinking: "The old man is some kind of wag."

✧

16 May

Lev Nikolayevich is ill. He did not drink any coffee this morning and has eaten neither lunch nor dinner. I went in for the letters after dinner. There were a great many of them and he had looked over them all.

"You're not feeling very well, are you, Lev Nikolayevich?"

"Quite poorly. I have heartburn and feel weak. That's the way it has to be. It's time now. . . ."

Why did I have to ask him!

17 May

Lev Nikolayevich is weak; he has not left his room today. Two peasants, to whom I had given some books, and an old Skopets [33] talked with him in his room. Concerning his conversation with the Skopets, Lev Nikolayevich said:

"I was rather taken aback at first. He said: 'If it is necessary to practice chastity, then what were we given that thing for?' But I have always said, and I say now, that life is not in the achievement of the ideal, but in the striving for it, and in the struggle against the obstacles the body raises. Genuine good and virtue are in continence. But those people are like the drunkard who didn't drink because he had no money, or because there was no tavern. That would certainly not be a moral act. I do not know how it is for others, but for me at least this notion has decisive significance. However, he is a holy man. And, you know, you do have to have strength to make a decision like that! To say nothing of depriving himself of a family, he is also subject to persecution. Why, he has spent thirty years in exile in Siberia!"

✧

20 May

Today after lunch we left Kochety and set out for home.

At lunch Lev Nikolayevich told us about having been at the village wisewoman's house—"an old crone."

"What struck me about her was her foolishness and her self-assurance. Seriously! Seeing her was for me a confirmation of the truth that success is attained by foolishness and effrontery. And that is not a paradox. I am more and more convinced of it."

"And how do you explain your success?" asked Chertkov amid the general laughter.

Lev Nikolayevich burst out laughing.

"I have no success," he said. "It's all a misunderstanding. I've

just had a letter from the wife of an ecclesiastical provost in which
she gives me a good scolding: she thought I was a such-and-such,
whereas in reality I am a so-and-so!"

And again he broke into genial laughter.

✦

21 May

Ekaterina Vasilyevna Tolstaya, Andrei Lvovich's second wife,
their little daughter, and Lev Nikolayevich's grandson Seryozha, a
high-school boy, and his French tutor have come to Yasnaya for a
visit. They all arrived today, and Sergei and Andrei Lvovich
left again this evening.

✦

I have been notified by V. V. Bitner, editor of *The Herald of
Knowledge*, that on a more detailed examination of *The Christian
Ethic* he has come to the conclusion that it is quite impossible to
publish it under the existing conditions of censorship. (Four chapters
are particularly "hazardous": "The Church," "The State," "Labor
and Property," and "Passive Resistance to Evil.") I shall have to
reconcile myself to the idea of burying the manuscript for a while
longer. I see no possibility of putting my work in acceptable form
for the censor.

I told Lev Nikolayevich about Bitner's letter and he just made a
hopeless gesture.

✦

"What are you writing now, dear Lev Nikolayevich?" asked
M. A. Schmidt ("Old Lady Schmidt," as Lev Nikolayevich's
daughters call her).

"Just imagine—nothing, Maria Aleksandrovna? And I'm quite
content," replied Lev Nikolayevich. "What do I have for Gorbunov
and Sytin? *For Every Day* and *Thoughts on Life*. This work is
necessary for me, and I flatter myself with the hope that it may
prove useful to others."

Maria Aleksandrovna asked him how he had spent the time at the Sukhotins'.

"Happily. I lived like a lord, in grand style, beautifully! But the grandeur hardly shows, because the hosts themselves are sweet, good. There they live under a constitution. Here, you know, we have a despotism, not a constitution as they have. They have good relations with the servants, are close to them. Consequently it's easy to live there."

✧

22 May

Today there was a misunderstanding with Sofya Andreyevna because of the Circassian watchman, who had refused to let some peasants pass through the estate to reach their work. It was settled to everyone's satisfaction.

Lev Nikolayevich has been working a great deal. His mood is good. He gave me his diary so that I could copy into it the thoughts he had jotted down in his notebook today.

A second telegram has been received from the sculptor Prince Paolo Trubetskoy asking whether Tolstoy is at home. He will probably come soon. They say he is very eccentric. A vegetarian. The fact that Trubetskoy reads nothing, as he himself admits, especially appeals to Lev Nikolayevich. During one of his former visits to Yasnaya Polyana he was asked whether he had read Tolstoy's *War and Peace*.

"I don't read anything!" Trubetskoy had answered, not in the least abashed by Lev Nikolayevich's presence, and, indeed, offended that they did not understand him and had not remembered such a simple thing as that he "didn't read anything."

He says that this is how he preserves the free growth and development of his creative individuality.

✧

23 May

Lev Nikolayevich has been working on the proofs of his book *Thoughts on Life*. I have helped him a little: arranged in sections the additional material on science, distributed throughout the various booklets newly collected thoughts of Dostoyevsky, Chernyshevsky, Lao-Tzu, Confucius, etc.

Many people here; noisy, confusing. Lev Nikolayevich finds this trying, I believe. There were: Andrei Lvovich; Skipetrov, whom Lev Nikolayevich likes; David Maksimchuk, a young Ukrainian who is thinking of refusing military service in the fall; M. V. Bulygin; Prince D. D. Obolensky; Goldenweiser; A. Sergeyenko. S. D. Nikolayev came in the evening and they sat on the terrace in the dark talking about Henry George.

"And here Andryusha is concerned about our consolidating the land——" Lev Nikolayevich began.

"And I shall continue to be concerned about it my whole life," Andrei Lvovich broke in.*

"—in the hands of landholders, so that the peasants become the same sort of robbers as the landlords are now," Lev Nikolayevich finished without raising his voice.

In the dining room at tea Sofya Andreyevna remarked that according to the newspapers, the ailing Field Marshal Miliutin has lost interest in everything and has completely retired into himself—in other words, his life is ending.

"On the contrary, his real life is just beginning," said Lev Nikolayevich quietly.

✧

---

* It is interesting to note that the late A. L. Tolstoy, who had assiduously defended Stolypin's land reforms in 1910 (toward which Lev Nikolayevich took a completely negative attitude), three years later, after becoming familiar with agricultural affairs as an official in the Ministry of Agriculture, became an opponent instead of a supporter of the November 9 law. V.B.

27 May

Aleksandra Lvovna and Varvara Mikhailovna have returned from the Crimea. And N. N. Gay, son of the celebrated artist, has arrived from Switzerland, where he resides permanently.

✧

28 May

✧

At dinner Lev Nikolayevich whispered to N. N. Gay, who was sitting next to him:

"I think that in fifty years people will say: 'Imagine, they could calmly sit there and eat while grown people walked around waiting on them—their food was served to them, cooked for them."

"What are you talking about?" asked Sofya Andreyevna. "About their serving us?"

"Yes," said Lev Nikolayevich, and repeated aloud what he had said.

Sofya Andreyevna began to protest.

"But I was only saying it to him," said Lev Nikolayevich, pointing to Gay. "I knew there would be objections, and I absolutely do not wish to argue."

✧

In the evening I left for my new, or rather my old, residence—Telyatinki.

29 May

There is a difficult family situation at Yasnaya. Dima Chertkov, who had ridden over there, told me about it. Sofya Andreyevna has been complaining to Lev Nikolayevich that she is sick and tired of everything, that she cannot go on with the management of the estate, and so on. Lev Nikolayevich suggested that she drop these boring activities, and if being at Yasnaya Polyana made it impossible for her to do so that she go away somewhere. This offended her and she walked out into a field and lay down in a ditch. They sent someone out with a horse and she was brought back. Lev Nikolayevich fears that she may harm herself. He is agitated, and this agitation has given rise to an irregular pulse.

I am very sorry for him; it is sad that in his old age, and with all his greatness, he is not spared such scenes.

30 May

I was at Yasnaya today. When I arrived they were all at lunch on the terrace. I went first to Sofya Andreyevna and then around the table greeting everyone.

"Just like a stranger," Lev Nikolayevich remarked with his kind smile.

There were new guests: the sculptor Prince Paolo Trubetskoy and his wife.

Later Lev Nikolayevich talked to me about Trubetskoy.

"He's a very interesting man. He really doesn't read anything, but is a thinker and clever. He's a vegetarian. He says that animals live better than most people today. It was very nice of him—he came simply for a visit, not to do any sculpture, but then he got carried away and is going to do something."

I asked Lev Nikolayevich how he was feeling. He answered as if divining my thought.

"Fine. Yesterday things were bad, but today everything is all right."

He gave me several letters to answer. Then he went off on horseback with Trubetskoy, he on Délire and the Prince on a small horse, although he is tall and very heavy.

Trubetskoy is indeed very original. His appearance is that of an actor playing the role of a noble father or a philosopher. He is clean-shaven and there is something about him that makes one think of an American. He speaks Russian poorly because of having lived in Italy and France since childhood. His wife is Finnish or Swedish, and, according to Varvara Mikhailovna, speaks Russian almost better than her husband. Conversation at the table was always in French.

31 May

Lev Nikolayevich is very cheerful. He is taken up with Trubetskoy and talks to him a great deal. He calls him "Your Highness."

"I shall call him 'Your Highness,' it suits him," he said, laughing.

I believe he does this simply because Trubetskoy is quite indifferent to his title, as becomes obvious very soon after meeting him, and he would probably forget about it entirely if he were not reminded of it.

While I was at Yasnaya, Lev Nikolayevich rode to Telyatinki with Trubetskoy, and later told us that the latter was full of admiration for the simple, cheerful, industrious life of the Telyatinki group headed by Dima Chertkov.

Trubetskoy is not wasting his time at Yasnaya: he has already painted a small portrait in oils and made two pencil drawings of Lev Nikolayevich. He drew a caricature of himself and his wife in his sketchbook. He cannot begin modeling yet as he had to order clay from Moscow and it has not yet arrived.

2 June

I was at Yasnaya this evening when a lady, a neighboring landowner, came "to pay a call." She seemed to be a very nice woman, but much too talkative—from shyness, in my opinion. She herself admitted that she was timid, and I saw how her hands trembled. She is well-bred, with good manners, and speaks French.

Lev Nikolayevich came into the "Remington room" where I was alone typing letters.

"That woman annoys me terribly!" he said. "Talk, talk—and for the sole purpose of not remaining silent. Verbal fornication."

✧

4 June

✧

Referring to the preface to *Thoughts on Life*, Lev Nikolayevich said:

"I think I will finish it soon now. Yes, yes, it seems even to me that it is good as it is. You know, somehow this developed of itself in me, these three points—efforts. Against the lusts of the flesh, the effort of self-denial; against pride, humility; against falseness, uprightness. This is right! Very important, good . . . I shall finish it! Well, good night!"

5 June

✧

Trubetskoy is working on his statue. It is coming out very like Tolstoy. The figure is incomparable—especially the head. You do not understand his look at first, but it makes you feel like gazing at him intently and then falling into the same sort of reverie. The expression of the statue reminds me a little of the expression I observed on Lev Nikolayevich's face in the train on our way to Kochety. Trubetskoy says that I have noticed the chief merit of his work: that the clay Tolstoy "even has eyes."

Lev Nikolayevich poses for the artist sitting in an armchair or standing and talking. Trubetskoy is so considerate that he does not make him move about, but transfers the stand with the statue from place to place. His movements are quick, heavy, awkward, but careful. Lev Nikolayevich mimicked him: twisting his arms and legs into a wheel and rocking from side to side he ran about a little then fell to laughing and stopped.

He seems to love Trubetskoy, this "big child" who is an extraordinary person.

12 June

Lev Nikolayevich finally made up his mind to go and visit V. G. Chertkov, who is living in the village of Meshcherskoe near the Stolbovaya station on the road to Moscow. He was accompanied by Aleksandra Lvovna, Dushan Petrovich, his servant Ilya Vasil-yevna, and me.

We decided to go by horseback to Tula and take the train from there. A wonderful morning.

We rode past the Tula jail.

"Gusev was in prison here," said Dushan Petrovich.

They recalled that several other "Tolystoyans" had served sentences in the huge white building with its gloomy windows, and we felt as if the prison were "our very own."

At Lev Nikolayevich's wish we approached the Kursk station by way of deserted back streets, so as not to attract attention, if I am not mistaken.

We traveled second class and were joined by the Japanese, D. P. Konisi, who had come to see Lev Nikolayevich at Yasnaya Polyana and was now returning to Moscow. The journey was pleasant. Lev Nikolayevich was in his own little compartment and the rest of us crowded into another one. . . .

When we got out of the train at Stolbovaya, Lev Nikolayevich was surrounded by the Chertkovs, who had come to meet us. A youth wearing a cap with a green band shyly approached me and asked me to give Tolstoy "greetings from a commercial-school student," which I did later.

Now we are at the Chertkovs'.

At dinner everyone sat down at the table together: hosts, guests, and servants. Our Ilya Vasilyevich huddled timidly in a corner: he is not used to such customs.

❖

After dinner Lev Nikolayevich sat down to play a game of chess with A. D. Radynsky, a young man who is one of V. G. Chertkov's colleagues in his publishing business.

"When Sukhotin and I play we are equally matched," he said, "only he plays calmly, whereas I, because of my youth, always get carried away."

13 June

❖

Lev Nikolayevich is very animated, gay, and ready to talk. He told us he had been reading Kuprin's *The Pit*, but had put it aside, unable to finish it.

"It's so obscene. Moreover, it is too long. It could all be much shorter; it's padded. Right now there are two young girls waiting for me at Yasnaya Polyana who came to ask me for work. One of them has a gift for writing. She has nothing of interest to say: she describes. She describes the fate of a girl. Very naturally. Her legs are twisted, like this" (he illustrated with his hands), "but she has such a lovely face, tender and sweet. Someone had seduced her and then deserted her. Now such a story makes a far more powerful impression than all the Pits in the world. As I said to those Prechistenky students" (he had in mind the worker youths from the Prechistenky classes in Moscow who had recently come to see him), " 'disregard all literature written during the last sixty years, don't read it—it's all a muddle!' I purposely said sixty years in order to include myself. 'And read everything written before that time.' And I say the same to you young people," he added turning to us.

"What then, Pushkin?" said Vladimir Grigorevich.

"Without fail! And Gogol, Dostoyevsky . . . And foreign literature. Rousseau, Hugo, Dickens . . . But what is usual now is the amazing urge to know what is the latest. That—what's his name? Grut—Knut—Knut Hamsun! Björnson, Ibsen——. But to know Hugo and Rousseau only by hearsay, or to read about who they were in the encyclopedia—and enough! By the way," he continued, "I recently looked up Formosa in the encyclopedia. Have you any idea what Formosa is? It's an island that the Japanese recently seized. Konisi goes there continually and told me about it. Imagine, you find cannibalism there! Yes! Trubetskoy very cleverly said that cannibalism is a kind of civilization. Cannibals maintain that they eat only savages. But they consider savages those tribes that don't live there and that live on fruits." And he went on telling us what he had learned from the Japanese.

14 June

Lev Nikolayevich went to a village not far from here, where, under the surveillance of a feldsher, fifty insane people from a nearby psychiatric hospital have been placed among the peasants. He talked with them and became interested in several. . . .

Dr. Karl Veleminsky,[34] a Czech from Prague, was here; he teaches German in a technical high school, as Dushan informed us. He came for the specific purpose of acquainting himself in detail with Tolstoy's pedagogical views. Lev Nikolayevich spent considerable time with him, in the course of which Veleminsky questioned him about his attitude to the various scholastic disciplines and to teaching in general.

Speaking of ethnography, Lev Nikolayevich said that its task is not the teaching of the external aspect of the life of known peoples, not how they dress or are housed, but what they believe in, what meaning they give to life.

Veleminsky asked his questions in German and Lev Nikolayevich answered him in Russian. The conversation took place in the dining room with everyone present. Four or more people took notes on what Lev Nikolayevich said, Vladimir Grigorevich and Aleksei Sergeyenko among others. . . .

Referring to a collection of articles by some Kiev students on the question of suicide, Lev Nikolayevich said:

"A naive collection. Presumptuous: 'We, the youth . . .' Young people used to be very nice when they were modest."

And he said:

"It's worthwhile working with children. I am not so much speaking of little ones as those from the age of fourteen. Out of a hundred there are usually two you can work with and from whom something will come."

The children from a neighboring orphanage came with flowers for Lev Nikolayevich. He thanked them and Vladimir Grigorevich gave them books and pictures of Tolstoy.

16 June

Lev Nikolayevich went with Chertkov to inspect the psychiatric hospital at Meshcherskoe. The director was their guide. He and all the doctors were very cordial. In the evening Lev Nikolayevich shared his impressions with us.

"I really thought it would make a more powerful impression on me," he said, "that it would disturb me more than it did. Perhaps it was less strong because we saw so many sick people at one time, and there were so many interesting ones. It would have been stronger had we seen only one."

He was struck by the good relations of the doctors, and those serving in a lesser capacity, with the patients. . . .

"But what is surprising," he said, "is that for these doctors the patients are not people whom they pity, but material with which they must work. And I suppose it has to be so, or they would become demoralized."

Lev Nikolayevich was interested in the attitude of the patients to religious questions. One, when asked whether he believed in God, replied: "I am an atom of God." Another said: "I do not believe in God, I believe in science." He was particularly impressed by the second answer.

On the way to the hospital he was stopped by a peasant.

"What do you want?" he asked the man.

"I've heard you tell fortunes," he replied.

He appealed to Tolstoy as to a sorcerer. Lev Nikolayevich did all he could to explain his conception of life to the peasant.

In general, since he has been staying with the Chertkovs, Lev Nikolayevich appears to feel very well. He is always very animated and eager to talk. I think this is a rest for him after the constant bustle of his own house. And it seems to me that the relative simplicity of the Chertkovs' way of life is much more in harmony with his own spiritual state than the "luxury" which has become so repugnant to him, and the unquestionable if not absolute aristocratic exclusiveness of the Yasnaya Polyana house.

17 June

Lev Nikolayevich has been working again on the preface to *Thoughts on Life* and almost every day it is recopied for him once or twice. He says it is finished now, but he still has to give it to Vladimir Grigorevich to look over.

"I think it's finished," he said, "which is a sign that my brain is working well."

After dinner (at one o'clock here), Lev Nikolayevich and Vladimir Grigorevich rode to the neighboring village of Troitskoe. On the road they met a lady, a summer resident, and Lev Nikolayevich doffed his hat and greeted her "like a marquis," Vladimir Grigorevich told us. He also remarked on Tolstoy's usual habit of riding where it is most difficult.

"He rode over every hill and crossed every ditch between Meshcherskoe and Troitskoe," Vladimir Grigorevich jested.

Someone began telling how a few days ago Lev Nikolayevich had made his way through an opening in a wattle fence, suddenly appearing before an astounded housekeeper as if he had risen "right out of the rubbish pit," as she said.

Lev Nikolayevich came in while we were all laughing, and Vladimir Grigorevich told him what we had been talking about.

"Well, I have a saying about taking the direct route," he said. "Do you know it? 'Take the roundabout way and you'll be home for dinner; take the direct way and, God willing, you'll get there by nightfall.'"

Everyone laughed still more. The saying suits him perfectly. I was reminded of his rambles around Yasnaya Polyana.

Vladimir Grigorevich showed Tolstoy a collection of *Songs of Free Christians* made by his wife, Anna Konstantinovna, who is here now. Lev Nikolayevich went to the piano, looked over the song *Hear the Word*, and I sang one verse to his accompaniment.

"Bravo, bravo!" he applauded, as he got up from the piano.

At dinner he repeated with a smile:

"You sing well. Really well. Such a fine voice!"

Everyone assembled for tea in the evening. I shall note an amusing conversation about a cockroach that took place at the table.

"Imagine, I have beetles in my room!" said Lev Nikolayevich. "I noticed it twice today."

"Good heavens! But only one?" exclaimed Vladimir Grigorevich with a horrified expression.

"I don't know whether there is only one—I saw it twice."

"And does this disturb you?"

"Why, not at all—if there is only one."

"It can be caught," someone suggested.

"I think we'd better not do that," said Vladimir Grigorevich, "or it might be discovered that there is more than one. Better to remain under an illusion. Is it brown?" he inquired.

Lev Nikolayevich tried to recall the color. Those who were competent in the matter explained that real beetles are big and black; if they are small and dark yellow, they are cockroaches.

"Mine is little and dark yellow," said Lev Nikolayevich.

"Then you have a cockroach, not a beetle," Vladimir Grigorevich concluded amid the general laughter.

"Yes, it must be a cockroach," Lev Nikolayevich agreed.

❖

19 June

Today Lev Nikolayevich finished the article he began yesterday, *To the Slavs,* written on the occasion of his being invited to participate in the Slavic Congress at Sofia. He has completed the preface to *Thoughts on Life,* but today again revised it slightly. The change he wanted to make, as he told me, is the following: he had written about "love for God and other beings." Chertkov, if I am not mistaken, suggested that he omit the words "love for God." Lev Nikolayevich agreed, but today decided to replace "love for God" with the words "consciousness of God."

"That's much clearer and stronger," he said to me, explaining the essence of this revision.

✧

Yesterday the little daughter of one of the workmen fell ill with smallpox, and all the members of the household were inoculated against the disease except Vladimir Grigorevich, who refused on principle, Aleksandra Lvovna, and Anna Konstantinovna, neither of whom is entirely well, and, of course, Lev Nikolayevich.

He remarked on the futility of these inoculations.

"There's no point in trying to escape death, you'll die anyway."

"But some people don't want to die," someone objected.

"And that's futile too."

A letter has come from M. A. Stakhovich saying that Stolypin has granted Chertkov permission to live in Telyatinki while his mother is visiting there. General rejoicing. . . .

20 June

This morning Lev Nikolayevich was very animated and gay. He has been writing earnestly. Aleksandra Lvovna tiptoed into his room and put on his table for correction the freshly typed letter to the Slavic Congress. There was not a sound from him. He was covering page after page of paper. Later he went out to her on the balcony and gave her a manuscript—it turns out he has written a story entitled *By Accident.*

✧

Visitors have arrived. S. Solomakhin and A. S. Buturlin, who are said to have been of help to Lev Nikolayevich in the editing and publishing of his *Union, Translation, and Investigation of the Four Gospels.* He was very cordial to his old friends.

It was an extraordinary evening. Lev Nikolayevich read aloud his article *To the Slavic Congress,* and the new story, *By Accident,* based on the life of a child. . . .

We talked for a long time afterward, sitting on the terrace, Lev Nikolayevich at a table with a lighted lamp on it.

Buturlin said of the artist Meshkov that he reads nothing.

"Good for him!" exclaimed Lev Nikolayevich.

"Good for him?" Buturlin was dumbfounded.

"Good for him!" repeated Lev Nikolayevich.

And he told him about Trubetskoy, who also reads nothing. At the same time he characterized Trubetskoy as a great talent and a child.

"The only thing I don't like about him is that he goes around naked in the presence of his wife."

Actually, when at Yasnaya Polyana Trubetskoy had gone bathing with his wife in the Voronka river.

"He's not an immoral man," said Lev Nikolayevich, "he does it as a matter of principle. He's a terrific vegetarian and animal lover. According to him, animals are much more moral than humans, and people should try to be more like them. I argued with him about this, and said that man cannot take an animal as his ideal. He can fall lower than an animal, but he can go even higher than the ideal of man that he envisions. Man has an innate shame which an animal lacks. And it is good that he covers with clothing everything that is unnecessary and leaves exposed only that which reflects the spiritual—his face. I have always had this feeling of shame; for instance, the sight of a woman with her breast bared was always disgusting to me, even in my youth. At that time there was another feeling mingled with it, but it was nonetheless shame."

✧

21 June

✧

On returning from his walk Lev Nikolayevich called me and gave me some letters to answer. He happened to mention in some connection the story he wrote yesterday in which he describes a husband who comes home in despair after losing heavily at cards.

"I tried to show, without particularly stressing it, that in his despair he wanted to forget himself, first by satisfying his sexual lust, and then, when his wife pushed him away, by smoking."

A couple of hours later I learned that he had written another short story: a conversation with a peasant lad. Apparently he is in the grip of a very successful creative impulse, which I am sure is the result of the quiet, peaceful life at Meshcherskoe, filled as it is at this time with rich impressions.

F. A. Strakhov, the actor Orlenev, and the Skopets Grigorev, who had visited Lev Nikolayevich at Kochety, have arrived.

After lunch pictures were taken. As at Kochety, Lev Nikolayevich was seated at a table in the garden looking over his letters with me. When the others joined him he began reading aloud the new article on suicides which he has been working on, and Mr. Tapsel had an opportunity to photograph an interesting group.

When Lev Nikolayevich first sat down he glanced at me and, alluding to the photographer, murmured with a chuckle:

"I can hardly resist playing a joke on him, like kicking up my leg, or sticking out my tongue."

After the picture-taking everyone went in for tea. Lev Nikolayevich remained to finish going through his correspondence, and I stayed with him. Raising his eyes from a letter he was reading he said:

"Although Belinky is critical of my talking about love all the time—he once said that he finds it necessary to rewrite everything

I write about love—nevertheless, the longer I live the more I am convinced that love is the most important thing, that it should fill our entire life, and is what we should strive for. It determines everything and gives happiness. If there is love, all is well: both the sun and the rain are good. Isn't that so?"

When he had finished the letters, he went for a walk.

✦

22 *June*

✦

He came late to the dining room. Vladimir Grigorevich, Dushan Petrovich, and the Skopets were there.

"What is it you have clipped out of the *New Times*, Dushan Petrovich?" asked Lev Nikolayevich, having noticed a torn copy of the Suvorin newspaper.

Dushan started to describe some sort of "Jewish swindles."

"Oh, that's a sin, Dushan Petrovich," said Lev Nikolayevich shaking his head. "A sin——"

"But, Lev Nikolayevich——"

"Yes, a sin, a sin, a sin! To give your attention to that! I don't understand it."

He drank some kefir, took the empty bottle and began peering into it, continuing to talk as he looked. He beckoned to me with his finger, laughing.

"Look at that!"

I looked into the bottle: a fly was climbing up its slippery side, trying to reach the opening at the top.

"Oh, the poor thing!" I involuntarily exclaimed.

"Yes," laughed Lev Nikolayevich. "I too thought: 'Poor thing!' Now it is reaching the top, but at that moment it was lost."

"Evidently you don't consider it necessary to exterminate flies," said the old Skopets, puzzled.

"No, it isn't necessary," answered Tolstoy. "Why exterminate them? They are living creatures too."

"But they are insects."

"It doesn't matter."

"We always exterminate them in this way."

"You know, I can't even look at that flypaper."

"How do you get rid of them, then?"

"You have to get rid of them somehow without killing: chase them out of the house, or keep things clean."

Lev Nikolayevich walked over to the old man and bending over him said:

"This was very well expressed by the Buddhists. They say that one must not kill consciously."

Lev Nikolayevich explained that having permitted himself to kill insects, a man can then permit himself to kill animals, then men.

Vladimir Grigorevich reminded Lev Nikolayevich that he had not always taken such pity on flies and had even affirmed the opposite of what he had just said.

"I don't know," replied Lev Nikolayevich, "but now this feeling of pity is not something I have invented, it is quite sincere. And I believe that if one of the children were to see this fly he would experience the same spontaneous feeling of compassion."

The Skopets remarked that not everyone is capable of this feeling. Lev Nikolayevich agreed.

"Why, I myself used to be a hunter," he said, "and I would kill a hare with my own hands. You know, you have to clutch it between your knees and cut its throat with a knife. And I did this and felt no pity whatever."

"And, if I may say so, Lev Nikolayevich," began the old man, "you were in the war too, were you not?"

"I was."

"You were?" the others exclaimed, dumbfounded.

"Of course—I was at Sevastopol."

"You were at Sevastopol?"

"I was."

And Lev Nikolayevich told us he had been lucky not to have had to kill anyone; that although the Fourth Bastion was considered the most dangerous place to be, the artillery stationed there was at the ready only in case of an assault by the enemy, which did not occur.

"And the grand duke came there?" asked the Skopets, who was evidently familiar with the history of the Crimean War.

"The grand duke came there. Mikhail Nikolayevich was there with me in the Fourth Bastion. He didn't waste much time there, however; things were not to his liking."

✧

In the evening F. A. Strakhov read his new article on compromise and the principle of "all or nothing," based on texts from the Gospels.

Lev Nikolayevich spoke against the obligatoriness of the Gospel texts, which are distorted.

"I don't like to say this, but I shall: in the same way that I formerly loved the Gospels, I now have no love for them."

They then read a beautiful passage from the Gospels in Lev Nikolayevich's exposition of them.

"I have fallen in love with them again," he said smiling.

After dinner, late in the evening when everyone had gone to bed, two rather strange and confusing telegrams came from Yasnaya Polyana concerning Sofya Andreyevna's nervous illness. Lev Nikolayevich is being summoned and must leave tomorrow. The mood of the household is depressed. Lev Nikolayevich bears the ordeal with meekness.*

* Tolstoy's final calvary, which took him to his grave, began with these two ill-fated telegrams received at Meshcherskoe on June twenty-second. His wife's prolonged nervous illness, the conflict between her and V. G. Chertkov, the affair of the will, and, in general, the complications which for various reasons had arisen in the Yasnaya Polyana house, where one misunderstanding was compounded by another until they formed a tangle that could not be unraveled, created an utterly impossible and harrowing atmosphere for Tolstoy. He himself always stood above all temporary difficulties and misunderstandings, trying to overcome them by the power of love; nevertheless these painful events had an agonizing effect on him. They moved ahead by fits and starts, intensifying till they led to the day (October twenty-eighth) when he decided to tear asunder the net he was enmeshed in. And he tore it, but at the cost of his life. V.B.

23 June

Yesterday F. A. Strakhov cited a parable from the Gospel of Luke about a king who estimated in advance whether he could count on the success of a campaign with the number of troops he had at his disposal. Strakhov related the meaning of the parable to man's carnal life, but I expressed the opinion that the parable could be applied to the spiritual life as well: in striving to incarnate the ideal, man must calculate his spiritual powers so as not to fall under the burden he takes upon himself.

Coming into my room this morning Lev Nikolayevich said:

"I agree with the remark you made to Fyodor Alekseyevich yesterday, that you can relate that text to the spiritual as well as the carnal life. That is quite true. As we were saying, in striving for moral perfection it is necessary to begin with easy things, not difficult ones, so as to develop the will. And this possibility of interpreting one and the same text in different ways again confirms my thought that one should not attribute an obligatory meaning to everything that is written in the Gospels."

✧

. . . Lev Nikolayevich read aloud to Vladimir Grigorevich, Molochnikov, Strakhov, A. Sergeyenko, and me a chapter from the article on suicides which he has just written. The excerpt he read was devoted to an explanation of the insanity of present-day society. He had taken a saying of Pascal's to the effect that a dream differs from reality in the incoherency of the phenomenon, and that if the phenomena of dreams were coherent, we would not know what was the dream and what was reality. To this he added that when a person commits an immoral act in a dream he is unconscious of both the immorality of the act and his responsibility for it. Contemporary man, whose life is insane, is in a state similar to that of dreams.

"If insanity were general," he said after reading this chapter to us, "we would not know what is sane and what is insane. With Pascal this is in time, with me, in space. It's interesting to me because it does away with blame. It's new, and I wanted to consult you . . . although, of course, it's not important . . . What I wanted to explain is the state of insanity in which the majority of people today find themselves."

We began to prepare for our six-o'clock departure. Everything was packed and we had only to get into the carriages and drive to the station. Several people were crowded into the narrow corridor downstairs when Lev Nikolayevich came out of his room, dressed for the journey and carrying a pail. At the last minute he had remembered the waste accumulated in the course of the day, and, faithful to his custom, was carrying it out himself.

"Sorry, sorry," he said as he made his way through our midst.

✦

We arrived at Yasnaya Polyana between ten and eleven at night, and learned from V. M. Feokritova the details of what had happened during our absence. It seems that Sofya Andreyevna had been very displeased that Chertkov had not invited her to Meshcherskoe, or had invited her in a rather vague way and without offering her a separate room, and on these grounds a morbid, hysterical irritation had sprung up in her, not only against Chertkov, but against Lev Nikolayevich as well. Every communication had had a grievous effect on her.

Despite the lateness of the hour, Lev Nikolayevich sat for a while with Sofya Andreyevna, who today, it seems, had gone back to bed for an hour and a half. Then he sent their daughter to her.

"For God's sake, be careful!" he implored her.

Later he said: "It is impossible to remain silent, and to speak is dangerous! . . . I shall try to sleep," he concluded and said good night to us.

My heart is wrung for this great and dear old man.

24 June

Aleksandra Lvovna left this morning for Tula to make inquiries about Chertkov's prospective return to Telyatinki. His mother, who has important connections in the highest circles, is petitioning for him in Petersburg.

I am staying at Yasnaya. In the morning Lev Nikolayevich gave me some letters to answer. He said he had slept little. When I was about to leave the room he looked at me, laughed for some reason, and asked:

"How are you—all right?"

"Yes, only I suffer for you, Lev Nikolayevich."

"No, today it's all right, it's better. She says: 'You won't forgive me for all the things I've said about you'—so she is aware of this—of her abnormality."

✧

"Today I feel as if I were seventy years old," he said as he was about to say good night.

"How do you mean that?" I asked, somewhat astonished. "Is that good?"

"No, on the contrary! As a matter of fact, I can in no way get used to the idea that I am an old man. And this teaches you humility. You keep wondering why people speak to you with respect when you are only a little boy—a mere child! What you were is what you have remained!"

26 June

Yesterday was again a bad day for Sofya Andreyevna. She neither ate nor slept. In order to soothe his wife, Lev Nikolayevich rode to Ovsyannikovo with her (he had intended going alone on horseback).

In the morning Lev Nikolayevich walked to the village to visit his friends N. G. Sutkovoy and his sister, and P. P. Kartushin, but he did not find them at home. . . .

In spirit, at least of late, Sutkovoy and Kartushin have been close to the teachings of Aleksandr Dobrolyubov,[35] who is known to be a mystic. . . . Their ideological path to Dobrolyubov was through Tolstoy, whose admirers they have long been. . . .

Talking of the arrival of the "Dobrolyubovites," Tolstoy spoke out against the mysticism in their leader's views.

"Whatever is unclear is weak," he said. "It is the same in the field of ethics. Only those ethical truths that are clear are firm. And whatever is absolutely clear is firm. We firmly know that two times two is four. Or that the angles of a triangle equal two right angles. Why, why this mysticism?"

He also spoke against their use of the word "brother" only in relation to those who share their views.

"They set themselves apart. All men are brothers."

"Nevertheless, their life is amazingly consistent and lofty," observed Belinky.

"Yes, of course!" exclaimed Lev Nikolayevich. "God grant there be more such people!"

Belinky later said that Lev Nikolayevich had tears in his eyes as he said this. I did not notice it because of my nearsightedness.

❖

27 June

Today V. G. Chertkov's mother was expected at Telyatinki. To everyone's surprise, he arrived with her. It seems that he was escorting her here by train, and when he got off at Serpukhov, the farthest point on the Moscow province boundary and the one beyond which he was not permitted to travel, he received a telegram granting him permission to remain at Telyatinki during his mother's stay there. The artfully worded telegram did not specify, of course, the time of his mother's stay in Telyatinki.

The prospect of Chertkov's presence is provoking Sofya Andreyevna's jealousy. She has been in a morbidly excited state in general recently, and now fears that Chertkov's "influence" on Lev Nikolayevich may increase as a result of his proximity.

I asked her how she was feeling.

"I've just been taken with a fever again—I can't breathe!" she said, leaving the room once more.

"You see how this has upset her," said Lev Nikolayevich, turning to Goldenweiser.

In order to appease his wife, Lev Nikolayevich has acceded to her request to go with her tomorrow to visit their eldest son, Sergei Lvovich, on the occasion of his birthday. While Lev Nikolayevich was at Meshcherskoe, Sofya Andreyevna had been occupied with repairs to the house, and she wants to "recompense herself," as she expressed it to Varvara Mikhailovna, for Lev Nikolayevich's visit to the Chertkovs.

S. L. Tolstoy's estate, Nikolskoe-Vyazemskoe, is in the province of Orlov, only thirty-five versts from Kochety. Thus Lev Nikolaye-vich, who has just returned from a trip to the Chertkovs and has only recently been to Kochety, is faced with the prospect of another rather long journey by rail and horse. The trip to Nikolskoe may be circumvented, however, if Tatyana Lvovna arrives tomorrow morning as expected; with the influence she has on her mother, she may be able to persuade her to remain at home. Lev Nikolayevich has asked me to spend the night here so that I can let Vladimir Grigorevich know whether he is going to his son's or not.

✧

28 June

A telegram came from Tatyana Lvovna informing them that she will not be able to come because of ill health. Consequently it has been definitely decided that Lev Nikolayevich and Sofya Andreyevna will go to Nikolskoe.

During his walk this morning Lev Nikolayevich met Chertkov, who is temporarily refraining from visiting the house as a result of the coolness in his relations with Sofya Andreyevna, and they had a talk. Yasnaya Polyana has turned into a sort of fortress, with secret meetings, parleys, and so forth.

❖

1 July

The story drags on. A controversy has arisen between Sofya Andreyevna and Chertkov over who is to have custody of the Tolstoy diaries (those from 1900, I believe). Lev Nikolayevich had given them to Chertkov, and they are now in his possession. Chertkov and those close to him believe that if they are turned over to Sofya Andreyevna she may strike out all the passages that she finds objectionable. Lev Nikolayevich is also opposed to transferring them to her. There is a general feeling of uneasiness.

Lev Nikolayevich is weak and languid today. He did not go horseback riding. When he sent for me to discuss some letters I found him lying on the couch in the drawing room.

❖

5 July

❖

This evening a large company assembled in the Yasnaya Polyana drawing room: Lev Nikolayevich, Sofya Andreyevna, Lev Lvovich, N. N. Gay, M. B. Bulygin, A. B. Goldenweiser, and, later, V. G. Chertkov.

We discussed some of the things Lev Nikolayevich had talked about today on our ride to Telyatinki: the brochure written by a learned student, the fire at M. A. Schmidt's house, and Repin. In connection with the latter's insanity, Lev Nikolayevich said that he had read thoroughly two-thirds of Professor Korsakov's big book on mental illness, which the doctors at the Meshcherskoe hospital had given to him, but that there were so many absurdities in it that he could not help laughing as he read it.

"Just imagine," he said, "there are eighteen different classifications of mental disorders, and they all contradict one another. And each classification has its own subsections and categories which don't go together either. He puts the question: what is the 'I'? And answers that there are sensations, that from these sensations concepts are formed, from the concepts reasoning, and this reasoning constitutes the 'I.' Well, who experiences the sensations? Must there not be an 'I' that perceives them? Total absurdity! And it's almost all like that."

Later Lev Nikolayevich gave a very interesting definition of insanity. He said:

"I do not agree with the scientists' definition of mental illness, insanity. In my opinion insanity is the lack of receptivity to other people's ideas: an insane person holds with certitude only to what has taken root in his own mind. He will not understand me. There are two kinds of men. One is distinguished by his receptiveness, his sensitivity to the ideas of others. He is in communication with all the wise men of the world—both the ancients and those living today. He gathers impressions from everywhere: from them, from his childhood, what his nurse told him. . . . And the other kind of man knows only what at some time occurred to his own mind. . . ."

11 July

✦

I spent the night at Yasnaya Polyana. When I got up this morning I learned that there had been a great commotion in the house last night. Sofya Andreyevna, persisting in her demand that Lev Nikolayevich take his diaries away from Chertkov, had created a stormy scene. First she had lain down on the floor of his balcony, and later had run out into the park. The pleas of Dushan, N. N.

Gay, and Lev Lvovich all failed to bring her back. She insisted
that Lev Nikolayevich himself come after her. In the end he went
out and she returned with him.

Lev Lvovich showed himself in a very bad light, rudely shouting
at his father and demanding that he go to the park after Sofya
Andreyevna.

Sergei Lvovich has come and a council was held by all the Tolstoy
children to decide how to protect Lev Nikolayevich from all
possible unforeseen freaks of behavior on the part of their sick
mother.

12 July

✧

It happened that I had to return to Telyatinki from Yasnaya
Polyana just at the time Sofya Andreyevna was setting out to visit
E. I. Chertkova. When she learned that I was going she kindly
offered to drive me there, and I accepted with pleasure. We went
by carriage with the trotters. She wore an elegant black silk dress
in honor of Chertkov's fashionable mother, who is a friend of the
Dowager Empress Maria Fyodorovna.

We took a detour along the highway to bypass the bad bridge
over the Kochak brook. Sofya Andreyevna wept the whole way
and was exceedingly pitiful. She begged me to tell Chertkov to
return the manuscripts of Tolstoy's diaries.

"Let him copy them, retype them," she said, "if he will just
return to me Lev Nikolayevich's original manuscripts! Why, all the
earlier diaries are in my custody—tell him that if he will return
them to me I shall be at peace. I shall be well disposed to him again,
he can visit us as before, and we shall work together for Lev
Nikolayevich and be of service to him. Will you tell him this?
Tell him, for God's sake!"

Weeping and trembling, Sofya Andreyevna gazed at me implor-
ingly. Her tears and agitation were absolutely sincere. For some

reason she did not believe that I would tell this to Chertkov, and kept imploring me over and over again.

I could not look at this weeping, unfortunate woman without feelings of deep compassion. I shall never forget those moments spent with her in the carriage.

I confess that I myself was seized with agitation and I longed for the return of peace to Yasnaya Polyana—whether at the price of the manuscripts' being given to Sofya Andreyevna or at any other price—a peace so necessary for everyone, but especially for Lev Nikolayevich! It was in this mood that I went in to see Chertkov when we arrived at Telyatinki.

Learning that I had a commission from Sofya Andreyevna, Vladimir Grigorevich, with an anxious, troubled look, led me into the room of his assistant and indispensable adviser, Aleksei Serge-yenko. We both sat down on the modest "Tolstoyan" bed and Sergeyenko, his face tense with curiosity, sat down in a chair opposite us.

I began telling them about Sofya Andreyevna's request that the manuscripts be returned to her. Vladimir Grigorevich became violently agitated.

"Do you mean to say," he broke in, fixing his large, light-colored, restless eyes on me, "that you came straight out and told her where the diaries were?"

And with these words, to my utter amazement, Vladimir Grigorevich made a hideous grimace and stuck out his tongue at me. I stared at him, suffering inwardly because of the preposterous position he had put me in. I did not know whether to feel humiliated for myself, or to feel sorry for this man who was inflicting such humiliation on himself. I imagine that Chertkov wanted to make fun of the helplessness I must have displayed when Sofya Andre-yevna had become so importunate with me in the carriage. He had probably noticed my agitation and was understandably irritated by my sympathy and compassion for her. I braced myself and, ignoring his vagary, replied:

"No, I could not tell her anything because I do not know where the diaries are."

"Oh, now that is wonderful!" exclaimed Chertkov, impetuously springing up from his seat. "Please go now," he said, opening the door to the corridor. "They are having tea there—you must be hungry. We want to have a talk in here."

The door slammed behind me and I heard the lock click. I went into the corridor, stunned by the reception shown me. Chertkov and Sergeyenko held a consultation.

Later I learned that it had been decided not to return the diaries.

14 July

There is an atmosphere of anxiety at Yasnaya. Sofya Andreyevna demands categorically, under threat of poisoning or drowning herself, that Lev Nikolayevich's diaries for the last ten years be taken away from Chertkov and given to her. Lev Nikolayevich is worried about her, but he bears this great trial very well. He is prepared to make any concession to calm his wife. It goes without saying that general peace and harmony are infinitely more important to him than any papers.

Today he wrote the following in a letter to Sofya Andreyevna:

(1) I will not give my current diary to anyone, but will keep it in my own possession.

(2) I will take my old diaries from Chertkov and keep them myself, probably in some bank.

(3) If you are troubled by the thought that those places in my diaries where I write under the impression of the moment concerning our disagreements and conflicts may be used by future biographers who are ill-disposed toward you, then, not to mention that such expressions of temporary feelings in both my diaries and yours cannot in any way give a true understanding of our real relations—if you fear this, I am glad of the opportunity to express in my diary, or, quite simply, even in this letter, my relationship to you and my evaluation of your life.

My attitude toward you and my estimation of you are this:

just as I loved you in my youth, so I have never ceased loving you, and love you still, despite various reasons for coolness. The reasons for this coolness were, first, my withdrawing further and further from the interests of temporal life and my repugnance for them, whereas you neither would nor could relinquish them, not having in your soul those principles that led me to my convictions—which is very natural and for which I do not reproach you. That is first, and the second (forgive me if what I say is unpleasant for you, but what is now taking place between us is so important that one must not be afraid to speak out and to hear the whole truth), the second is that your disposition in recent years has become more and more irritable, despotic, and lacking in self-control. The manifestation of these traits of character could not but cool, not my feeling itself, but the expression of it. That is the second reason. The third and main reason was that fatal one for which neither of us is to blame— which is our absolutely contrary understanding of the meaning and purpose of life. Everything about our conception of life has been completely antithetical: the way of life, relations to people, even the means of living—property—which I consider an evil and you consider a necessary condition of life. I have submitted to a way of life which was difficult for me in order not to part from you, while you have taken this as a concession to your views, and the misunderstanding between us has grown greater and greater. There have been other reasons for my coolness, for which we have both been guilty, but I shall not speak of them now because they are beside the point. The point is that despite these misunderstandings, I have not ceased loving and esteeming you.

My estimation of your life is this: I, a debauched man, deeply depraved in the sexual sense and no longer in my first youth, married you, a pure, beautiful, clever eighteen-year-old girl, and, my vile, dissolute past notwithstanding, you have lived with me for almost fifty years, loving me, living a hard, industrious life, bearing children, nursing them, rearing them, caring for them and for me, and not succumbing to the temptations that might easily have enticed any other strong, healthy, beautiful woman in your position. You have lived in such a way that I have nothing to reproach you for. I do not, cannot, reproach you for failing to follow me in my unusual spiritual movement, for each man's spiritual life is a mystery between him and God, and no one can require anything different of him. And if I have made demands on you, then I was mistaken, and in this I am guilty.

So here you have a true description of my relation to you and my estimation of you. And as for what can be found in the diaries, I only know that nothing harsh, nothing that would be contrary to what I am now writing, will be found there.

So that is (3), concerning what might, but should not trouble you about the diaries.

(4) is this: if at the present moment my relations with Chertkov are painful for you, I am prepared not to see him, although I can say that this will be harder for him than for me. But if it is what you want I will do it.

And now (5), which is that if you do not accept my conditions for a good, peaceful life, then I will retract my promise not to leave you. I will go away. I will go, but certainly not to Chertkov. I shall even set as an indispensable condition that he not come to live near me, but I shall leave without fail, because it is impossible to go on living as we are now.

I would be able to go on living in this way if I could endure your suffering with equanimity, but I cannot. Yesterday you went away agitated and suffering. I wanted to go to bed and sleep, but I began not so much thinking about you as being aware of you, and could not sleep but kept listening until one o'clock, two o'clock, then woke up again and listened; I even dreamed about you.

Think it over calmly, dear friend, listen to your heart, be sensible of it, and you will decide everything as it should be. For my part, I will say that this is how I have decided everything, and that for me it *cannot, cannot* be otherwise. Stop torturing, not others, but yourself, my darling, for you are suffering one hundred times more than anyone else. That is all.

Morning, 14 July, 1910   Lev Tolstoy

On Lev Nikolayevich's instructions, Aleksandra Lvovna went to Telyatinki for the diaries and remained there for a long time. As I later learned from Varvara Mikhailovna, there assembled with Chertkov in Sergeyenko's room (the same room where the day before yesterday my conversation with Chertkov had taken place) all those closest to him—his *alter ego* A. Sergeyenko, O. K. Tolstaya (Anna Konstantinovna's sister), Aleksandra Lvovna, the Goldenweisers, both husband and wife—and hastily copied out of Lev Nikolayevich's diaries those passages which compromised Sofya Andreyevna and which in their opinion she might destroy. Then the diaries were packed up and sent to Yasnaya Polyana. Chertkov, standing on the porch of the Telyatinki house, with mock solemnity made the sign of the cross three times over Aleksandra Lvovna with the packet of letters, and then handed them to her. It was not easy for him to part with them.

At Yasnaya Polyana Sofya Andreyevna was waiting with similar excitement and impatience. According to Varvara Mikhailovna, she flung herself on the dairies with such vehemence that they had to call M. S. Sukhotin to help prevent her from damaging the notebooks. They were subsequently taken away from her and put under seal.

✧

15 July

✧

The story of the diaries seems to be drawing to a close. Lev Nikolayevich yielded to Sofya Andreyevna in taking the diaries from Chertkov; he decided, however, not to allow them to become

an object of contention by granting them to either side and will
keep them in a neutral place, that is, in some Tula bank.

As I was saying good-bye before going home, Sofya Andreyevna
asked me to convey an invitation to Vladimir Grigorevich to visit
them this evening.

I had already been given a letter for him by Lev Nikolayevich,
who also asked me to tell him to be as circumspect as possible with
Sofya Andreyevna, not to mention a word about the diaries, and
to refrain from tête-à-tête conversations with him in his study and
to talk to him only in the common rooms.

He took from his pocket a letter from Vladimir Grigorevich
and showed me a passage in it where the latter had asked whether
it would not be better to keep the diaries at Yasnaya Polyana so
that they would be available in case they were needed for work.

"How can he possibly say such a thing? Please tell him not to
say a word about the diaries! It could provoke an inconceivable
explosion! Diaries, you know, are precisely the subject to unhinge
the mentally deranged!"

16 July

✧

This afternoon the "great event" took place: Tatyana Lvovna
(recently arrived from Kochety) together with Sofya Andreyevna,
has finally taken Lev Nikolayevich's old diaries to Tula and
deposited them in the Tula branch of the State Bank. It has been
arranged that they can be given only to Lev Nikolayevich or, by
his power of attorney, to M. S. Sukhotin.

✧

19 July

✧

Lev Nikolayevich has written a conclusion to his short story *From My Diary*, which was recently published in the newspapers. Chertkov suggested sending it to the newspapers with a note in his name to the effect that Tolstoy considers it desirable that this should be published. Lev Nikolayevich has changed Chertkov's note to say that he, Chertkov, considers the conclusion worth printing and is therefore sending it to the editors' offices with Tolstoy's permission.

"I'm shifting it onto him," he said to me. "I write that he considers this piece worth printing—because I myself do not. Show my note to Vladimir Grigorevich: if he likes it he can send it, if not, let him leave it as it was."

Sofya Andreyevna came in during this conversation, and seeing a sheet of paper in Lev Nikolayevich's hand began questioning him about it. He tried to explain it to her, but she understood nothing of what he said. "Is that a letter from Chertkov? Why Chertkov? May I make a copy of it? Why this sheet of paper to Chertkov and not my copy of it?" and so forth, a stream of questions ending with: "I still don't understand."

"I am very sorry," replied Lev Nikolayevich in a tired voice, adding when she had gone: "As soon as it has to do with Chertkov everything gets so confused in her head that she doesn't understand anything, and God knows what she thinks!"

Dr. D. V. Nikitin and the psychiatrist G. I. Rossolimo have come from Moscow to examine Sofya Andreyevna.

At dinner Rossolimo and Lev Nikolayevich discussed the cause of suicide. Lev Nikolayevich gave lack of faith as the chief cause. Rossolimo cited the economic, cultural, physiological, and biological causes as well as the possibility of a lack of faith, in other words (and this he said in his own language), "the want of a fulcrum on which one might lean." He could in no way reach an understanding with Lev Nikolayevich, and, no wonder: they speak different languages, inasmuch as Tolstoy has a skeptical attitude toward medicine as a science.

In the evening Lev Nikolayevich went out to the terrace for tea. Sofya Andreyevna was still in her room with the doctors.

"They have prescribed a good medicine for me," he said, "and one that I will swallow with pleasure—to go to Kochety."

The doctors had not yet reached any conclusions today and consequently will remain till tomorrow.

In view of the fact that relations between Sofya Andreyevna and Chertkov continue to be strained, Lev Nikolayevich has decided to give in to her in the hope that this will calm her and to ask Chertkov not to visit Yasnaya Polyana for a while. Late in the evening he rang for me. I went to his bedroom, where Dushan was bandaging his aching leg.

"You'll be going to Chertkov's tomorrow," he said, "so tell him about all of our adventures here. And tell him that what is most difficult for me in all this is—he. It is truly difficult for me, but tell him that for a while I must give up seeing him. I don't know how he will take it."

I expressed confidence that if Vladimir Grigorevich knows that this is necessary for Lev Nikolayevich then, without doubt, he will readily accept and endure the temporary deprivation of seeing him.

"And how very necessary this is for me, how necessary!" he continued. "But his letters have always been so truly friendly and loving. I am not troubled for myself, but I feel terribly grieved for him. And I know it will be hard for Galya * too. Yet to think that these threats of suicide, which sometimes are no more than idle threats but then—who knows?—to think that it might happen! And if I were to have that on my conscience! What is going on now—for me, this is nothing. That I have no leisure, or have less—never mind! Besides, the more external experiences you have the more material you have for the inner work. Tell that to Batya.** We probably shan't see each other in the morning."

* A. K. Chertkova.
** The name used for Chertkov by the members of his family. V.B.

22 July

I brought to Lev Nikolayevich a long letter about God that I have written to one of his correspondents, a convinced atheist, to whom I wrote once before. Lev Nikolayevich read the letter and approved of it. I happened to have touched on the question of the essence of spiritual love: how to formulate it, what exactly constitutes this feeling? I put the question to Lev Nikolayevich.

"I have already formulated it many times. Love is the joining of souls separated from each other by the body. Love is one of the manifestations of God, just as understanding is one of them. There are probably other manifestations of God as well. We apprehend God by means of love and understanding, but the essence of God is not revealed to us in all its fullness. It is beyond human understanding and, as you have written, it is through love that we strive to apprehend the divine essence."

He further said concerning this letter:

"It is good that you have answered his objections directly. Point out that though he does not want to use the word 'God,' he nonetheless recognizes this essence. Even if you call this essence a bush, it exists all the same."

He sat on the balcony, very weak and exhausted. Things are going badly with Sofya Andreyevna again, and there is a state of tension in the house. Any minute there may be a flare-up and the tensions will erupt into something unforeseen and difficult. It is unbearably painful for Lev Nikolayevich; I feel this today especially for some reason.

He wanted me to go to Telyatinki as quickly as possible to tell Chertkov, who intended to resume his visits to Yasnaya Polyana, not to come today.

"You had better go and tell him this. Otherwise I am sure there will be more scenes," he said.

But just then a young Finnish girl who had come from Tel-yatinki to have a talk with Lev Nikolayevich happened to be going back, and he gave her a letter for Chertkov. As it turned out, she and Chertkov missed each other on the way. There are two roads between Telyatinki and Yasnaya Polyana: she took one and he the other. So Vladimir Grigorevich, suspecting nothing, appeared at Yasnaya.

At first he talked with Lev Nikolayevich on the balcony of his study. Later everyone, including Sofya Andreyevna, went out to the terrace for tea.

Sofya Andreyevna was in a dreadful state. Nervous and upset, she was rude and antagonistic not alone to the guest but to everyone present. The effect this created was understandable: everyone was strained and dejected. Chertkov looked as if he had swallowed a poker: he drew himself up and his face turned to stone. The samovar boiled cheerily on the table, the bowl of raspberries stood out like a bright red patch on the white tablecloth, but those sitting around the table looked as if they were serving a prison sentence and hardly touched their tea. No one stayed very long, however; soon they had all gone their own ways.*

* When I think of that evening, I am amazed at Sofya Andreyevna's intuition: she seemed to feel that something awful and irreparable had just happened. And, in fact, as I learned only later, that very day Lev Nikolayevich had signed a secret testament in the forest near the village of Grumont, assigning the rights to all his works to the public domain. His youngest daughter is nominally the executrix of his will, but V. G. Chertkov will be the actual administrator. (The latter appointment was stipulated in a separate "covering document" drawn up by Chertkov himself and signed by L. N. Tolstoy.) The witnesses to the signing of the will were A. P. Sergeyenko, A. B. Goldenweiser, and one of the members of Chertkov's household, a youth by the name of Anatol Radinsky. In the morning I had seen in front of the porch of Chertkov's Telyatinki house three horses saddled for these people and was very surprised when Radinsky, whom I questioned, refused to tell me where he was going. As it happens, he had been drawn into signing the testament quite unexpectedly and did not himself know what he was signing. The whole affair was conducted in absolute secrecy. I was purposely not brought into it because they feared that with my constant contact with Sofya Andreyevna I might betray the secret. And so, an act had been committed which Sofya Andreyevna had dreaded above everything: the family, whose material interests she had so jealously guarded, was deprived of the literary rights to Tolstoy's works after his death. V.B.

26 July

Yesterday for the third successive day Lev Nikolayevich was not well.

Sofya Andreyevna, excited as usual, suddenly decided to leave Yasnaya Polyana and go to Moscow, "perhaps forever," as she said. Then she immediately grew calmer, and having formally taken leave of Lev Nikolayevich and everyone in the house left in the carriage for Tula, intending to take the express train from there. We all thought she meant this quite seriously, that she very likely felt the need of finding peace somewhere away from home. But today she unexpectedly returned from Tula with Andrei Lvovich and his family: his second wife Ekaterina Vasilyevna (the divorced wife of the Tula governor, Artsimovich), and their two-year-old daughter, Mashenka, the only child that Lev Nikolayevich (in his own words) "could not love." He had opposed Andrei's divorce from his first wife, Olga Konstantinovna, and somehow, in his heart, has never accepted his second marriage. This, of course, does not prevent him from being chivalrously polite to Ekaterina Vasilyevna whenever they meet.

Sofya Andreyevna said that she had met Andrei Lvovich in Tula quite by chance and had persuaded him to return with her. There is no doubt that she has told her son in detail about all she has been through. This is obvious from the fact that Andrei Lvovich's mood is what is called "aggressive." He is very hard on Lev Nikolayevich.

I believe that both Sofya Andreyevna and Andrei Lvovich are plagued by suspicions about the will. . . .

✦

28 July

I told Lev Nikolayevich that Vladimir Grigorevich sends his regards and asked me to say that he would like to hear from him.

"Tell him that I have meant to write to him in detail, but that

I have no time now. Tell him that there is peace in the house—I don't know whether this is the lull before the storm—that I continue to feel poorly, really quite poorly: my liver, my bilious condition . . . and that Sergei Lvovich has come. You have seen that this is pleasant for me, because he is closer to me. And there was a letter from Tanya."

Lev Nikolayevich rode off with Dushan but forgot something in his room and came back. As he passed through the "Remington room" he said to me:

"As to Tanya's letter, tell him that I do not agree with it."

He seemed to be in a hurry and walked away quickly, but then he came back again.

"She writes that he should go away. But I think this is absolutely unnecessary, and I do not wish it."

✧

1 August

✧

Toward evening Lev Nikolayevich and P. I. Biryukov had a long talk alone in the study. This was a conversation of great importance, as I later learned, concerning the extraordinary event that recently took place at Yasnaya Polyana, that is, Tolstoy's drawing up in secret from his family his last will and testament, by virtue of which all his works, both literary and philosophical, pass into the public domain after his death.

When this was made known to Biryukov (by Lev Nikolayevich himself, if I am not mistaken), he pointed out to him what an unsavory construction would be placed on this as a result of the conspiratorial way in which the will had been made. To gather all the members of the family together and announce to them his wishes might better correspond to Lev Nikolayevich's general spirit and convictions.

For Lev Nikolayevich, placed as he is in the midst of these various currents in his intimate circle, this conversation, coming on

top of another unpleasant episode with Sofya Andreyevna, has not
been without effect.

✧

2 August

✧

Sofya Andreyevna has taken to her bed. Vladimir Grigorevich
is still not visiting Yasnaya Polyana, nor is Lev Nikolayevich going
to Telyatinki. They correspond either through me or A. B.
Goldenweiser.

Both Aleksandra Lvovna and Chertkov are very much disturbed
by Biryukov's statement yesterday. In their opinion, without
having gone into all the complications of the question, he has very
clumsily interfered in the matter, and has given Lev Nikolayevich
advice which has only upset him. From what I understand, his
remarks really have made an impression on Lev Nikolayevich.

✧

3 August

✧

This evening there were again painful, nightmarish scenes.
Sofya Andreyevna exceeded all limits in showing her lack of respect
for Lev Nikolayevich, casting insane aspersions on his relations
with Chertkov, of whom she is jealous, and citing a certain entry
in the diary of his youth.

After this conversation in the drawing room with her, I saw
Lev Nikolayevich when he rapidly passed through my room on his
way to his bedroom, holding himself erect, his hands thrust under
his belt, and his pale face frozen with indignation. There was a
click of the lock after he closed his bedroom door. Then he went
from the bedroom to the study where he locked the door leading to

the drawing room, thus immuring himself in his two rooms as in a fortress.

His unfortunate wife ran from one door to the other, beseeching him to forgive her and open the door ("Levochka, I won't do it again!"), but he did not answer.

God knows what feelings of outraged dignity he was suffering behind those doors!

4 August

At Yasnaya a telegram was received from V. G. Korolenko: "Would be happy to pay you a visit, please let me know whether I would be disturbing Lev Nikolayevich." Sofya Andreyevna replied: "Everyone will be delighted to see you, come."

V. G. Chertkov asked me to give Lev Nikolayevich his regards, as usual, and to tell him that he could imagine nothing better for him than that he should leave Yasnaya Polyana and go to Tatyana Lvovna's in Kochety.

"Yes, I've been thinking of that myself," Lev Nikolayevich replied vaguely when I gave him Chertkov's message.

5 August

I was sitting in Lev Nikolayevich's study with him.

"Sofya Andreyevna is not well," he said. "If only Vladimir Grigorevich could see her as she is today! One cannot help feeling compassion for her—and to treat her as severely as he does, he and many others, myself included——. She does these things without any reason! If there were some reason, she would not be able to keep it to herself, she would express it. But as it is she is suffocating here, she cannot breathe. It's impossible not to feel pity for her, and I rejoice when I succeed in feeling it. I have even made a note concerning this."

He felt in his pocket for his notebook, took it out, and began reading from it. Sofya Andreyevna walked in unexpectedly to bring him some apples. She said something to him about them and he left off reading to answer her. She went out apparently annoyed by my presence in the study and suspicious of something. Lev Niko- layevich continued reading.

This is the thought he read to me:

"All men are in a constant process of growth, and therefore it is impossible to reject anyone. But there are those who are alien to such a degree, who are so far gone in the condition they may be in, that you can only treat them as you do children, loving, respecting, and protecting them, but not putting them on the same level as yourself and not demanding of them an understanding of that which they lack. There is one thing that impedes such a treatment of them, which is that instead of the inquiring mind and simplicity of the child, these children manifest an indifference and negation of what they do not understand and—and this is the most trying—self-assurance."

Then he added, pointing to the door:

"And how many such children there are among the people surrounding us! By the way, here is some work for you, to copy this—see how much has accumulated—into the diary."

This meant that I was to copy the rough draft of thoughts from the notebook into his diary.

And then he, the great Tolstoy, gray and bent, climbed on a stool, reached behind the bookshelf, and took down the copybook diary which he had hidden from his wife.

We agreed that I should do the copying downstairs in Dushan's room, wait for Lev Nikolayevich to return from his walk, and then give him the notebook.

"Though there is really nothing special in here," he said, leafing through the notebook.

6 August

While Lev Nikolayevich was resting after his ride, V. G. Korolenko appeared. He had come on foot from Zaseka, where he got off the train not knowing there would be no cabs there. I received Vladimir Galaktionovich and took him into the drawing room. Sofya Andreyevna, informed of his arrival, came in at once.

V. G. Korolenko is an imposing, gray-haired old man. He is short and stocky, with a handsome, serene face, a broad, thick beard, and kindly eyes. His movements are unhurried, gentle, and deliberate. He was neatly and simply dressed in a dark lounge suit.

Lev Nikolayevich came in before dinner.

"I was prepared to say: 'Too bad you didn't notify us of your arrival—you wouldn't have wasted three rubles on a cab.' I know, I know, you walked here from the station."

"Glad to find you in good health, Lev Nikolayevich," said Korolenko.

As might be expected, Lev Nikolayevich immediately began talking about Vladimir Galaktionovich's article on capital punishment (*An Everyday Occurrence*). Korolenko mentioned that thanks to Lev Nikolayevich's letter to him about the article it had in fact received tremendous attention. Lev Nikolayevich said that if this were so it was entirely owing to the merit of the article itself.

We sat down to dinner and during the conversation it became apparent that Korolenko is rather deaf. Later he explained that he had been ill recently and that his ears were stopped up from quinine.

They began talking about decadence in literature and painting. Korolenko sought a deeper reason for it than mere affectation or the attempt to be original. He told us about a painter of his acquaintance who purposely "blued" his paintings, that is, concealed the definite forms and colors of his pictures under dark spots— deliberately, as he said, so that the rich people who bought his paintings could not see their real beauty.

"I don't know!" exclaimed Lev Nikolayevich in uncertainty. "I admire the discretion you display in your attitude toward decadence—I admire it, but I myself am not capable of it. Art has always served the wealthy classes. It is possible that a new art is emerging that does not cater to the gentry, but nothing has come of it yet."

They talked about music, and Lev Nikolayevich said:

"Real art ought to be accessible to everyone. Present-day art is only for the corrupt classes, for us. However much I love Chopin, I do not believe that he will live; he will be dead for the art of the future. There is no real art yet."

In talking about the November ninth law, Korolenko expressed himself cautiously. Lev Nikolayevich definitely stated his view that land is something that must not be privately owned.

✧

Korolenko turned out to be very talkative and altogether a splendid storyteller. His reminiscences of a life rich in events furnish him with an abundance of material. Where has fate not taken him! At one time he lived as an exile in the province of Perm; at another time he was "sent even farther away" to the Yakut region; he went to America to see an exposition in Chicago; he visited London; and there were times when, walking stick in hand, he wandered through Russia with one of his "comrades" (he always says "with a comrade, my comrades," which gives a partial picture of his world-view) to the most out-of-the-way corners, visiting monasteries, living among sectarians, etc.

✧

What is astonishing is that here at Yasnaya Polyana he was able to hold his own as a man of letters. He remained completely himself and only himself. As a rule Lev Nikolayevich draws everyone into his own sphere of interests, religious in the main. Korolenko, besides keeping the general attention concentrated on his stories of everyday life and his own experiences, also contrived to lead Lev Nikolayevich into a purely literary conversation, which is something almost no one ever succeeds in doing. The literary discussion arose late in the evening, just before everyone parted for the night.

"One young critic says," began Korolenko, "that in Gogol and Dostoyevsky there are types, but that in your works there don't seem to be any types. I, of course, do not agree with this; first of all because you do have types, but there is a certain truth in it. I think that in Gogol the characters are presented in a static state, in that they are already developed, fully formed. But with you they develop throughout the entire work—with you it's dynamic. Like Pierre Bezukhov, Levin: they are not yet formed, they develop, take shape. And in my opinion it is precisely in this that the artist's greatest difficulty lies."

"Perhaps," said Lev Nikolayevich, "but above all, the artist must not reason, but discover the type through spontaneous feeling. What a variety of characters there are in life! There exist so many mixtures and combinations of character traits! And certain of these combinations are typical. All the others come under them. Now, when I grow up and become a writer, I shall write about the type. I'd like to do that. But now, as the old fellow says, 'I've already been in.' "

❖

7 August

Having spent the night at Yasnaya Polyana, Korolenko went to Chertkov's in the morning with Aleksandra Lvovna, where he was undoubtedly informed of every aspect of Sofya Andreyevna's sick and malevolent behavior.

At three o'clock he set off for Tula to take the train from there. Lev Nikolayevich was unfailing in his courtesy and consideration. He had me ride out to the Tula road, leading his Délire by the reins, and he followed a little later with Korolenko in the droshky. As I looked back and saw the two old men with their white beards sitting side by side in the approaching droshky, for a moment I could not tell one from the other. They drew up to me and stopped, and Lev Nikolayevich got out and said good-bye to

Korolenko for the last time. I too took my leave of him and the carriage rolled on, taking Vladimir Galaktionovich to Tula.

✧

10 August

✧

While Lev Nikolayevich was resting after his ride, a soldier came to the house. Two battalions of soldiers were bivouacked near the village today, pitching their tents in the field just in front of the entrance to the Tolstoy estate. The officers had been quartered in huts. On their arrival, the commander of the detachment had summoned the platoon commanders and ordered them to see that none of the soldiers attempted to reach Tolstoy, "that enemy of the State and the Orthodox Church." And here was a twenty-one-year-old Jew from Kiev, Isaak Vinorsky, who had taken two mess-tins and set off, supposedly for water, and made his way to Tolstoy's house by back ways. He had said to his platoon commander that they could put him under arrest if they liked, but he was going to see L. N. Tolstoy. As I told him, unfortunately Lev Nikolayevich could not come out to see him. I had a talk with him.

"At least I've seen Lev Nikolayevich's house," he said.

Taking advantage of the fact that no one was at home, I took the soldier into the house, showed him the drawing room, then gave him a postcard with a picture of Tolstoy on it, which he hid in his boot-top. He left very happy, taking with him two apples from the Tolstoy orchard to give to the platoon commander who had let him come to see Tolstoy.

11 August

✧

Lev Nikolayevich told us that last evening four soldiers from the detachment in the village came to see him. One of them was Vinarsky, one a Russian, and the other two were Jews.

"If I were to take the patriotic view," said Lev Nikolayevich, "I would let Jews enter the universities and schools without restraint, but I wouldn't let one of them enter the army. The ones who came to see me, because they are intelligent, feel nothing but horror and repugnance for soldiering. The other one, the Russian, I suppose feels the same. Books? They are permitted to read only the books in the regimental library. And since it contains only the stupidest books, and the people are now above that level, they don't read them."

He also told us that he had learned that three of the soldiers who had come to see him had been arrested and given a three months' sentence for absence without leave.

12 August

✧

Sofya Andreyevna, who was present at dinner, kept interrupting Lev Nikolayevich with her remarks. She disagreed with almost everything he said. Schopenhauer's apothegm about God and the spiritual origin of man—a statement which for Lev Nikolayevich is one of the fundamental convictions of his life and the basis of all his thinking—she dismissed outright as "no more than a witticism." Lev Nikolayevich soon went off to his study.

"Sinner that I am, I left," he said, "because there is no possibility whatever of holding a conversation, a serious conversation, in Sofya Andreyevna's presence."

✧

15 August

Tomorrow Lev Nikolayevich, Sofya Andreyevna, Tatyana Lvovna, and Dushan Petrovich are leaving for Kochety for an indefinite stay of one to three weeks or more. I suddenly fell ill with rheumatic fever and am staying at Telyatinki.

V. G. Chertkov has received permission to live permanently at Telyatinki. Khiryakov, who was just released from prison, where he spent eight months for having written the poem *Peaceful Marseillaise,* has come here with his wife.

✧

13 September

I went to Yasnaya Polyana to collect some books and mail them to the addresses sent to me from Kochety. Only Varvara Feokritova has been living there. We talked for a long time about the tragedy of Yasnaya Polyana. . . .

Sofya Andreyevna was expected to arrive by midnight tonight: lights were burning in the drawing room and tea was prepared.

She arrived looking exhausted. She complains that Lev Nikolayevich refuses to tell her anything definite about the date of his return.

Looking ahead there seems to be no end to this sad story.

14 September

Sofya Andreyevna (completely distraught) wanted to show me the place in one of Lev Nikolayevich's early diaries on which she bases her morbid jealousy of Chertkov, but I refused to read it, explaining to her that I cannot do such a thing, that it would be very hard for me. I love and respect Lev Nikolayevich too much to allow myself, without his permission, to examine his diaries, or to look for something in them that is discreditable to him. Sofya Andreyevna accepted my refusal with good grace and said she understood me. She simply believes that I wish to preserve certain illusions, when in fact I have no illusions, only a deep conviction of Lev Nikolayevich's moral integrity and purity.

As usual she complained of Chertkov's unkind and at times even rude treatment of her. On one occasion he is supposed to have said to Lev Nikolayevich in her presence: "If I had a wife like yours I would shoot myself." And at another time he said to her: "If I had wanted to, I could have dragged your family through the mud, but I haven't done it."

I do not know how accurate Sofya Andreyevna was in quoting Chertkov,* but it is clear to me that there are times when, as a sick and elderly woman, she should be treated with more consideration than is shown her by Chertkov and Aleksandra Lvovna. I am sometimes astonished that they do not see how the anger and irritation aroused in her by this conflict with them are inevitably vented on Lev Nikolayevich, who takes no part in the struggle, but stands outside it.

Both Vladimir Grigorevich and Aleksandra Lvovna suffer from a sort of blindness in this regard. The former aims at the moral destruction of Tolstoy's wife in order to get control of his manuscripts. The latter is either in conspiracy with him or, with typical female antagonism toward the mother, devotes herself to the struggle as to a kind of sport. Whatever the reason, it does her no credit. Varvara Mikhailovna pretends to be equally devoted to both mother and daughter, yet repeats every unfortunate, hysterical word that Sofya Andreyevna utters, thereby inciting Aleksandra Lvovna to further "acts of war." Both Goldenweiser and Sergeyenko support Chertkov.

It is an appalling, disheartening picture. The one hope is that Lev Nikolayevich can overcome all this petty squabbling among

---

* I subsequently became convinced that she had been entirely correct in what she said. V.B.

those nearest him by the greatness of his soul and the power of the vital love he has for them and for others—for everyone and everything.

18 September

When I arrived at Yasnaya Polyana, I did not find M. M. Klechkovsky, a close friend of Tolstoy's and Chertkov's, a lawyer by training and a teacher at the conservatory by profession, who is responsible for several of the articles on education in *The Intermediary*'s publications. He is a very kind and sensitive man, though perhaps somewhat emotional.

Immediately upon his arrival, he had encountered Sofya Andreyevna. She decided, as usual, to initiate the visitor into the affairs of Yasnaya Polyana, and began telling him such dreadful things about Chertkov, and plunged him into such filth, that the poor man was horrified. He burst into tears then and there, sprang up from his chair, and rushed out of the house like a man who had been scalded. He fled to the woods, where he wandered about for almost the entire day, after which he turned up at the Chertkovs' in Telyatinki.

Klechkovsky is a very impressionable man who loves Lev Nikolayevich with all his heart. He had no idea that life at Yasnaya Polyana was as difficult for him as this meeting with Sofya Andreyevna led him to conclude, and he was terribly upset by such a revelation.

No doubt he had expected to find solace at the Chertkovs'. But here in turn A. K. Chertkova and Vladimir Grigorevich, pouring out all the excruciating vicissitudes of their struggle with her, slandered Sofya Andreyevna so despicably that Klechkovsky was reduced to an even worse state of distraction. I believe that he almost went out of his mind that night.

Contrary to his custom, he declined their hospitality, refusing even to stay the night, and returned to Moscow the same evening.

It happened that I was preparing to go to Moscow that night on business of my own, and we were driven to the station in the same carriage (though we traveled in different coaches, as we were not going by the same class). On the way to the station he was silent and complained of a headache. We exchanged only a few words. I confess it was painful for me, too, to touch on the subject of what was going on at Yasnaya Polyana.

"My God! How can they fail to take care of Lev Nikolayevich? How can they do this? How reckless they are!"

From time to time his involuntary exclamations broke the silence as he sat beside me staring abstactedly before him into the darkness of the night.

This last exclamation was overheard by Misha Zaitsev, a village lad in Chertkov's employ who was driving us to the station.

"Yes," he remarked, "Sofya Andreyevna sure is reckless!"

At the Chertkovs' he naturally had heard all about the state of affairs at Yasnaya Polyana.

"She is not the only one who is reckless!" retorted Klechkovsky.

"Well, who else is?" Misha asked, turning to us in bewilderment.

"He knows who," Klechkovsky said, nodding toward me.

He was astounded at the atmosphere of hatred and malice surrounding the great Tolstoy, so much in need of peace in his old age. And having stumbled on this knowledge unwittingly he was shaken. The unexpected revelation filled this very sincere, natural, and loving man with bitter resentment and fear for Tolstoy.

Yet for a long time after his departure they continued to speak of him at Telyatinki and Yasnaya Polyana with condescending, contemptuous smiles: "He's a queer one . . ."

21 September

On my return from Moscow I found a letter addressed to me from Aleksandra Lvovna, sent from Kochety on the seventeenth of September, which said:

"... What can I tell you about us? We live peacefully and quietly here, but when I think of what awaits us, my heart sinks. However, during this time there has been a change—a change which in my opinion is very important—in Lev Nikolayevich himself. Even he now feels—to some extent influenced by letters from good friends *— that it is no longer possible, considering the harm it does to his conscience and work (?) to put up with the situation when doing so, strange to say, neither pacifies nor engenders feelings of love as it ought to, but on the contrary, only intensifies hatred and increases malicious acts. Meanwhile Father stands firm in his intention not to yield, but to pursue his own course. God give him strength to so continue. It is the only way to establish a feasible life together for Father and Mother.

"Yesterday Father wrote to Chertkov—not quite accurately— about my wanting to return home. What I want is that Father should not yield to Mother, but do what is best for himself. Before her departure he said to her: 'When do you want me to come?' She said: 'Tomorrow.' 'No, that's not possible.' 'Well then, the seventeenth.' 'Even that is too soon!' 'Then do as you wish.' And Father said: 'I'll come by the twenty-third.' So if we don't leave on the twenty-third there'll be a scene; she'll have hysterics and carry on, and Father may not be able to stand firm. You understand, it will be better for him to do as he chooses than to be at her beck and call. This is why I want to go. Explain this to Vladimir Grigorevich."

Chertkov gave credence to this letter, but I must confess I was far from pleased with all it contained. One felt Aleksandra Lvovna's indomitable nature, her desire to urge her father on in the *struggle*

---

* While at Kochety, Lev Nikolayevich had received a letter from A. B. Goldenweiser in which he had enclosed typewritten extracts from the private diary of V. M. Feokritova, which put Sofya Andreyevna in a very bad light. In reply, Lev Nikolayevich sent a very cool letter to A. B. Goldenweiser, in which he said, among other things: "In what V.M. has written, and in what you yourself express on the subject, there is a great exaggeration of the sinister aspects, a disregard for the fact that she is sick, and a mixture of good and bad sentiments." V.B.

with his wife, as if he himself did not know what he must do in this or any other situation.

22 *September*

A note from Lev Nikolayevich:

Thank you, dear Valentin Fyodorovich, for your letter and for sending your article and the story by Kudrin. The article is beautifully written. And the story is very good. I read it aloud here and it made a strong impression. Perhaps I shall see you before you receive this letter. I expect to arrive on the twenty-second. Greetings to all our friends.

20 September   Lev Tolstoy

In the evening I set out for Yasnaya Polyana to await Lev Nikolayevich's arrival. Sofya Andreyevna seemed to be exceedingly agitated. In her present mood she is hostile not only to Chertkov, but even to her husband. She said outright that she no longer loves him and considers him "almost a stranger." From what she says, she has been awaiting his return without her customary feelings of joy.

"And it's all because of Chertkov! Whose fault is it? He meddled in our domestic life. You know, before he appeared, such a thing had never happened," she said.

I tried to intimate that a reconciliation might be possible at some future time, saying that Lev Nikolayevich could never forget Chertkov; but I could see that even the thought of such a thing is inconceivable to her. The dissension between them has gone so far that it is evidently too late to mend matters. It now becomes clear to me that the tragedy of Yasnaya Polyana will be of long duration; or it will end quite suddenly, but in a way that nobody has foreseen.

Lev Nikolayevich, Aleksandra Lvovna, and Dushan arrived at half-past twelve. It was a cold night and Lev Nikolayevich wore

a huge bearskin coat that had been sent to the station by Sofya
Andreyevna—after she had been reminded of it by Ilya Vasilyevich.
To my inquiry about his health, Lev Nikolayevich replied that he
was feeling very well.

"Wasn't it cold?" asked Sofya Andreyevna.

She had come downstairs to greet him only after he had taken
off his things.

"No, they put seven articles of clothing on me—I counted."

He went upstairs with his wife, and the rest of us went to
Aleksandra Lvovna's room. Perhaps a quarter of an hour had passed
when Sofya Andreyevna came to her daughter and announced:
"Papa feels dull without you," and invited us all to come upstairs.
She seemed to be upset; obviously her conversation with Lev
Nikolayevich had not gone the way she would have wished. She
retired to her own room and did not appear in the drawing room
for some time.

Aleksandra Lvovna, Varvara Mikhailovna, Dushan Petrovich,
and I went up to the drawing room. Lev Nikolayevich greeted
us with the words:

"Always the same . . . always the same . . . terribly excited."

"Well, shall we go away again tomorrow?" asked Aleksandra
Lvovna.

"Yes . . . yes . . . Ah, the unfortuate woman!" He shook his
head, deeply distressed. "So unfortunate!"

We sat down to tea and Lev Nikolayevich began telling us
about his stay at Kochety.

❖

23 September

❖

"When you go to Chertkov, tell him—he will certainly be
interested—that Sofya Andreyevna is intensely disturbed. So many
conversations, so many reproaches! Yesterday there was a terrible

scene. But she is so pitiful—extremely pitiful! I was truly sorry
for her. Thank God, I succeeded in acting as I should. I was silent
the whole time, and said only one thing, but that one thing upset
her. She asked me why I had not returned sooner, and I said:
'Because I didn't want to.' And that 'didn't want to' provoked her
and brought forth goodness knows what! One has to be so careful
not to upset her!"

"It's difficult for you, isn't it, Lev Nikolayevich?"

"No . . . When one strives to act as he should, then it is easy.
Yes . . . I had written to Vladimir Grigorevich that we would see
each other—but tell him that I shall wait a little. I should have
liked to have it come from her. I was thinking of suggesting it to
her when I found her in a receptive mood; but I have not found
such a moment, so I shall wait."

I told him that it seemed to me that even the thought of renewing
relations with Vladimir Grigorevich was inconceivable to Sofya
Andreyevna.

"I wanted to take this up with her," he said. "It's really
ridiculous—to live practically next door to each other and never
meet. For me this is a great loss. I sometimes need to talk things
over with him and ask his advice. And I know it's important for
him too."

✧

Today is the Tolstoys' forty-eighth wedding anniversary.
Contrary to her usual custom, Sofya Andreyevna got up early, put
on an elegant white dress, and went for a walk in the park. She said
she had gone to bed at four o'clock in the morning and had not slept
a wink.

"May I offer my congratulations?" I said, after greeting her.

"On what?" she asked, giving me her hand. "It's such a sad——"

She did not finish but walked away, covering her face with her
hand and weeping.

After lunch I took pictures of her with Lev Nikolayevich. She
had prevailed upon him to have these pictures taken on the occasion
of their anniversary. It was an extremely painful procedure. Sofya

Andreyevna was flurried and nervous, and though plainly not wanting to vex him repeatedly asked him to change his pose. Knowing Lev Nikolayevich's dislike for having his picture taken, it was not hard to imagine what he was feeling during all this. I felt embarrassed to look at them while taking the pictures, and mechanically squeezed the camera bulb, counting aloud as Sofya Andreyevna had instructed me: "One—two—three!" This had to be repeated four times. And then it turned out that the pictures were underexposed; there was not enough light in the room and all four pictures turned out very badly. And besides, Sofya Andreyevna had approached her objective most injudiciously.

A little later Lev Nikolayevich came into the "Remington room."

"What is it, Lev Nikolayevich?"

"Nothing," he replied and smiled. "How good it is to live in the present! To have in mind only what must be done at the present moment. To stop thinking about the future."

I understood him, and felt that what he said referred to the recent instance of the picture-taking, when he had succeeded in "acting as I should" in a situation that might have called forth only irritation. And apparently he was glad that he had not offended another human being and had himself avoided feelings of ill-will.

"And I want to give up games altogether."

"What games?"

"Solitaire, chess . . ."

"Why?"

"Because in games too there is concern for the future: how the game will come out."

"But after all, that is just a glimpse into a not very distant future—almost the next moment."

"It's good discipline. It breaks one of the habit of being concerned about the future. Very good discipline. I recommend it to you."

"I have exactly the same attitude toward letters: I always look forward with terrific impatience to the arrival of the mail from the station," I confessed.

"You see—it's the same thing! And the newspapers, too . . . One must work on this. Well, but you're still a young man!"

"You know, Lev Nikolayevich, what Belinky does in order to cure himself of such impatience: when he receives a letter he leaves it unopened till the next day, and only then does he read it."

"Wonderful—he is right! How much spiritual effort goes into that! . . . Amazing people, these Jews! And here's a letter from Molochnikov that came today . . . and there was a letter from Gusev," he smiled. "He's in jail for being absent without leave. They, the exiles, the youth, formed a conspiracy not to ask permission for leave, since they do not consider themselves subject to the government. Such a letter is cheering! He's probably been released by now; the sentence was for two weeks."

Being photographed with Sofya Andreyevna was not without consequences for Lev Nikolayevich: having yielded to one side, he fell under a storm of reproaches from the other, that is, from Aleksandra Lvovna. She resented not only his acceding to his wife's request, but also his failure since his return from Kochety to replace the photographs Sofya Andreyevna had removed from the wall of his study. Above the table there had hung two large photographs: one of Chertkov with Ilyushka Tolstoy, and the other of Lev Nikolayevich with Aleksandra Lvovna. Sofya Andreyevna had removed them—the first had disappeared behind the window curtain and the second was hung in his bedroom; in their place she had hung portraits of herself and of Tolstoy's father. Insane pettiness!

Aleksandra Lvovna resented her father's not having replaced the photographs and now, to make matters worse, he had allowed himself to be photographed with Sofya Andreyevna! This resulted in his having a painful scene with his daughter.

Aleksandra Lvovna was in the "Remington room" vociferously criticizing her father to Varvara Mikhailovna, who, of course, sympathizes with her in everything, when suddenly Lev Nikolayevich came into the room.

"What's the matter with you, Sasha, shouting like that?"

Aleksandra Lvovna recited her grievances to him too: it was wrong of him to be photographed with his wife after she had made him promise never to be photographed at Chertkov's; it was inconsistent of him to sacrifice the interests of both his friend and his daughter to a harebrained woman, to allow her to rearrange his photographs, and so forth and so on.

Lev Nikolayevich shook his head in reply. "You're becoming just like her!" he said, and went back to his study.

A few minutes later his bell was heard: one ring, the signal for Aleksandra Lvovna to go to him (two rings were for me). Still resentful, she did not respond.

I went to Lev Nikolayevich. I had hardly left his room after fulfilling some small request when he again rang for Aleksandra Lvovna. She did not move. Then he sent me to get her, and she went to him.

What took place between Aleksandra Lvovna and her father, according to what she told me later, was this: Lev Nikolayevich said that he wanted to dictate a letter. She had no sooner sat down at the table than the old man suddenly let his head fall onto the arm of his chair and broke into sobs.

"I don't need your stenography!" he exclaimed through his tears.

Flinging herself into his arms she asked his forgiveness, and they both wept.

✧

24 September

This morning Lev Nikolayevich told me that yesterday he had hidden his "most private" notebook and could not remember just where he had put it.

"You know, in one notebook I jot down the thoughts which will go into my diary. The diary is read by Chertkov and Sasha, but this little book is absolutely private, and I never let anyone read it. I've searched everywhere and can't find it. It's possible that Sofya Andreyevna has found it." *

---

* This was the notebook in which Tolstoy kept his "Diary for Myself Alone." It had been found by Sofya Andreyevna in his boot-top and not returned to him.

"Was there anything in it——"

"Yes, of course! I write candidly. Well, never mind. That means it was meant to be. Some good may come of it."

I went to the study again later in the morning. Lev Nikolayevich said that he had been looking over *The Circle of Reading*.

"What splendid, powerful thoughts on vegetarianism! I am reminded of the time when goose was served at Kochety, and it was set down on the table near me. This seemed to me so barbaric! I could not conceive of that carcass being cut up and eaten. How powerfully Plutarch has expressed it!"

And he read Plutarch's thought:

" 'You ask me on what grounds Pythagoras abstained from the use of animal flesh? I, for my part, do not understand what kind of feeling, thought, or reason guided the man who first decided to defile his mouth with blood and permit his lips to touch the flesh of a slaughtered creature. I wonder at the man who will allow on his table the mutilated forms of dead bodies, and use for his daily sustenance what only a short time before had been a living being endowed with movement, a voice, perceptivity.' "

✧

I rode with Lev Nikolayevich to Zaseka. There we met M. A. Schmidt, who was setting out for Yasnaya Polyana in a cart. Lev Nikolayevich stopped to talk to her.

"Well, and how is Sofya Andreyevna?" asked Maria Aleksandrovna. "Is she all right?"

"Yes, more or less," answered Lev Nikolayevich. "When we came back she made a terrible scene. But then the next day she was unusually loving. You know, it's all so abnormal. But that is

---

After reading this personal diary, she had pasted a sheet of paper in it on which she had written: "With an aching heart I have copied this lamentable diary of my husband's. How much of what it says about me—and even about his marriage—is unjust, cruel, and—God and Levochka forgive me—untrue, distorted, and fabricated! Let people read the diary he kept when he was courting me: 'I am in love as never before. . . . I'll shoot myself if it goes on like this,' and so on. That was my Levochka, then and for a long time. Now he is Chertkov's. Sofya Andreyevna." V.B.

her affair. I try only to act as I should, because what I do is between me and God, and what she does is between her and God."

✧

At dinner Sofya Andreyevna remembered that somewhere on the way back from Kochety Lev Nikolayevich had forgotten his overcoat.

"Whoever finds it probably needs it more than I do," he remarked.

When the soup was served and the plates handed round, he suddenly said:

"No, you couldn't wash a baby in that soup!"

And in response to the general perplexity he recounted an incident that had been told to him by a feldsher at the Kochety hospital. In the hut of a peasant woman who had just given birth, there was no hot water for washing the infant, nothing on the stove but soup. But it was such a thin, watery soup that they washed the baby in it.

✧

Sofya Andreyevna did not appear for tea this evening. The reason, it seems, was another misunderstanding with Lev Nikolayevich.*

---

* Under this date in Lev Nikolayevich's "Diary for Myself Alone" appeared the following entry: "The beginning of the day was peaceful. But then at lunch a conversation arose about *The Wisdom of Children,* which Chertkov, who is a collector of material, has compiled. She wondered what he would do with my manuscripts after my death. I somewhat heatedly asked her to leave me in peace. Things seemed to be all right. But after dinner she began to reproach me for shouting at her, saying that I ought to take pity on her. I was silent. She went to her room and now it is ten o'clock and she has not come out. I feel depressed. A letter from Chertkov full of reproaches and accusations. They are tearing me to pieces. Sometimes it seems to me that I must get away from all of them." V.B.

25 September

❖

We read in the newspapers about the revolution in Portugal and the proclamation of a republic. At lunch I asked Lev Nikolayevich what he thought of this.

"Well, of course, it's cause for joy. . . . In any event, the activity is cause for joy."

Sofya Andreyevna again pleaded with Lev Nikolayevich to have their pictures taken together: their forty-eighth wedding anniversary had to be commemorated, and the last time, because of my inexperience, the pictures had not turned out well. Lev Nikolaye-vich gave his consent.

Aleksandra Lvovna, who is generally intolerant of people who disturb Lev Nikolayevich to take his picture, even when it happens to be Chertkov, at once expressed her disapproval of her father's compliance. Besides, it seemed to her that his yielding in this particular instance was wrong because it would have an effect on Sofya Andreyevna's condition.

"Well, but after all, it takes only a minute," he rejoined to his daughter's objections.

Again it was I who had to take the pictures. This time it was to be out of doors under the drawing-room windows. Sofya Andreyevna had marked with a peg the place where she and Lev Nikolayevich were to stand. Earlier she had counted the steps between this spot and the place for the photographic equipment.

As he came downstairs for the picture-taking Lev Nikolayevich looked at me and smiled. Then he stood on the spot pointed out to him and thrust his hands under his belt. Sofya Andreyevna took his arm. I made two photographs of them.

❖

"I want you to go to Chertkov," Lev Nikolayevich said to me on the way back from our ride. "Give him my letter. Tell him that my problem is now very difficult, and that Sasha is further complicating it."

He had in mind Aleksandra Lvovna's resentment and reproaches because of his being photographed with Sofya Andreyevna.

"And also, that I am thinking about how to resolve this problem."

I took advantage of his having mentioned personal matters to ask his permission to tell him what had been confided to me by Aleksandra Lvovna and V. M. Feokritova, which was that Sofya Andreyevna had announced to her daughter that she would no longer give Chertkov the rough drafts of Tolstoy's manuscripts. "Perhaps Lev Nikolayevich will change his attitude toward Chertkov," she had said, "and will give all his manuscripts to me." It was in this statement that Lev Nikolayevich's daughter and her friend had discerned the "mercenary motives" that they wanted to call to his attention.

"I don't understand, I don't understand!" said Lev Nikolayevich on hearing this. "What does she want the manuscripts for? And why is this mercenary?" He was silent for a moment. "There are certain people, like Sasha, who ascribe everything to self-interest. But this is a very much more complex matter! These forty years of life together . . . There are habits, and vanity, and pride, and jealousy, and her illness. . . . She is in a dreadful, pitiful state! I am trying to extricate myself from the situation. But what is particularly difficult is Sasha—when you feel in her this egoistical—when you feel this egoism, it hurts."

"I told Aleksandra Lvovna that there must always be renunciation and sacrifice of one's personal interests," I said.

"Exactly!"

Lev Nikolayevich rode on in silence.

"I confess," he said, "that just now I was actually praying as I rode along: I prayed that God would help me to free myself from this situation." We crossed a ditch. "Of course, I prayed to that God which is within me."

We entered the spruce grove, the customary place for the residents of Yasnaya Polyana to ride. As we approached the house Lev Nikolayevich said:

"I was thinking today—I even remember the very spot where I

was standing in my study near the bookshelf—how singularly difficult my position is! . . . Perhaps you will not believe me, but I say this in absolute sincerity," and he put his hand on his breast. "It seems that I ought to derive satisfaction from my fame, but I am at a loss to understand why people see anything remarkable in me when I am exactly the same as everyone else—with all the same human weaknesses! And the respect shown to me is not rated simply as the respect and love for a kindred human being, but some special significance is attached to it."

"Are you saying this, Lev Nikolayevich, in connection with what we were just talking about, or simply in general?"

"In connection with what?"

"With what you were saying about your domestic affairs—about Aleksandra Lvovna and Sofya Andreyevna?"

"But of course in connection with that! There is Sofya Andreyevna's fear of losing my regard. And my writings and manuscripts provoke a contest for their possession. You can have simple, natural relations only with people you are very close to. And now Sasha has fallen into the same pattern. I should like so much to be like Aleksandr Petrovich, just to roam about and be given food and drink by good people in my old age . . . but this exceptional position is a terrible burden!"

"It's your own fault, Lev Nikolayevich—why did you have to write so much?"

"Exactly! Exactly!" he responded with a laugh. "My own fault. I'm to blame! As guilty as a man who has brought children into the world, and if the children are stupid and give him trouble it's his own fault! . . . But I simply cannot comprehend that special attitude toward me," he began again. "They say people are afraid of me in some way. It seems to have been true even of Chekhov—he came to see me, but then felt intimidated."

"And Andreyev, Lev Nikolayevich; he too was afraid in the beginning, and couldn't come. Perhaps that can be attributed to your insight."

"Yes, yes, that's what I've been told."

✧

M. A. Schmidt told me that while at Kochety Lev Nikolayevich had begun a work of fiction on a theme he has frequently discussed in the past: *None Are Guilty in the World*.* He has already written the first chapter. She gave me a brief summary of the story.

"You know, a charming, rich family, like the Sukhotins. And then the contrast with a village hut . . . But it's impossible to work now. There's no peace. . . ."

A. M. Khiryakov came this evening.

"Wasn't it tedious, being in prison?" asked Lev Nikolayevich.

"No, it wasn't tedious."

"What are the good aspects of being in prison?"

"There are none."

"None? Absolutely none? And here I'm always envying——"

"There's nothing to envy."

"And haven't you written your impressions of prison? That's always so interesting—personal experiences."

❖

Speaking of the revolution in Portugal he said:

"Appalling, this superstition of the state! The youth is now beginning to understand it. Revolution is inevitable in these present-day states. As in Portugal. It's like a fire—the light from it will ignite everything. The time is coming when all those kings will be sitting in cellars.** And how aware the people are of the injustice of state systems! You know, there is a saying among the peasants at Kochety: 'The kingdom of heaven is the Lord's—the kingdom of the earth, the lords'.' And to think that this has really happened in our time! The upheaval in Portugal is in any case a definite step. . . . No servility, no tyranny of the individual."

During the day the atmosphere of the house was quite alarming, and by late evening it had resolved into a perfect tempest between Sofya Andreyevna and Aleksandra Lvovna.

It should be remarked that for the past few days Sofya Andre-

* This story remained unfinished. V.B.
** I had told Lev Nikolayevich the previous day that the newspapers stated that the king of Portugal, having fled the palace, spent two hours sitting in a cellar. V.B.

yevna has been relatively calm. Lev Nikolayevich and Chertkov have not seen each other and there seems to have been no cause for irritation. Such an occasion arose, however, when Lev Niko-layevich, wishing to appease Aleksandra Lvovna and give her pleasure, asked her to rehang in their former places in his study all the photographs that Sofya Andreyevna had taken down.

When this had been done, he went riding with Dushan Petrovich, and Aleksandra Lvovna and Varvara Mikhailovna set off in the carriage to spend the night with O. K. Tolstaya at the Taptykovo estate outside of Tula.

I was sitting in the "Remington room" with M. A. Schmidt when all at once Sofya Andreyevna rushed into the room in a state of extreme excitement and announced that she had burned Chertkov's photograph.

"The old man is trying to kill me! I have been completely well these last few days—but he purposely rehung Chertkov's portrait and then went off for his ride!"

She left the room only to return a few minutes later to say that she had not burned the photograph but had "prepared it for burning." After another brief interval she appeared carrying the torn scraps of the despised photograph in the hollow of her hand.

"I am going to throw it into the water closet!" she said, and went out.

The subsequent events developed with extraordinary speed and unexpectedness.

Suddenly we heard a shot * from the direction of Sofya Andre-yevna's room; despite the faintness of the sound, Maria Aleksan-drovna was impelled to rush to the room, where Sofya Andreyevna explained to the terrified old lady that she had fired a shot (at whom she did not say) and missed. She had succeeded only in making herself deaf in one ear. Then she ran out of the room saying that she had "attempted" to shoot.

When Lev Nikolayevich came home we told him the whole story. After he had gone to his room to lie down and rest, another

* Sofya Andreyevna had fired a toy gun. V.B.

shot was heard from Sofya Andreyevna's room. Dushan was
bandaging Lev Nikolayevich's sore leg at the time and told us that
although Lev Nikolayevich had heard the shot he did not go to
his wife's room. Maria Aleksandrovna was with her at the time
and said that Sofya Andreyevna had made another "attempt" and
fired into the cupboard. An amazing choice of place for this
enterprise—the home of the elderly Lev Tolstoy!

At the conclusion of her shooting practice, when she saw that
no one was coming to plead with her to be calm, she set out for
the park. Night was coming on and it was getting cold and dark.

After about half an hour, Dushan went out and asked her to
come in. He found her pacing the quadrangle of old lime trees not
far from the house; she was not dressed warmly enough and had
nothing on her head. His mission was unsuccessful: Sofya Andreyevna would neither put anything on nor return to the house.

Maria Aleksandrovna persuaded me to go out, which I reluctantly
consented to do. I had no wish to take part in what to me appeared
to be playacting, and I did not know what to say to her in any case.

She finally returned to the house, but only after the ill and
elderly Maria Aleksandrovna, weak, bent, and supported by a cane,
had gone out after her. However, it would have been unthinkable
to let her stay out in the cold.

Dinner and evening tea passed quietly. After everyone had
retired for the night, I sat alone in the "Remington room" working.
I was thinking about Maria Aleksandrovna having sent a note to
Aleksandra Lvovna informing her of the shooting episodes and
asking her to return at once instead of spending the night at
Taptykovo. Before leaving, Aleksandra Lvovna had instructed her
to do this, fearing that her mother might in some way take
advantage of her absence. But now it was midnight and she had
not yet arrived; apparently she was not coming. Perhaps it was
just as well. On the one hand, I felt sorry for her; she was nervously
exhausted from her life at Yasnaya Polyana: she never got away,
and she was constantly with her mother. It would be good for her
to have even this one day of rest at Taptykovo. And besides, the
house was now quiet and the immediate need for her presence had

passed. I went on to finish my work and gave no further thought
to Aleksandra Lvovna and Sofya Andreyevna.

However, the note unfortunately accomplished its aim, and
when it was already quite late at night the two young women
returned. Seeing the light of my lamp, they noisily descended on
the "Remington room." Close on their heels came Sofya Andreyevna,
who is always up late.

A dreadful scene took place. Dismayed and incensed by the
unexpected return of her daughter, she did not know whom to
vent her wrath on: Aleksandra Lvovna, Varvara Mikhailovna, or
Maria Aleksandrovna, who in all innocence had sent for them. In
the end she let it fall on all three. Maria Aleksandrovna, who had
been asleep in her bed behind the bookcases in the library when
they arrived, completely lost her head, poor thing, and tearfully
entreated Sofya Andreyevna to forgive her.

Aleksandra Lvovna—I shall never forget her—burst into the
room with a little cap pushed back on her head and both arms raised
in front of her in semicircles as if she were about to enter into
single combat with someone. I involuntarily recalled her mother's
characterization of her on one occasion: "Is that a well-bred young
lady—or is it a coachman?"

While Sofya Andreyevna was railing at everyone and upbraiding
the two young women for disturbing the peace of the house,
Aleksandra Lvovna, looking imperturbable, sat motionless and silent
on the sofa behind the desk, her lips compressed in a cold, mocking
smile.

Varvara Mikhailovna was terribly unnerved; in her voice there
was a note of repressed outrage and humiliation, and a resentment
that had long been seething within her.

I was sitting facing Aleksandra Lvovna, in the armchair on the
other side of the desk, listening and observing. And I kept thinking
that there in the next room the great Tolstoy, probably roused
from sleep by the shouting, lay listening to all this. These women
had to make this scene so close to him! And not only close to
him, but because of him. How incongruous!

In the course of the wrangle Sofya Andreyevna came out with: "I'll put you out of the house!" to her daughter. And as for Varvara Mikhailovna, she told her straight out to leave tomorrow. The result was that they both decided to leave in the morning and go to live in the little house at Telyatinki that belongs to Aleksandra Lvovna.

"I shall come to see Papa every morning all the same," said Aleksandra Lvovna.

She immediately went to inform her father of her decision.

"It all leads to the same end," was his response.

27 September

This morning Lev Nikolayevich came out to the staircase in his dressing gown to call Ilya Vasilyevich.

"Good morning, Papa," said Aleksandra Lvovna, going to him and kissing him. "I'm leaving now."

Lev Nikolayevich nodded his head in silence. Later, in the study, he said to her that her going was "for the best: it brings everything closer to a solution."

Aleksandra Lvovna and Varvara Mikhailovna were soon ready to leave. By twelve o'clock, when Sofya Andreyevna appeared as usual, they had gone.

When Lev Nikolayevich came to the "Remington room" shortly after this, I could not help mentioning their departure.

"Not my will but Thine be done; not what I wish but what Thou wishest; not how I wish but how Thou wishest. That is what I think," replied Lev Nikolayevich.

❖

He discussed with Khiryakov the latter's essays on the origins of the Christian teaching, which deal with the fact that there were more than four Gospels.

"It's a pity that I have forgotten your essays," said Lev Niko-layevich. "After all, I did read them. This is very important now, especially in a popular exposition. Today, you know, even educated people believe that there were four Apostles who wrote four Gospels, and almost no one knows that there were many of these Gospels, and that from among them were chosen those containing the fewest absurdities in the opinion of those who selected them. I now feel especially keenly the enormous harm done by the Church."

The conversation turned to education and training. Lev Nikolayevich pointed out the singular importance of travel descriptions in this connection. Someone spoke of the need for introducing the subject of literature into the field of education, and Lev Nikolayevich observed:

"Writers of fiction must be very fine, otherwise they are abominable."

The Portuguese revolution was discussed and I said that the provisional government of Portugal had issued a decree on the separation of church and state. Lev Nikolayevich recalled reading in a newspaper that in Portugal it was forbidden for priests to appear in public in clerical garb.

"That was in connection with the separation of church and state, of course," he added. "It's a good thing: they will be less conspicuous."

Dushan said that in Spain the liberals are in conflict with the priests because of their weak faith, but that they still need them. He did not make himself very clear on this point.

"No," objected Lev Nikolayevich, "I think they are striving to free the people from the influence of the clergy, and in this lies their great merit."

✧

28 September

There was a visitor this morning. Speaking of him Lev Nikolayevich said:

"Oh, that officer, that officer! I should write it all down at once.

A colonel, no less, and on the staff. Very elegant—and terribly confused! Great excitement at first—a whole hour of it: I am unable to get a word in. Then he begins to talk about the necessity of free action, free action—and what does free action mean? It means that people must be helped, people live in darkness. 'You acknowledge physiology,' he said. 'Yes, yes, physiology . . .' Then I say to him: 'How can you talk of the necessity of helping people when you bear the weapons of destruction? First of all, you ought to examine yourself. You would do better,' I say, 'to direct your attention to my works, not to me; I've covered a lot of paper with my scribbling, and there you'll find everything that I can say.' I was very short with him. At first, in my stupidity, I thought that he felt oppressed because of serving in the army, or something of the sort."

Shortly after the officer had gone, Aleksandra Lvovna arrived from Telyatinki, stayed for an hour, and left before lunch. She spoke very sharply to Sofya Andreyevna, who greeted her but would not kiss her.

"What for? It's only a formality!" she said nervously in response to Aleksandra Lvovna's salutation.

"It certainly is," agreed the latter, "and I'll be very glad to dispense with it."

In a conversation alone with her, Lev Nikolayevich told her that the step she had taken in leaving, the fact that she was incapable of controlling herself and had gone away, he considered bad, but that for him in his weakness, the consequences of this act were welcome.

"The worse it is, the better," he added.

She told her father that Chertkov had reproached her for leaving, mainly because Lev Nikolayevich would miss her keenly.

"No, no, no!" he protested.

The consequence of this move to Telyatinki, which Aleksandra Lvovna and, to some degree, Lev Nikolayevich expected, was evidently the sobering effect it would have, and has already had, on Sofya Andreyevna.

At one o'clock Lev Nikolayevich came out of his study for lunch. We sat down at the table with Dushan. Lev Nikolayevich slyly glanced at me and said with a chuckle:

"Well, how do you find your 'dragoonian service'—difficult?"

"No, not at all, Lev Nikolayevich. It's fine! The more work, the better I like it——"

Just then Sofya Andreyevna came in. When she left the room, Lev Nikolayevich said:

"When I spoke to your 'dragoonian service' I meant something else . . ."

"Yes, I understood you, Lev Nikolayevich," I said. "Of course it's difficult, but isn't it even more difficult for you?"

"For me it's very difficult, terribly difficult!"

This conversation grew out of the following episode.

Earlier in the day, when Lev Nikolayevich had come into the "Remington room" to speak to me about something, he found Sofya Andreyevna there. She had been standing next to my desk for some time talking incessantly about her past, the childhood of her daughters, the good and bad governesses who had lived with them, and so forth.

When Lev Nikolayevich came in, she turned to him and said:

"I was just telling Bulgakov about Madame Seiron, how one day she drank too much red wine and slapped Masha's face. And all I said to her was: 'We are getting ready to go to Yasnaya now'— we were living in Moscow at the time—'your trunks are packed, but when the rest of us go to Yasnaya, you shall remain here in Moscow!' I didn't say another word to her. I said nothing more than that!"

Lev Nikolayevich let her finish, and after asking me whether a letter had come from Tatyana Lvovna, turned and went back to his room in silence. And then at lunch he jested about my "dragoonian service."

✧

After lunch he went with Dushan to see M. A. Schmidt, who happened to be present the other day during the distressing family quarrel and had become involved in it by force of circumstance. Lev Nikolayevich has tried in every way to soothe the completely distraught old lady.

At dinner the other day as the third course of four (not including dessert) was being served, Lev Nikolayevich said:

"We really ought to reduce our daily meal by one course. Why have this? It's quite superfluous."

"Very well then," retorted Sofya Andreyevna, patently displeased, "I'll order the cook to prepare only three courses."

Four-course meals continue to be served, however. Today Lev Nikolayevich ate almost nothing for dinner; he is not feeling well; he coughs, is listless, and in low spirits.

◇

29 September

Aleksandra Lvovna drove over again this morning. Sofya Andreyevna's attitude toward her has unexpectedly changed: today she asked not only Aleksandra Lvovna but Varvara Mikhailovna to return to Yasnaya and promised to forget their recent falling out. But Aleksandra Lvovna is obdurate. She continues with the work of settling into her cottage, where extensive repairs are being made. Her furniture, horses, dogs, and even the parrot in its cage, have all been sent from Yasnaya to Telyatinki.

Such a radical change in their relations has noticeably upset Sofya Andreyevna. As for Lev Nikolayevich, the departure of his favorite daughter leaves him quite alone at Yasnaya, and this may affect his mood. Today he feels very well physically and mentally; he is brisk and cheerful.

Sofya Andreyevna spoke of her doubts about publishing the fourteenth volume of Tolstoy's collected works: *Union, Translation, and Investigation of the Four Gospels*. Those competent to advise her are of various opinions. Lev Nikolayevich's advice is that since the text would never be passed by the censor, the entire volume should be printed as ellipses.

He brought from his study a book sent to him from Belgium: *Révélation d'Antoine le Guérisseur* and spoke very highly of it, saying that he found it in complete agreement with his views. After waiting for some time for Sofya Andreyevna to return from the other room where she had gone for some reason, he read aloud the article in the last issue of *Russian Wealth* about the need for illustrated books for convicts.

In general Lev Nikolayevich has been very affectionate and attentive to Sofya Andreyevna today. This has shown itself in all sorts of trifles. He brought her a pear while she was talking, and in the course of the conversation asked her several questions about the management of the estate, a subject in which he never shows any interest and treats as being entirely outside the sphere of his concerns. At dinner he offered her kvas, and in the evening advised her to go to bed early. Her uniform calm of the last few days has evoked this spontaneous and kindly attitude toward her. Moreover the absence of his daughter makes it possible for him to forget the tactics enjoined by her, which are obviously unnatural to him, of being "severe and unyielding."

After he had gone to his room, Sofya Andreyevna came through the "Remington room," and stopping at the door in the dark corridor said to me:

"It's a godsend for us having you here."

"Why?"

"Because it's less dull with you here—Lev Nikolayevich feels less dull. You are very tactful. And whenever I question you, you always answer tactfully, if evasively. I understand you: you say only what you can say. I know you are trying to keep peace. Do you think I don't see it? I've learned to understand people a little in sixty-five years, thank God!"

It is quite true that I still manage, though with difficulty, to maintain the same policy of noninterference in the events that have been occurring here. In this respect the attitudes of dear Dushan Petrovich and M. A. Schmidt serve as an example to me. I feel nothing but deep gratitude to absolutely everyone surrounding Lev Nikolayevich for their kindness to me. With whom should I contend, and whose side should I take? No, I definitely wish to remain outside the struggle and try to do only one thing: to serve and be of use in every way possible to the infinitely good Lev Nikolayevich.

Thank God Sofya Andreyevna has always understood me and was not angered by my replying "evasively" to her questions concerning matters which, though they happened to come to my knowledge by chance, might have annoyed her and further aggravated family dissensions. I have become a diplomat of necessity: now I am almost the only person who can freely visit both camps— Yasnaya and Telyatinki—and be welcome in both. I have to be on guard against bearing tales from one place to the other. My position is an awkward one.

✧

At dinner Lev Nikolayevich expressed his surprise that again a superfluous course was served. Sofya Andreyevna justified it on the grounds that a vegetarian table needs variety. How strange these petty differences are! I am quite convinced that for the most part she is acting in his interests in insisting on a more elaborate diet; at the same time it is obvious that he will always demand the exact opposite—moderation and simplicity.

During the evening he again read aloud from *Culte Antoiniste. Révélation.*

"A strange and remarkable book," he said. "The details are a muddle, but the fundamental ideas are very deep. Of course, an intellectual philosopher would reject this book."

And he went on reading, translating Antoine's biography into Russian for my benefit.

" 'It is possible to believe in God. We can be conscious of Him in ourselves. One must recognize that God is oneself; recognize that one wills, therefore one can.' "

Lev Nikolayevich turned to me and said:

"Isn't that enough to convince you of the profundity of the book?"

He continued reading till he came to a passage on loving one's enemies.

"That's hypocrisy!" said Sofya Andreyevna. "I don't understand it!"

"Not understanding something doesn't disprove it," said Lev Nikolayevich.

He cited the example of the composer Chaikovsky and another musician, both of whom were unable to understand differential calculus. Chaikovsky remarked, very wittily in Lev Nikolayevich's opinion: "Either it is ridiculous or I am."

Later he brought out a little book of Russian folk sayings and read aloud the best of them.

30 September

Lev Nikolayevich wrote a rather sharp letter to a high-school girl.

"She's one of those who seeks the answer to the question of the meaning of life in Andreyev, or in Chekhov," he said, "And what they offer is—pap. If this is so with such advanced people, what are we to do? The usual reasoning. It's a great pity!"

Late in the evening he came into the "Remington room" from his bedroom, having already taken off his belt. Excusing himself he began looking for something on the table.

"Are you looking for the letter to the young lady?" I asked, thinking that he wanted to make some further change in the letter he had only just amplified and signed.

"Yes . . . It's really not necessary . . . not necessary to send it. I have been seriously thinking about it. . . . Never mind, it will only hurt her."

He asked me to send the young girl nothing but the booklets *For Every Day*, and to write her that she would find in them the answers to her questions.

"And throw that letter away!" he said, smiling sheepishly but probably feeling satisfied with what he had done. After apologizing once more for making me waste my time copying the letter he disappeared into his bedroom.

✦

He read P. A. Sergeyenko's article about his childhood this evening and said that he enjoyed these reminiscences very much. The arrival of Aleksandra Lvovna and her story about Marcus Aurelius also delighted him.

It seems that she and Varvara Mikhailovna were sitting at home in Telyatinki wondering how things were with Lev Nikolayevich and growing despondent at the thought of not knowing, when Annushka, the peasant woman who is helping them to arrange their new place, said to them:

"You should read Marcus Aurelius, then all your sorrows would cease."

They were thunderstruck. "What do you mean, Marcus Aurelius? Why Marcus Aurelius?"

"You know," replied Annushka, "there's a little book the count once gave me, and it says in it that we shall all be reconciled. And if you think of death, it becomes easier. That's what I always do when my soul is sorrowful. Ay, children, read Marcus Aurelius! Do what he says, and all sorrows cease!"

The story touched Lev Nikolayevich, and he kept recalling it and repeating: "Ay, children, read Marcus Aurelius!"

"You see, we never know the fruits of our actions," he said.

Today I made a copy of the inscriptions made by visitors to Yasnaya Polyana on the columns of the little summerhouse in the park. Many have been effaced, but I list here those that remain.

INSCRIPTIONS INSIDE THE SUMMERHOUSE
IN THE GARDEN OF YASNAYA POLYANA

1. Down with capital punishment!
2. May the life of Lev Nikolayevich be prolonged for as many years again.
3. In token of visiting Count Lev Tolstoy, a man with an intellect as large as a lion, I affix my signature.
4. Come, all you who have grown weary in the struggle, and here you will find peace.
5. This hallowed hut was visited by a student of the Moscow Geodetic School. (*signed*)

6. A humble pilgrim offers his respects.

7. Respects to L. Tolstoy from one more visitor to the summerhouse. (*signed*)

8. Greetings to Count L. N. Tolstoy from the Tula realists.

9. An admirer of the talent of Count Tolstoy, now and forever.

10. Esteem to the great and celebrated elder.

11. Glory to the great one, glory!

12. Sow ye reason, good, eternal, sow in darkness and foul weather.

13. No one knows the truth, not even Tolstoy.

14. God is not in force but in truth.

15. Glory to you who have shown us the light.

16. Workers of the world unite and render homage to a genius.

17. After long dreaming, we at last have visited the genius of the human mind.

18. "Those born to creep cannot fly." What can I write? All are so pale and dull compared to you that words fail me.— A Social-Democrat.

19. This lowly abode was visited by a pilgrim. (*signed*)

20. To the Hercules of Russian thought, to the ideal of nonresistance to evil, our heartfelt thanks.

21. Glory to the genius of Tolstoy.

22. We have visited this wondrous nook. (*signed*)

23. "Young Russia." The All-Russian Union of Students of Middle Schools.

At her request I gave Sofya Andreyevna a copy of these inscriptions. She placed it on the piano, where it was seen by Lev Nikolayevich in passing. He read it, dropped it indifferently as he turned to go, and said:

"Not interesting."

2 October

Goldenweiser came today, as well as Tatyana Lvovna, Sergei Lvovich, and P. I. Biryukov. At lunch they discussed the latter's impending trial for the possession of Tolstoy's writings. Biryukov has engaged a lawyer to defend him, as he does not consider himself capable of going into all the formalities of a lawsuit.

Apropos of this Lev Nikolayevich said:

"I really don't know how it is possible to discuss this seriously. It's as if I were to try to talk seriously about the quarreling and arguing of children, or of drunken men after one had given the other a punch in the jaw. What articles of law are in question in such a case? None whatsoever. One has simply punched someone in the jaw—played a dirty trick on him—and that's all. It's better not to get mixed up in such drunken company."

"Yes," remonstrated Goldenweiser, "but when a man is threatened with eighteen months in prison——"

"I understand," said Lev Nikolayevich. "Well then, tell one drunken man to take it up with the other drunken men. . . ."

✧

Sergei Lvovich told about his conflict with a neighbor, a landowner by the name of Sumarokov, "over the wolves." Sumarokov had taken the liberty, without Sergei Lvovich's permission, to hunt "his" wolves in "his" forest. In one of the liveliest moments of this account, Lev Nikolayevich suddenly asked his son:

"And the wolves know nothing about this?"

Sergei Lvovich was taken aback, but then laughed good-naturedly and replied:

"No, they know nothing about it."

Later Lev Nikolayevich was carried away by his son's story to the point of grunting his disapproval of Sumarokov. The description of the fashionable hunt being led into the forest by that ill-fated Sumarokov and then being sent packing by Sergei Lvovich captured his interest.

✧

3 October

✦

Lev Nikolayevich fell asleep after his ride. We waited till seven o'clock and then sat down to dinner without him. Having ladled out the soup Sofya Andreyevna rose from the table and once again went to his door and listened to hear whether he was up. She came back and said that as she approached his room she had heard the striking of a match, and when she went in had found him sitting on the bed. He asked what time it was and whether we were at dinner. It seemed to her that something was wrong: his eyes had a strange look.

"They look vacant, as they do before an attack. He will lose consciousness—I know it. His eyes are always like that before an attack."

She took a little soup, then pushed back her chair and again went to his study. Her children, Tatyana Lvovna and Sergei Lvovich, exchanged a look of annoyance: why did she disturb their father?

When she came back her face was white.

"Dushan Petrovich, go to him, quickly! He is unconscious—he lies there mumbling something—God knows what!"

We all jumped up as if we had received an electric shock. Dushan, with everyone following, ran through the drawing room and study to the bedroom. The room was dark. Lev Nikolayevich lay on the bed. His jaw was moving as he made queer, inarticulate, lowing sounds.

Horror and despair pervaded the room. The candle on the little table at the head of the bed was lit. They took off his boots and covered him with a blanket. His eyes were closed, the brows contracted, and his lips moved as if he were chewing something.

Dushan sent everyone out of the room except Biryukov, who remained, sitting in an armchair in the corner opposite the bed. Sofya Andreyevna, Sergei Lvovich, Tatyana Lvovna, Dushan, and I went back to the dining room, shaken. We tried to resume our interrupted dinner; just as dessert was served, Biryukov rushed into the room.

"Dushan Petrovich, he's in convulsions!"

Again we all ran to the bedroom. When we got there the attack was over. Biryukov said that his legs had suddenly begun to move. He thought that Lev Nikolayevich wanted to scratch his leg, but when he went to the bed, he saw that his face was distorted by the convulsion.

"Hurry—go down and get hot-water bottles to put on his feet. We must put a mustard plaster on his calf. Coffee, hot coffee!"

Someone was giving orders, I think both Dushan and Sofya Andreyevna. The rest of us obeyed and, together with those giving orders, did whatever had to be done. Dushan, cool and noiseless as a shadow, moved among us. Sofya Andreyevna was pale, her brows knit, her eyes almost closed, as if the lids were swollen. It was heartbreaking to look at the face of this unhappy woman. God knows what was going on in her soul, but she did not lose her self-possession: she placed the hot-water bottles around his feet, went downstairs and herself prepared the solution for an enema, and put a compress on his head—after an argument with Dushan.

Lev Nikolayevich had not yet been undressed. Dushan and I, with the help of Sergei Lvovich or Biryukov—I did not even notice who—undressed him. We held him while Dushan, with the greatest possible care and words of tender persuasion—although the sick man was still unconscious—removed his clothing. At last he lay quiet.

"Society . . . Society concerning three . . . Society concerning three . . ."

Lev Nikolayevich was delirious.

"To make a note . . ."

Biryukov gave him a writing pad and pencil. Lev Nikolayevich covered the pad with a handkerchief and then moved the pencil across it. His face, as before, was dark.

"Must read . . ." he said, and several times repeated: "Wisdom . . . wisdom . . . wisdom . . ."

It was a grievous and unnatural sight to see a man of his superior and luminous intelligence in this condition.

"Levochka, stop, darling! What are you writing? See, this is a handkerchief, give it to me."

Sofya Andreyevna tried to take the writing pad from his hand, but he shook his head in refusal and persisted in moving the pencil over the handkerchief.

And then began a strange succession of convulsive seizures, after which his whole body lay prostrate, twitching and quivering, on the bed. He threw his legs about so violently that it was only with difficulty that we were able to hold them. Dushan clasped his shoulders, and Biryukov and I massaged his legs. There were five attacks in all. The fourth was particularly violent: his entire body was thrown almost crosswise on the bed, his head rolled off the pillow and his legs hung over the other side of the bed.

Sofya Andreyevna fell to her knees and embraced his feet, pressing her head against them. She remained in that position for some time, while we tried to straighten him out on the bed. She was altogether terribly pitiful, raising her eyes heavenward and crossing herself with quick little movements as she whispered:

"Lord! Only let it not be this time! Only let it not be this time!"

But she did not do this in the presence of anyone: I happened to go into the "Remington room" and found her praying there.

To Aleksandra Lvovna, who had been summoned by a note from me, she said:

"My suffering is greater than yours; you lose a father, but I lose a husband of whose death I am guilty!"

Aleksandra Lvovna appeared outwardly calm, but said that her heart was pounding terribly. Her pale, thin lips were resolutely compressed.

After the fifth seizure, Lev Nikolayevich lay quiet, but he was still delirious.

"Four . . . sixty . . . thirty-seven . . . thirty-eight . . . thirty-nine . . . seventy . . ." he mumbled.

Late that night he regained consciousness.

"What are you doing here?" he asked Dushan, and was surprised to learn that he was ill.

"Did you give me an enema? I don't remember anything. I shall try to sleep now."

A little later Sofya Andreyevna went into the bedroom to look for something on the little table next to the bed and accidentally knocked over a glass.

"Who is that?" he asked.

"It's I, Levochka."

"What do you want?"

"I just came in to see you."

"Ah . . ."

He lay quiet. Evidently he was fully conscious.

Lev Nikolayevich's illness affected me deeply. Wherever I happened to be during the night, there arose before me that pale, ghastly, harrowed face, with its knit brows and resolute, indomitable expression. The significance of that expression was so clearly and vividly defined in his features that standing at his bedside, I was afraid to look at his face. Even the thought of it wrung my heart. When I looked at him and saw only the pitiful, moribund body, it did not seem so terrible to me, even when it was in the throes of convulsions, for there lay before me only a suffering body. But if I glanced at his face, I could not bear it; it was a face on which lay the imprint of a mystery—the mystery of a great act, a great struggle, where, as it is commonly expressed, "the soul leaves the body."

Shcheglov, the doctor from Tula, arrived late at night. But he did not see Lev Nikolayevich. Dushan explained the illness to him as poisoning of the brain by the gastric juices. To our question as to the cause of the convulsions, the visiting physician replied that they could have been induced by Lev Nikolayevich's recent nervous condition, which is connected with his arteriosclerosis.

It was after two when we went to bed, Dushan and I close at hand. Biryukov sat up in the bedroom till three in the morning.

4 October

The danger has passed. Lev Nikolayevich slept through the night. In the morning he awoke fully conscious. When Biryukov told him what he had said in his delirium, that he had uttered the words "soul, wisdom, statehood," he was satisfied, according to Biryukov.

Sofya Andreyevna says that Lev Nikolayevich's illness has been a lesson to her; she realizes that her own condition might be one of the causes of this illness.

Tatyana Lvovna told me that when she went in to her father this morning, he said, among other things, that he "strove with Sofya Andreyevna with love," and that he hopes for a victory, and even now sees a glimmer of hope.

At Lev Nikolayevich's request, his daughter read him the letters that came today. He told her which ones had to be answered. He rang for me (not forgetting the stipulated two rings), and after giving detailed instructions, entrusted me to answer one of the letters. He lay there absolutely calm, clear, and rational.

In the course of the day there occurred another joyous event: Sofya Andreyevna made peace with her daughter.

In the evening Lev Nikolayevich asked Sofya Andreyevna to send me to him. As she left the room she reminded him that he was not to tire himself.

"In any case, I can't help thinking," he replied. "So you're still at work, still tapping away?" he said to me as I entered the room, referring to my typing in the next room.

"I'm doing a little work, Lev Nikolayevich. Does the sound disturb you?"

"No, I only meant to say that you are constantly working: everyone else is chattering, but you keep busy."

He asked me not to make a fair copy of one of the letters, as he wanted to dictate a quite different reply.

Later he called me to ask:

"And are you sleeping there?" he pointed to the wall that separates his bedroom from the "Remington room."

"Yes, Lev Nikolayevich, right in the next room. Please, call me as often as you wish. I am always at your service."

"Thanks, thanks . . . Well, good night!" and he extended his hand as briskly and firmly as when he was well.

The joy over his recovery is as great as was the fear of his death last night.

5 October

✧

This evening P. A. Sergeyenko arrived. Lev Nikolayevich came to the dining room and took part in the general, and very animated, conversation. Sergeyenko spoke of the attitude of science to vegetarianism. I told him about the experiment in vegetarianism made by the son of one of the first Tolstoyans, my friend Rafael Butkevich. His mother was reduced to a state of despair by his decision to give up eating meat, and was reassured only after a physician had acknowledged that this was not harmful to her son.

"What is important," said Lev Nikolayevich, "is that in the beginning vegetarianism is undertaken on a religious basis, and later analyzed scientifically. Science will capitulate only when it cannot do otherwise. It's the same with other questions. Chastity, for instance. Here science argues that without chastity the earth would be overpopulated."

Sergeyenko spoke about the former chairman of the first State Duma, S. A. Muromtsev, who died only recently. He admired his superior moral character, but expressed surprise that, for all that, Muromtsev was not a religious man.

"With him the principle was the same," said Lev Nikolayevich, "but some people are unwilling to acknowledge this, though they unconsciously live according to it. The principle is the same— truth. They find religion to be mystical. They are reluctant to name God, but they are conscious of Him."

A telegram came from the editor of the *Petersburg Gazette* asking to be informed of the state of Lev Nikolayevich's health.

"What shall I say?" asked Sofya Andreyevna.

"Say that I'm dead and buried," replied Lev Nikolayevich with a laugh.

They began talking about Guy de Maupassant.

"He had a tendency toward deep thought, side by side with that sexual licentiousness. And he had an amazing ability to depict the emptiness of life, and that can be done only by a man who has some knowledge according to which life does not have to be empty. Like Gogol, for instance. An amazing writer."

✧

6 October

✧

I am planning to take advantage of Lev Nikolayevich's recovery to set out on foot tomorrow for a journey of some forty versts. . . . I have definitely decided to withdraw officially from the university. While there I intend to read a statement to the students, taking a stand against the university, which continues to threaten me with complications in connection with my being called up for military service. And after that I want to see my friends and say good-bye to them.

Lev Nikolayevich has been told of my absence, which will be of several days' duration.

✧

22 October

I have returned from Moscow, where I spent more than a week. I submitted my application for withdrawal from the university, and after I had registered it, read my paper *On Higher Schools of Learning and on Science* in a student meeting.

From the station I went first to Telyatinki, and in the evening set out with Radynsky for Yasnaya Polyana. I shall never forget this evening and the welcome shown to me.

They had just finished dinner when we arrived. Lev Nikolayevich was still sitting in his accustomed place on Sofya Andreyevna's right at the end of the table. Radynsky and I were greeted with exclamations of joy. I went first to Sofya Andreyevna, but I was conscious only of him, and my heart overflowed with joy. Then I turned to him: he greeted me, held out his hand and drew me toward him. I bent down and kissed him, looking into his beaming, infinitely kind, dear, aged face.

It was a very special evening. Radynsky too remarked on it later. Such blissful, quiet happiness, such complete harmony and brotherly love, seemed to reign among those present.

Lev Nikolayevich eagerly questioned me about my journey, about my paper, whom I had seen, how I had spent my time. He told me about the books he had received in my absence, about interesting letters and visitors who had come.

"The peasant Novikov was here. Have you heard about him? Ah, such a clever man! I'm sorry you didn't meet him."

He talked about Novikov's book *The Concept of God as the Absolute Principle of Life.*

"This is a remarkably conscientious work. He has not left out a single authority on any question that might explain his views or define his attitude to these questions. Amazingly conscientious work! And withal, such clarity! He has been working on it for fourteen years. And, of course," he added sadly, "no one will talk about it and no one will read it."

It must be said that P. P. Novikov's book was written under the obvious and very powerful influence of Tolstoy. When, apropos of a certain section of the book, I mentioned this, Lev Nikolayevich smiled and said:

"Yes, I keep forgetting what I have written, and then I enjoy finding out."

✧

26 October

✧

I brought Lev Nikolayevich a letter from V. G. Chertkov. It was not of a personal nature; when he gave it to me, Vladimir Grigorevich let me know that it was not confidential.

The letter concerned a book by P. P. Nikolayev; Chertkov wrote that it contains a summary of Tolstoy's views on the Unitarian faith, a subject Lev Nikolayevich had expressed an interest in only a few days ago in a conversation. He finds that the Unitarians, like other Christian sects of this kind, such as the Baptists and the Malevans,* do not carry their rationalism through to the end.

On learning that I had brought a letter from Chertkov, Sofya Andreyevna immediately began asking Lev Nikolayevich to disclose its contents to her. He told her that it was of a business nature, and that on principle he could not let her read it.

"Everything he writes is good," Lev Nikolayevich said to me on returning from his ride, "both what he says about Nikolayev and the other matter."

This was in the "Remington room." He must have been tired after his ride, for he walked slowly and with a stoop as he went into his bedroom and closed the door after him.

Unfortunately, even the threat of another attack does not persuade Sofya Andreyevna to keep her promise not to disturb his peace of mind. Again her jealousy of Chertkov, again scenes with Lev Nikolayevich and clashes with her daughter! And what is even worse, she persistently questions him as to whether he has made a will, and demands a special memorandum assigning the rights to his literary works to her personally. What with her suspicions, spying, and eavesdropping, the atmosphere of the house is troubled and uneasy.**

* The Malevans were a Baptist sect led by Kondraty Malevany who, in 1884, left the Orthodox Church to convert to Baptism. He later became preoccupied with the mystic origins of the Holy Ghost. V.B.
** Only after Tolstoy's death was it known that not long before this his private diary had fallen into Sofya Andreyevna's hands. She had learned from it that

Among those close to Lev Nikolayevich, talk of the possibility of his leaving Yasnaya Polyana in the near future grows more and more insistent. I was shown in great secrecy the text of the following letter, which he recently sent to the peasant Novikov, who lives in the village of Borov in the Tula province.

Mikhail Petrovich:

In connection with what I discussed with you before you left, I wish to make the following request: if it should happen that I were to come to you, would it be possible for you to find me a little hut in your village—no matter how small as long as it is warm and private—so that I should not be forced to impose on you and your family for too long? I also want to let you know that in the event that I should have to telegraph you, I shall do so not in my own name, but in the name of T. Nikolayev.

I await your reply, and press your hand in friendship.

Lev Nikolayevich

Bear in mind that this should be known to no one but yourself. L.T.

◇

28 October

I spent the night at Telyatinki. This morning I was summoned to the dining room, where Vladimir Grigorevich was waiting to see me. I found him seated on a stool, his back against the long dining-room table, with a note in his hand. His face expressed joy and excitement.

"Listen, Bulgakov, you must go at once to Yasnaya Polyana. They've sent for you. Lev Nikolayevich went away last night, with Dushan, and no one knows where he has gone."

he had made a secret will; the contents of this will were still unknown to her, however. V.B.

It had happened! What lately had been so much talked of, what had been expected almost daily, what many had wanted so much for Lev Nikolayevich, had actually happened! Tolstoy had left Yasnaya Polyana—and there could be no doubt—forever.

Although the news was not entirely unexpected, it was profoundly, overwhelmingly thrilling. It had been too difficult for Lev Nikolayevich to live in the midst of family squabbles, and the bitter struggle of those close to him for influence and the possession of his manuscripts, to say nothing of the constant, tormenting awareness of the incongruity of the external conditions of his life with the creed of love for the workingman, with the equality, simplicity, repudiation of luxury and privilege, that he professed.

Lev Nikolayevich went away in the following circumstances. The evening of the twenty-seventh had found the household of Yasnaya Polyana in an especially strained and difficult state. Around midnight Lev Nikolayevich, who was in bed in his room, saw a light through the crack of his study door and heard the rustling of papers. It was Sofya Andreyevna, who, tormented by the her suspicions, was searching for proof of the existence of the will. This visitation at night was for Lev Nikolayevich the drop that overflowed his cup of patience. His decision to go away was formed suddenly and irrevocably.

In the middle of the night Aleksandra Lvovna and Varvara Mikhailovna heard a knock on their door.

"Who's there?"

"It's I, Lev Nikolayevich."

Aleksandra Lvovna opened the door. Lev Nikolayevich stood on the threshold with a candle in his hand.

"I am leaving at once—for good. Come and help me pack."

As Aleksandra Lvovna described it, his face had an extraordinary and beautiful expression of resolution and inner clarity. She and Varvara Mikhailovna hastily dressed and rushed upstairs to Lev Nikolayevich's study, where, with D. P. Makovitsky, they began packing Tolstoy's clothes and manuscripts. Lev Nikolayevich himself took a hand in the packing. He refused to take with him anything that he did not consider absolutely necessary, such as the apparatus for an enema (which is indispensable for him at times), a fur coat, a flashlight. Only at their insistence was he finally persuaded to take these things.

He had written a letter to his wife, which he entrusted to Aleksandra Lvovna to give to her mother. In it he said:

> My departure will distress you. I regret this, but please understand and believe that I cannot do otherwise. My position in this house has become unbearable. In addition to everything else, I can no longer live in these luxurious conditions, and I do now what is commonly done by old people my age who leave the worldly life in order to spend their last days in peace and solitude.
>
> Please understand this and do not come after me, even if you find out where I am; this would only worsen both your position and mine, and would not alter my decision.
>
> I thank you for your honest forty-eight years of life with me, and ask you to forgive me for everything I am guilty of before you, as I, with all my heart, forgive you for everything you may be guilty of before me. I advise you to reconcile yourself to the new conditions of life which you will face with my departure, and to bear me no ill will.
>
> If you wish to communicate with me, tell Sasha; she will know where I am and will send me anything that is necessary; but she cannot tell you where I am, because I have exacted her promise to tell no one.
>
> 28 October.   Lev Tolstoy

All that Lev Nikolayevich had told Aleksandra Lvovna was that he probably would go first to see his sister Marya Nikolayevna, a nun at the Shamardino monastery in the province of Kaluga. They have preserved a great friendship, despite their differences on questions of faith.

When the packing was done, Lev Nikolayevich himself went

to the stables to order the harnessing of the horses. But in the darkness he mistook his way, lost his cap in the bushes, and returned to the house bareheaded. Only then did he remember the flashlight. . . .

The hands of the coachman, Adrian Eliseyev, trembled as he harnessed a pair of horses to the old droshky, and the sweat ran down his face. Lev Nikolayevich became agitated and began to help him, bridling one of the horses himself. The postilion Filya lit a torch, as the night was extraordinarily dark, and prepared to accompany the two travelers on horseback.

At half-past five in the morning the droshky set out. Adrian drove Lev Nikolayevich and Dushan to the Yasenki station, where they were to take the eight-o'clock train south.

When I arrived at Yasnaya Polyana at about eleven o'clock, Sofya Andreyevna had just got up. She looked into Lev Nikolayevich's room and not finding him there rushed to the "Remington room" and from there to the library, where she was told of his departure and handed the letter.

"My God!" she exclaimed in a whisper.

She tore open the envelope and read the first lines: "My departure will distress you . . ." and could not go on. She flung the letter onto the library table and ran to her room, whispering:

"My God! What is he doing to me!"

"Read the letter—there may be something in it—" Aleksandra Lvovna and Varvara Mikhailovna called after her, but she would not listen.

A moment later one of the servants rushed in, shouting that Sofya Andreyevna had run out to the park in the direction of the pond.

"Go after her, you have boots on!" Aleksandra Lvovna said to me and ran to put on her galoshes.

I hurried out to the park, where I caught glimpses of Sofya Andreyevna's gray dress through the trees: she was rapidly approaching the pond. I followed her, trying to keep out of sight behind trees. Then I began to run.

"Don't run so fast!" shouted Aleksandra Lvovna from behind.

I looked back. By now several people were following us: Semyon the cook, Vanya the footman, and others.

All at once Sofya Andreyevna turned, but she was still making for the pond. She disappeared behind the bushes. Aleksandra Lvovna rushed headlong past me, her skirts rustling, and I started to run after her. There was not a moment to lose: Sofya Andreyevna was at the very edge of the pond. She looked back and saw us. Having descended the slope she was moving rapidly along the plank to the jetty (near the bathhouse where the clothes are washed), when all at once she slipped and fell on her back with a crash. She clutched at the plank, crawled to the edge of the jetty, and rolled over into the water.

The moment Aleksandra Lvovna reached the jetty, she too fell when she stepped on the slippery place on the plank. By then I was there. Having taken off her warm knitted jacket as she ran, Aleksandra Lvovna instantly jumped into the water. I did the same. From the jetty I had seen Sofya Andreyevna's body lying face up and open-mouthed in the water, her arms spread helplessly as she sank. Suddenly she was completely submerged.

It was fortunate that Aleksandra Lvovna and I could touch bottom. Had Sofya Andreyevna not slipped and fallen where she did, but had thrown herself into the pond from the end of the jetty, it would have been impossible for us to stand. The middle of the pond is very deep and people have drowned there. Near the bank, where we were, the water was only chest high.

We pulled her out of the pond and got her onto a log trestle and from there onto the jetty. By that time the footman Vanya had reached us, and with difficulty the three of us lifted her, soaking and heavy, and carried her up onto the bank.

Aleksandra Lvovna ran back to change her clothes while Vanya, Semyon, and I gently led Sofya Andreyevna toward the house. It was hard for her to walk. At one point she sank weakly to the ground.

"I just want to sit for a moment . . . Let me sit . . ."

But this was out of the question: it was imperative that she get out of her wet clothing as soon as possible. Vanya and I made a cradle with our arms and Semyon and the others helped her to sit in it and be carried by us. But she soon asked to be set down.

At the door of the house she ordered Vanya to go to the station and find out for what destination Lev Nikolayevich had bought tickets. Then, with the help of Varvara Mikhailovna and the housekeeper, she changed her clothes. But she came downstairs again to see whether Vanya had left and gave him a telegram to be sent to train No. 9, which said: "Return at once. Sasha." Vanya showed the telegram to Aleksandra Lvovna, not out of flunkyism, but out of his sincere sympathy and attachment to Lev Nikolayevich. In general the servants do not like Sofya Andreyevna.

Aleksandra Lvovna sent a telegram along with her mother's in which she told Lev Nikolayevich to trust only those telegrams signed "Aleksandra."

Meanwhile, Sofya Andreyevna kept reiterating that she would find other ways of doing away with herself. We had to take from her by force a penknife, some opium, and several heavy objects with which she had begun to beat herself on the breast.

Not an hour had passed when they rushed in to say that she had run away again and was going toward the pond. I caught up with her in the park and almost forcibly led her back to the house. On the threshold she burst into tears.

"Like a son . . . like my own son!" she cried, embracing and kissing me.

Vanya returned from Yasenki and reported that four tickets had been sold for train No. 9: two second-class tickets to the Blagodatnoye station (from which there is a road leading to Kochety, where the Sukhotins live), and two third-class tickets to the Gorbachev station (where one has to change for Shamardino, where M. N. Tolstaya is). This information was rather vague; Lev Nikolayevich might have gone to either station.

Aleksandra Lvovna sent for Andrei Lvovich, Sergei Lvovich, and Tatyana Lvovna. She also sent to Tula for a psychiatrist for

Sofya Andreyevna, whose condition is alarming. By chance M. A. Schmidt has arrived from Ovsyannikovo and will remain here.

Before the day was out, Andrei Lvovich arrived from Krapivna, where he happened to be. He confidently promised Sofya Andreyevna that by tomorrow morning he will tell her where Lev Nikolayevich has gone. He had intended taking action through the governor of Tula, but later his ardor cooled.

29 October

I did not sleep, but sat up all night in the "Remington room" on duty. Varvara Mikhailovna went to bed only at three o'clock, as Sofya Andreyevna could not be left alone for a moment. They had put her to bed in Lev Nikolayevich's room instead of her own. She scarcely slept, however, but kept walking about the room lamenting over Lev Nikolayevich, saying that she could not live without him and would die. Toward morning she declared that it would be impossible to be in greater torment than she was, that she was conscious of her guilt toward Lev Nikolayevich, and of her helplessness to do anything about it now.

In the course of the day Sergei, Ilya, and Mikhail Lvovich arrived, as well as Tatyana Lvovna. There were conferences among Lev Nikolayevich's children the whole day. With the exception of Sergei Lvovich, they all want Lev Nikolayevich to return to Yasnaya. But what would his life here be now?

Ilya, Andrei, and Tatyana Lvovna wrote a letter to him to this effect, which Aleksandra Lvovna is to take to him. Sergei Lvovich wrote a brief note to his father in which he told him that in his opinion he did the right thing; that the situation was hopeless, and in leaving he had chosen "the true way out."

I was very much surprised by Lev Nikolayevich's youngest son, Mikhail Lvovich. Sitting at the piano and playing bravura waltzes, he announced that he was not going to write.

"Everyone knows that I don't like to write! Tell him," he

called over his shoulder to his sister, without taking his hands off the keys, "that I agree with Tanya and Ilya. . . ."

His father had fled from his home, perhaps endangering his life, and this son could not spare the time to write to him!

In the evening Prince D. D. Obolensky appeared. He announced at once that he had come not as a correspondent, but as a friend of the family. A few minutes later, however, he asked their permission to write for the newspapers everything that had happened at Yasnaya Polyana.

"All Tula is talking about this!"

And he did, in fact, report the news, quite accurately conveying the details of yesterday's event.

"I believe," said the Prince (or "Mitasha," as the Tolstoys call him behind his back), "that I am entitled to write about this. I am fortunate in that the count has always been more than frank with me."

The poor Prince! He is evidently deluded about the nature of his relations with Lev Nikolayevich. . . . But now, with this report about Yasnaya Polyana, he was able to give the signal for the uncalled-for hue and cry that has arisen in the press around Tolstoy's name. This was probably unavoidable after Sofya Andreyevna had talked to him and given him the text of Lev Nikolayevich's last letter.

The attitude of Sofya Andreyevna herself toward Lev Nikolayevich, which is inevitably deduced from her expressions of it, is now characterized by duplicity and insincerity. On the one hand she will not part with his little pillow, covers it with kisses and presses it to her bosom, all the while lamenting:

"Dear Levochka, where are you laying your little head now? Hear me! After all, distance means nothing!"

And on the other hand, her criticism of her husband is full of malice.

"He is a brute," she was heard to say, "he could not have acted with greater cruelty—he wanted to kill me!" And remarks of a similar nature.

30 October

Last night at midnight, Aleksandra Lvovna and Varvara Mikhailovna left to go to Lev Nikolayevich, taking a roundabout way through Tula in order to cover their tracks. Only Tatyana Lvovna, M. A. Schmidt, and I knew about their proposed journey.

Yesterday Ilya and Mikhail returned to their own homes, and today Sergei Lvovich left for Moscow. Of Lev Nikolayevich's children, only Tatyana Lvovna and Andrei Lvovich have remained at Yasnaya.

Correspondents from the various newspapers have come, but Andrei Lvovich was rather short with them, peremptorily sending them about their business wthout giving them any information.

In the course of the day, I paid a visit to Telyatinki. There I learned that Chertkov had sent Aleksei Sergeyenko to Lev Nikolayevich at the monastery of Optina Pustyn (on the road to Shamardino). He returned only today with the report that Lev Nikolayevich is in good health and spirits and has seen his sister, who is in complete sympathy with his decision to leave Yasnaya Polyana. Though he was distressed by the news Sergeyenko brought him about Yasnaya Polyana, on no account did he wish to return.

During the day Sofya Andreyevna repeatedly implored me to go with her in search of Lev Nikolayevich, but I refused, reminding her that in his farewell letter he had asked that no one try to find him. In the evening she sent for a priest so that she could confess and take communion. And she asked me if I would go tomorrow to Telyatinki and tell Vladimir Grigorevich to come to her: she wants to be reconciled with him "before death," and to ask his forgiveness for any wrong she may have done him.

31 October

A telegram has come from Gorbachev, unsigned, but obviously from Lev Nikolayevich: "We are leaving. Do not try to find me. Will write."

There was also a telegram from Paris from L. L. Tolstoy: "Disturbing news in Paris newspapers, please telegraph."

The Moscow newspapers which came today already contain reports of Lev Nikolayevich's departure, and even certain details.

Dr. Berkenheim, the psychiatrist Rastegayev, and a nurse have arrived for Sofya Andreyevna. Dr. Berkenheim, an experienced physician and a kind and clever man who thoroughly understands the domestic relations of the Tolstoys, is specially welcome.

Sofya Andreyevna has eaten nothing since Lev Nikolayevich left; she is growing weak and says she wants to die. If the doctors attempt to use a probe for artificial feeding, she says she will fall on the knife ("like this—in one movement"), or will kill herself by some other means.

One of the servants, Ilya Vasilyevich, told me something interesting about Sofya Andreyevna, but asked me not to mention it to anyone at this time. It seems she had attached a little holy image to the foot of Lev Nikolayevich's bed where it could not be seen. After his departure she removed it: its influence apparently was the very opposite of what she had wished.

Once again she asked me to convey to Chertkov her request that he come to see her, and to tell him that the invitation was without "ulterior motive." Again, as on that memorable day, the twelfth of June, when she had appealed to him through me to return the manuscripts and consent to a reconciliation, I went to him with the secret hope that this time the reconciliation would take place. But, alas, my hopes were in vain. Chertkov was true to his nature: shrewd and alien to sentiment. After hearing her request, he at first agreed to go to Yasnaya Polyana, but then changed his mind.

"Why should I go?" he asked. "So that she can humble herself before me, ask my forgiveness? It's a ruse to get me to send a telegram for her to Lev Nikolayevich."

I confess that such a reply both surprised and pained me. Only the want of any desire for a reconciliation and a deep antipathy to Sofya Andreyevna could have prompted such an answer. The fear that she would ask him to send some sort of unsuitable telegram to Lev Nikolayevich? Oh, that was indeed a feeble excuse for not going! He could have been reconciled to her and still have maintained his position. How is it that I could have refused to go with her in search of Lev Nikolayevich and yet have preserved my good relations with her? No, the enmity between the persons closest to Lev Nikolayevich is unfortunately too deep. And now that one of them has made the attempt to extend a hand to the other, he has refused to take it. Yet it is impossible to say how everything would have changed for Lev Nikolayevich, how relieved he would have been, had this reconciliation been effected! Of course they are at fault for not having brought it about earlier; but there is less justification for the one who spurned it, and now, in the face of such grave and alarming events. This guilt is the more unpardonable in a man who considers himself a follower of Tolstoy.

With the obvious aim of palliating the effect of his refusal, Vladimir Grigorevich asked me to tell Sofya Andreyevna that he was not angry with her, that he was kindly disposed toward her, and would send her a letter this evening with a circumstantial reply to her invitation. These were mere words, unsupported by the one step which could and should have been taken in these circumstances.

At Yasnaya Polyana everyone was astounded when I returned alone. It was inconceivable to them that Chertkov could refuse to grant her request for a meeting and a reconciliation. They decided to say nothing to her about his reply, in fact, not even to let her know of my return for the moment, as she was impatiently awaiting his arrival and in a highly agitated state.

In an attempt to ameliorate the situation, Dr. G. M. Berkenheim was called upon to go to Chertkov and persuade him to come. He set out for Telyatinki, where he spent a rather long time. But even his exhortations were of no avail: Chertkov still refuses to come. He merely gave the doctor a letter for Sofya Andreyevna, written in the most tactful, diplomatic terms, in which he repeated his refusal to come to Yasnaya at this time. The letter was read to her.

"Hollow moralizing!" was her comment on this letter, with all its verbiage. And perhaps she was right.

She immediately wrote an answer and sent it to him. By then it was evening. It is also characteristic of her that she had already composed a telegram to Lev Nikolayevich: "Have taken communion. Reconciled with Chertkov. Growing weak. Forgive and farewell."

It was impossible to send such a telegram! Although it is true that she has reaffirmed her wish to send for a priest, there has certainly been no reconciliation with Chertkov.

1 November

This morning Brio, the assistant editor of *The Russian Word,* an elderly gentleman with mild, courtly manners, was at Yasnaya. Sofya Andreyevna received him herself, though she was still in her morning dress. She granted him this favor after reading a laudatory article about herself written by Doroshevich in the issue of the paper that came today.

Describing the recent events from her own point of view, she gave Brio a very ugly picture of what had happened. But more of that. She had seen certain articles in the newspapers condemning her and extolling Lev Nikolayevich's act and she is beside herself. She made a hideous scene in Brio's presence, flying about the room in her lilac-colored morning dress with her hair in disorder, and denouncing both Lev Nikolayevich and Chertkov. It was very difficult to calm her.

Brio also interviewed Tolstoy's children, M. A. Schmidt, me, and several other members of the household, before leaving in haste to write his article and get it into print.

In the evening a disturbing telegram was received at the Chertkovs'. Lev Nikolayevich has a fever and is unconscious. His temperature is 39.8° C. He is apprehensive about Sofya Andreyevna's coming, and is calling for Vladimir Grigorevich.

It seems that he had left Shamardino and was on the road

to Rostov-on-Don, intending to visit his relatives the Denisenkos, in Novocherkass, when he fell ill and was obliged to leave the train at the Astapovo station on the Ryazan-Ural railroad.

Chertkov has decided to go to him today. Meanwhile, Sofya Andreyevna again asked him to come to Yasnaya Polyana—and of all times, tonight! He excused himself on the grounds of having to go to Tula on urgent business. He felt that he was not committing a sin against truth, as he and Aleksei Sergeyenko are going to Astapovo by way of Tula.

I spent the night at Yasnaya. The Tolstoy brothers, several of whom are here again, have asked me to remain for a while. They thanked me for my sympathy and help to the family in this difficult time.

2 November

Vladimir Grigorevich sent a telegram to Telyatinki stating that Lev Nikolayevich is in comfortable conditions, but that he has bronchitis. Later, another telegram was received from him saying that Lev Nikolayevich is suffering from pneumonia.

Yasnaya is absolutely deserted. A telegram addressed to Sofya Andreyevna from the editor of *The Russian Word* disclosed Lev Nikolayevich's whereabouts. Orlov, one of the newspaper's correspondents, had tracked him down in the course of his journey. At eight o'clock in the morning, the whole family, including Sofya Andreyevna, her psychiatrist and nurse, having assembled once more at Yasnaya Polyana, set out for Tula, where they will take a special train that has been chartered for them to Astapovo.

7 November

On the Tolstoys' departure from Yasnaya, I moved to Telyatinki. When he left for Astapovo, Chertkov had asked me as a friend to oblige him by staying with his sick wife, who has been shocked and exceedingly distressed by all that has happened, and to help her in any way I could, should the need arise. Consequently, I again find myself tied down here, while knowing that many of Lev Nikolayevich's friends and relations have gathered at Astapovo. And I had such a strong desire to go there, if only to have a momentary glimpse of my dear teacher!

An opportunity unexpectedly arose for me to go: warm clothing and certain other articles needed for the patient had to be taken to him. A. K. Chertkova had decided that I should take them there, and I was to have left in the evening. I was happy knowing that I would soon see Lev Nikolayevich. Then, at about eleven o'clock in the morning when I was sitting in Anna Konstantinovna's study reading to her, the door opened and Dima came in. Holding out his arms to his mother, he quickly went to her.

"Mamma . . . darling . . ." he said in a sorrowful voice, obviously at a loss for words. "What are we to do? . . . It evidently had to be . . . It happens to everyone, Mamma . . ."

I heard what he was saying without understanding.

Meanwhile, Anna Konstantinovna had risen from her chair, her face white as a sheet. Peering into her son's face she uttered a faint scream and fell unconscious in his arms.

I ran out to the corridor to call for help . . . and only then did I realize . . .

Tolstoy was dead.

Notes

1. *For Every Day,* also called *Thoughts on Life,* was a series of booklets of sayings of the wise, compiled from the works of writers whose views were in harmony with those of Tolstoy. This was to become his last important work. The title ultimately given to it was *The Way of Life.*

2. *The Intermediary,* a publishing house founded in 1884 by V. G. Chertkov for the distribution at modest prices of literary and popular writing as well as material in various fields of knowledge. Tolstoy was an active contributor, writing certain works, such as *How Much Land Does a Man Need?*, specially for it.

3. Baron d'Estournelles de Constant (1852–1924) was a member of the French Parliament, and founder of the *Comité des Intérêts Nationaux.* He was in Moscow in 1910 as head of a peace movement. Tolstoy was invited to become a member of this organization, but refused.

4. The title of the story was *Carelessness.*

5. During the coronation ceremonies of Nicholas II, two or three thousand people were trampled to death in a stampede on the Khodynka parade grounds outside Moscow. Tolstoy's story *Khodynka* was left in an unfinished state and published posthumously.

6. The title was changed to *Vanity* in *The Way of Life.*

7. The title was changed to *Inequality* in *The Way of Life.*

8. It is probably to these visitors that Tolstoy's note in his diary refers: "I saw off some Cossacks and a sailor, as well as a Ukrainian alcoholic and his wife."

9. Yakubovich-Melshin (1860–1911), revolutionist and poet. For his participation in the People's Freedom movement in 1887 he received the death sentence, which later was commuted to eighteen years of penal servitude. On his return he became an editor of *Russian Wealth.*

10. *Reprints* was a publishing house set up for the purpose of printing works of Tolstoy banned before 1905. It lasted only a year. One of the publishers was imprisoned for six months.

11. Nikolai Vasilyevich Chaikovsky (1850–1926), Russian populist, one of the leaders of a group known by his name. The group was abolished in 1873

and Chaikovsky was exiled. In the '70's he escaped and settled in London, where he founded *The Free Russian Press Fund.* He returned to Russia in 1905, was arrested, and acquitted in 1910. After the October Revolution, he became a White emigré, and one of the most rabid enemies of Soviet power.

12. Vladimir Sergeyevich Solovyov (1853–1900), a Russian philosopher, mystic, and poet. Tolstoy became acquainted with him in 1875 and they met often in the '80's and '90's. There were profound disagreements between them on philosophical and religious questions.

13. Aleksei Stepanovich Khomyakov (1804–1860), a Russian poet, philosopher, and theologian. Tolstoy was acquainted with him and with his work, but was not in sympathy with it.

14. Fyodor A. Strakhov (1861–1923), philosopher and author of *The Search for Truth,* a collection of essays published by *The Intermediary* in 1911. Tolstoy read the work in proofs, liked it, wrote to the author, and his letter was used as a preface to the book.

15. For reasons of censorship, this booklet was not published in *The Way of Life.*

16. The title was changed to *False Faith* in *The Way of Life.*

17. Aleksandra Andreyevna Tolstaya (1817–1904), a second cousin of Tolstoy, maid of honor at the Imperial Court. Despite deep differences in their views, they were close friends and carried on an active correspondence up to the time of her death. His letters and her memoirs were to be published.

18. The title was changed to *Thought* in *The Way of Life.*

19. The title was changed to *Self-Abnegation* in *The Way of Life.*

20. These titles were changed to *Veracity* and *Life in the Present* in *The Way of Life.*

21. Arvin Ernfelt (1861–1932), Finnish writer. He shared Tolstoy's religious and philosophical views and was in correspondence with him from 1895.

22. Henry George (1839–1897), American economist and land reformer, who popularized the idea of the single tax.

23. *Our Revolution: Violent Rebellion or Christian Liberation?* by V. G. Chertkov, with an afterword by L. N. Tolstoy. In this brochure, Chertkov wrote against the revolutionary struggle, to which he opposed the idea of Christian service to man, nonresistance to evil, and renunciation of practical action.

24. These thoughts from Leskov were not included in *The Way of Life.*

25. The reference is to Tolstoy's play, *The First Distiller, or How the Imp Earned a Crust of Bread,* written in 1884.

26. The chapter *The Hunt* is in all the published editions of *Childhood.* Apparently a manuscript version was being read by Sofya Andreyevna, which was different from the published version.

27. Ivan Ivanovich Gorbunov-Posadov (1864–1940), a friend of Tolstoy's and sympathizer with his views. He was one of the publishers of *The Intermediary* and a writer of stories and folk tales. In 1909 he was tried and acquitted for publishing a work by Herbert Spencer which advocated distributing land to the workers.

28. This was called *Intemperance* in *The Way of Life*.

29. Aleksandr Modestovich Khiryakov (1863–1940), liberal journalist and author of books and articles on Tolstoy. In 1909 he was sentenced to a year in prison for editing *The Voice,* a Petersburg newspaper.

30. *The World's Chinese Student Journal,* published in English.

31. O. D. Durnovo had made an analysis of the four Gospels, treating them as literal truth. He was the author of a book called *Thus Spake Christ.*

32. There are about one hundred manuscript versions of this preface in the archives of the Tolstoy Museum.

33. Skopets: a member of an ascetic religious sect that practiced castration.

34. Dr. Karl Veleminsky, a Czech educator, translator of Tolstoy's pedagogical writings into Czech.

35. Aleksandr Dobrolyubov (1876–1930), one of the first Symbolist poets, who early discovered the French Symbolists. He later became the leader of a religious sect and disappeared from view.